Mending the Broken Bough

Most Berkley Books are available at special quantity discounts for bulk purchases for sales promotions, premiums, fund-raising, or educational use. Special books or book excerpts can also be created to fit specific needs.

For details, write to Special Markets, The Berkley Publishing Group, 200 Madison Avenue, New York, New York 10016.

Mending the Broken Bough

Restoring the Promise of the Mother–Daughter Relationship

Barbara Zax, PH.D.
Stephan Poulter, PH.D.

BERKLEY BOOKS, NEW YORK

This book is an original publication of The Berkley Publishing Group.

MENDING THE BROKEN BOUGH

A Berkley Book / published by arrangement with
the authors

PRINTING HISTORY
Berkley trade paperback edition / July 1998

All rights reserved.
Copyright © 1998 by Barbara Zax, Ph.D., and Stephan Poulter, Ph.D.
Text design by Leslie Phillips.
This book may not be reproduced in whole or in part,
by mimeograph or any other means, without permission.
For information address: The Berkley Publishing Group,
a member of Penguin Putnam Inc.,
200 Madison Avenue, New York, New York 10016.

The Penguin Putnam Inc. World Wide Web site address is
http://www.penguinputnam.com

ISBN: 0-425-16318-0

BERKLEY®
Berkley Books are published by The Berkley Publishing Group,
a member of Penguin Putnam Inc.,
200 Madison Avenue, New York, New York 10016.
BERKLEY and the "B" design
are trademarks belonging to Berkley Publishing Corporation.

PRINTED IN THE UNITED STATES OF AMERICA

10 9 8 7 6 5 4 3 2 1

This book is dedicated to Stan, Marlene, Andy, Lauren, Holly, Madison, and Jonathan
For their love and inspiration

Acknowledgments

This book has been through many versions and transformations. Each alteration was the result of something we learned from the women who came to us, seeking help to improve their relationships. Without these women—our clients, our group members, and our workshop participants—there would be no book.

A book, we have discovered, is a team effort and the following people have been key players on our team:

Jane Dystel—our agent, who cheered us, consoled us, and never lost faith in us. Her encouragement to do more than we thought we could helped make this book a reality.

Richard Trubo—our tireless and unflappable editor. His knack of asking just the right questions kept us on track and his ability to soothe our "writer's angst" kept us sane. Richard was our book's midwife and we couldn't have completed it without him.

Denise Silvestro—our wonderful, and always accessible, editor at Berkley. Her incisive suggestions and editing made this book what you see today. We are indebted to her for her enthusiasm and commitment to this project from the beginning. We are also grateful to her indefatigable assistant, Martha Bushko, for fielding our phone calls and requests with patience and good humor.

Laudii Jahromi, Mandy Sherman, and Melissa Boutielle—our research assistants. The hours they spent in the library and at the printers gave us more time to write, and we are grateful for their help.

Linda Preuss—our imperturbable computer consultant, who made house calls at weird hours and dealt with hard drive crashes, lost data, and balky software with equal aplomb. Her assistance was invaluable.

Laura Golden Bellotti—author and editor, who not only guided us through our book proposal but taught us to "think like Laura." Her expertise helped us initiate this project.

Our colleagues—Drs. Marion Solomon, Rita Lynn, Winston Gooden, Eileen Tonic, Lo Sprague, Russell Hunter, Trudy Moss, Jim Gottfurcht, and Marvin Koven. Their contributions and feedback inspired us. Our respect for them and their contributions to our field is enormous and we are grateful for their help and encouragement.

Our pals—Sandy Pressman, Nancy Jacobson, Elaine Wynn, Bonnie Fuller, Evie Spound, Chip Fisher, Bob Henke, Bob Brodie, and Bob Sharples. They laughed with us, cried with us, and cheered us on. Sometimes they even made us come out and play.

And last, but most important, our families—Albert Slepyan, Stan and Marlene, Andy, Lauren, Holly Jo, Madison, Jonathan, the Slepyans, the Poulters, the Clarks, the Zaxes, and the Millers. They put up with missed dinners, late phone calls, abbreviated weekends, shortened vacations, and mood swings. In return they gave us smiles, hugs, words of endearment, encouragement, inspiration, and unconditional love. We couldn't have done this without them.

Was will das Weib?
What is it that the female wants?

SIGMUND FREUD

What is it that the female wants? In every
likelihood it is a paradoxical package: a close
identification with the person of her mother and
her loving permission to separate and go her
way into full autonomy as a sexual and creative
woman in her undisputed right.

NINI HERMAN
*Too Long a Child:
The Mother Daughter Dyad*

Contents

Introduction   1

1. The Power and Legacy of the
   Mother/Daughter Relationship   16
2. A Girl's First Love—Her Mother   43
3. Mothering Styles   70
4. Understanding the Family You Came from
   and the Family You Are Creating   98
5. Shaking the Family Tree: Three Generations
   of Mothers and Daughters   134
6. Rules We Learn from Our Mothers   164
7. Leaving Home—Can I Take My Mother
   with Me?   195
8. Sticking Points and Immovable Objects   229
9. The Psychology of Mending Moves:
   Moving Beyond Diagnosing and Blaming   259

Bibliography   287

Introduction

If you're like most women, the impact that mothers and daughters have on one another's lives is a topic of endless fascination. During the past few years, when women learned that we were writing a book about mothers and daughters, we got the following range of responses:

"Wow, what a great subject!"

"Heavy!"

"I could really use a book like that."

"Tell me how to get my daughter to read it."

"I thought I was the only person who worried about that stuff."

"Do you think it would help me with my mother?"

"When will it be published? I need it *now!*"

As you can see from these responses, this is a subject that never fails to provoke strong emotions, ranging from tenderness, ambivalence, and neediness, to frustration and rage. We believe that a relationship that has the power to create such potent reactions deserves to be explored in depth. Our goal in this book is to investigate the way mothers and daughters interact with one another—from infancy through adulthood—and the impact these interactions have on the way each of them functions as women, in the workplace and in relationships.

Since every woman is somebody's daughter, we are going to explore the important connections not only between *two* generations of women, a mother and daughter, but also the impact of the *multigenerational* family on the relationships between daughters, granddaughters, and great-granddaughters.

While the focus of this book is on the roles and rules of women in families, we do not mean to diminish the importance of fathers and grandfathers. In every mother's and daughter's story, there is always a "man in the room." We are cognizant of the importance of these men in the lives of the women we write about. We are well aware of the influence of fathers on the emotional development and self-esteem of growing daughters, and of husbands on their wives in their role as mothers. The particular focus of this book, however, is on the process of being a mother and being a daughter, and how the lives, behavior, and beliefs of each woman's mother and grandmother affect who she is and how she feels about herself today.

Whether your relationship with your mother or your daughter is "fine," "tolerable," or "absolutely impossible," we believe that you, like most mothers and daughters, want to know and understand each other better. Regardless of how you feel about your mother or your daughter, there is usually a longing for greater insights into and, perhaps, a clarification of the bonds that connect you. Even when there is plenty of love available, daughters and mothers sometimes slip "off track," and yearn to get back in sync. This book will show you how.

The Intricacies of This Special Relationship

As you'll discover in these pages, the mother-daughter relationship is certainly a powerful one. The way a mother interacts with her daughter, and how she "models" for her what it means to be a woman, has a strong influence on how her daughter lives, loves, and works. When a daughter looks out at the world, much of what she sees is colored by what she has learned and absorbed from her mother. Her mother's moods, behavior, and point of view can alter not only how a daughter views the outside world but how she sees herself.

On the other hand, a mother may look at her grown daughter with awe, pride, or trepidation—sometimes all three. She may question her own effectiveness as a parent: Has she been the best kind of role model? It can be unnerving to hear herself echoing words that she knows she heard from her own mother: "I always promised myself I would never say that." And yet, where else was she going to learn about mothering if not from her own mother?

For each woman, the early relationship with her mother is the foundation upon which she will build *all* of her future relationships. A young girl may bask in the bright sun of mother's approval and internalize those good feelings, which, in turn, become a positive part of her self-image. Or she may habitually get the message that mother is disappointed in her, which also becomes a part of how she views herself. As a child grows, each interaction with mother, both positive and negative, has the power to impact a daughter's emerging self-portrait.

One of our aims in writing this book is to help you unravel the mystery of why your relationship with your mother or daughter may not be working the way you want it to. We will help you get this crucial relationship back on track. We are very fortunate because the women we have worked with, both individually and in groups, have shared with us remarkable stories and insights about their relationships with their mothers and daughters. We think their experiences can inspire you to begin the process of mending and reworking your own relationship.

Before we begin to explore the stories that our clients have shared with us, we think it is important to share with you part of our *own* histories, and the way we each became involved in the subject of mothers and daughters.

Barbara's story

I come from a long line of martyrs on my mother's side of the family. I realize that is a pretty strong statement, so let me explain what I mean by martyr.

Everyone has a healthy need for attention and validation. But when the needs of the women in my family were not met in a positive way, they learned to get attention by either creating or exaggerating emotional pain. They were masters of the art of convincing those around them that they were long-suffering, exhausted, and deprived of love.

These women were not just your "garden variety" martyrs. My grandmother could have easily won the world martyrdom Olympics. As a small child, I used to watch how she manipulated her four children—including my mother, who was her oldest—with the awesome power of her anguish and her ability to self-flagellate.

I remember my grandmother sitting on the porch of her farm, tears rolling down her face, surrounded by her four grown children. As she mournfully complained that none of them loved or appreciated her, these four adults sat at her feet and begged her not to cry. They told her how much they loved her, how wonderful she was. I was impressed. I may not have understood what she was doing, but at the tender age of six, I certainly recognized what power was when I saw it.

My mother never quite matched my grandmother's ability to elicit guilty responses from her children. She was only a talented amateur in comparison with my grandmother. Still, she had the power to control my brother and me with her mood swings and manifestations of worry and self-sacrifice. My younger brother developed an effective defense against her emotional machinations: He simply tuned out. It was as if he created a protective cloud around himself that made him completely oblivious to her behavior.

I, on the other hand, bore the full brunt of my mother's mood swings. When she appeared sad and depressed, I reacted immediately. I would ask her what was wrong. She would sigh and reply, "Nothing." Even as a small child, I recognized that she was lying.

Young children are highly sensitive to the nuances of the adults around them. My mother was intelligent, sweet, loving, and totally devoted to her family. However, when one of her dark moods hit, and she began to feel unloved and unappreciated, I would mobilize into action. I would be good. Actually, I would be better than good—I would be wonderful. I would ask her if I could help. I would pick up my clothes without being asked. I would set the table. I would stop hitting my brother. I would do anything to bring my adored mother back to "normal," back to feeling loved.

I became like a tuning fork. I could sense when she was on the road to a bout of martyrdom. I learned to be quiet. I learned to listen. Listening was the key to assessing her moods. I would intervene if I thought my father or my brother might do something that would have a negative effect on her. This did not make me exceptionally popular in my household. But it did contribute to my sense of safety. As long as my mother felt loved, I would feel loved, and that was that.

About the time I entered high school, my mother became profoundly depressed. There was nothing I could do about it. I was incapable of making her feel better. As a result, I became angry and defiant. Every emotion that I had repressed as a child in service of my mother came out with a vengeance.

I told myself I didn't care how she felt—"let her be depressed if she wants!" I acted out because I didn't know what else to do; my repertoire of behaviors to bring my mother back to me didn't work anymore. I vacillated between sulky silence and outrageous behavior that was guaranteed to cause her discomfort. (I should note here that, in comparison to today's standards, my "awful" behavior seems almost quaint. At the time, however, it did the job.)

So how did this sad yet common family scenario of martyrdom and depression contribute to the woman, mother, and professional I am today? For starters, it contributed to some important reality checks in my life as a young mother.

It is hard to remember all of the feelings I was bombarded with in the daily care of my own young children. I know I must have had some blue days, some frustrated days, and probably, some absolutely frazzled days. The first time, however, that my four-year-old son asked me, "Mommy, what's wrong?" and I found myself answering, "Nothing," I had a flash that something was happening that felt painful, familiar, and very, very wrong.

Some productive work in my personal therapy gave me a handle on the process I had begun to play out with my children. I saw how the impact of my relationship with my mother was coloring my responses, my attitudes, and my behavior, not only with my children but with myself.

At the same time I also found my calling. The skills I had developed as an attentive listener and empathically attuned caretaker—the instincts that I had honed being sensitive to my mother's behavior and pain—led me to my career as a therapist.

Thus it was the love, frustration, and pain in my relationship with my mother that motivated me to do the kind of work I do today. I often wonder what my mother would think if she could see me now. How would she feel if she attended one of my workshops, and listened to me speak on the topic of mothers and daughters? I'd like to think that she would be proud of me.

Hopefully, my mother would also be pleased to know how hard I worked to apply the lessons of our struggle together to the parenting of my own children. In addition to my son,

I am the mother of two daughters. When my oldest daughter was born, I began, once again, to assess my relationship with my mother. I had dreams for my daughter, and I wondered if my mother had ever had dreams for me. Did they extend beyond what she herself had personally experienced? If so, why had she never shared them with me? What kind of dreams had she had for herself? Did she ever want more out of life than being a housewife and mother? Did she dare to share her dreams with her own mother? If so, what would my grandmother have thought of my mother's ambitions?

When I was twenty-eight years old, just after the birth of my oldest daughter, my mother began to develop the early symptoms of Alzheimer's disease. Six years later she died. I never had the opportunity to ask her the questions that nagged at my heart after I had become a mother. These questions, which I have asked myself, my friends, my colleagues, and ultimately my clients, are at the core of my interest in this subject, and have provided the motivation for this book.

Stephan's Story

On a hot Monday night in late June, my mother walked into the backyard and began to sob. I was watering the rosebushes and almost flooded the yard as I watched her crying. I was fifteen years old at the time. Two days earlier, my dad had unexpectedly moved out. Although my mother and I were both in shock, what was more alarming to me was her uncharacteristic display of emotion. The sense of hopelessness that we both felt that day filled the house for the next ten years.

I remember standing there in the backyard as if time had stopped. My mom was crying about things that I could not express. But somehow, deep down, I knew the truth about my family like I knew the back of my hand.

My father left the same summer that Nixon resigned from

the presidency. I remember being unable to understand why I was so depressed about his resignation, but these two events will be forever emotionally joined for me. I did not have the words to explain how devastated I felt that summer. And even if I had the words, I had no one to talk to.

Many years later I realized that at that time my mom and I were in a similar place emotionally. I was fifteen years old and my mom was in her early fifties. Neither of us knew how to handle the situation in which we found ourselves. I was about to enter my sophomore year in high school with enormous ambivalence about my future, my family, and my life. My mom was entering the prime of her life, feeling worthless without a man. What was frightening to me was that, at a young age, I was so in touch with the depth of my mother's pain. Yet I could not fathom the idea that neither of us knew how to stop the pain or what to do with it.

That summer came and went, but the deep-seated fear in the bottom of my stomach stayed with me well into my adult life. The question that jumped out at me that summer, and in the ensuing years, was, "How am I going to become a productive, competent, complete individual without parents to emotionally support me?"

After that summer my mom never really left our backyard. My dad, although he returned to the house, never really "came home." For years my mother was afraid to leave the house, afraid to grow, afraid to change, afraid to pursue her own dreams. I vowed that I would not inherit her fears.

I think I started writing this book that summer, even though the mother-daughter relationship was certainly not foremost in my mind. I wanted to understand how women like my mom—people who appear to be emotionally mature—are held back by their fears. And I needed to understand, as well, my own feelings of guilt surrounding my mother's unhappiness. Although she encouraged me to make my own decisions, I never felt her support as I attempted to create my own life. My attempts to move forward and develop myself were experienced by my mother as abandonment. The seemingly endless struggle to move away from home, without a dark cloud of guilt looming overhead, took me the next sixteen years to complete.

My older sister was away at college when my father moved out. I had hoped that she would help me give Mom the emotional support she needed. My sister, however, could not comprehend the crisis. She was preoccupied with her own needs, foremost of which was her need to be married. She was panicked by the idea that no one would marry her. For her, marriage meant the illusion of safety, as it had for my mother.

I wondered why my sister wanted deliberately to make the same mistake my mom had made by putting her life in the hands of another person, and allowing him to direct it. Why did she feel that she had no other choice but to follow in my mother's footsteps? Why would this young, attractive, and intelligent woman deny or ignore her deepest dreams and potential? Was it something in her relationship with our mother? I didn't have the answers to these questions then, as I painfully watched her go through a series of failed relationships with men who, to my mind, were less than suitable for her.

Now, many years later, as a psychologist, husband, father of a daughter and a son, as well as a son and a brother, I understand the family dynamics underlying my own family's crises, and the relationship between my mother and my sister. Today, I see so many daughters look to their mothers for permission to go out into the world. Back then, as a young man, I wanted my own mother and sister to turn that corner and move ahead with their lives.

The dream of having my mother and sister expand their horizons and live fulfilled lives propelled me into this field— and this book. The desire of both my wife and me to see our daughter move out into the world with a sense of hope and confidence motivates my work as well. This book shares my observations about the challenging, often painful, process of becoming an individual. As you read about the experiences of others, my hope is that you will find the courage to explore your own mother-daughter relationship and grow to be the person you choose to be.

In each chapter of this book, we will highlight what we believe to be the essential elements, or building blocks, of the mother-daughter relationship. In *Chapter One,* we will begin to examine the issues and underpinnings that are vital to understanding the essence of this very complex relationship. For example:

- the connection between a woman's self-image and her relationship with her mother
- how the self-esteem of both daughters and mothers is influenced by their relationship
- how both daughters and mothers develop self-defeating behavior patterns
- the origins of anxiety and depression in both mothers and daughters

Your own mother-daughter relationship is dependent upon how both of you manage your "separateness" and your "connectedness." Coming together and moving apart are steps in the dance that the two of you do together throughout your lives. In Chapter One, you'll be introduced to the notion of mending and redefining your relationship in ways that promote growth for both of you.

In *Chapter Two,* we'll discuss the fundamental concept of attachment. Your initial attachment to your mother has a direct bearing on the way you, as an adult, form attachments with other people. If this crucial first attachment to your mother is not secure, for whatever reason, later separations—be they from your mother or from anyone else you love—have the potential to create tremendous stress and anxiety.

Some of the key areas that we will explore are:

- What happens in those first interactions between mothers and daughters?
- How does each mother's style of attaching influence her daughter's development?
- How is the ability to form trusting relationships as an adult rooted in one's early attachment to mother?

Chapter Two can help you understand how to transform an internalized, insecure view of the world, which had its genesis in infancy, into a secure one that promotes both individual growth and awareness for both mother and daughter.

Chapter Three will explore how a daughter's self-image evolves during the course of her interactions, from birth to adulthood, with her mother. The particular style of mothering practiced by a woman and experienced by her daughter has an enormous impact on how the daughter feels about herself and how she views the world. A mother's daily interactions with a growing daughter set the tone for how her daughter forms future relationships, deals with career options, and manages the myriad life choices that come her way.

We will examine different styles of mothering, using case histories to illustrate the impact of each style on a daughter's developing sense of self. We will also explore how these mothering styles develop and how they affect not only the daughter's self-esteem but her mother's feeling about herself.

Your family is the first place you learn how to trust and form relationships. *Chapter Four* will explore how styles of relating among family members impacts the mother-daughter relationship.

Each of our families functions on a continuum. At one end of this continuum there is an "enmeshed" style of relating; at the other end lies a "disengaged" way of interacting. The members of an enmeshed family are very closely connected, leaving little room for individuality; in a disengaged family, members have little or no emotional contact with one another. Most of our families fall someplace between these two extremes.

As you will read, the ways that enmeshed and disengaged families interact have a negative effect on the mother-daughter relationship. Neither provides the appropriate environment in which a child can develop self-esteem. Both extremes short-circuit a daughter's potential to become a separate person in a healthy manner. They also inhibit a mother's ability to be supportive of her daughter's process of growth. In this chapter, you'll get a better understanding of the nuts and bolts of these opposing styles of relating and their impact on how mothers and daughters relate to each other and to the world outside the family.

We will begin *Chapter Five* by looking at the evolution of three generations of mothers and daughters, and how they are influenced by the culture they live in. By examining a woman's life from a multigenerational perspective, we can better understand how her life today has been affected by the times in which she was raised.

The dramatic changes in women's roles over the past thirty years have had a profound effect on both mothers and daughters, altering their observations and expectations of themselves and one another. A multigenerational perspective of family life will allow you to take a closer look at the evolving nature of this relationship. In addition, by looking at the connections and disconnections between the generations, you can better understand the emotional context in which your mother and grandmother were raised. This understanding can enable you to have a new perspective about your own development as an individual and the life choices you have made. At the same time, by viewing your own family "snapshots"—those mental pictures of our families that all of us hold in our minds—you will have a better sense of the context from which you evolved.

Chapter Six will take a further look at women's roles by

exploring the "rules" that hold these roles firmly in place. The rules a mother learned from her own mother often come into direct conflict with the younger woman's dreams and wishes for herself. Thus, her relationship with her own daughter often becomes the battlefield on which this conflict is played out. Both mother and daughter feel the confusion and tension that can arise from this predicament. Frequently, daughters find themselves ignoring their own needs in order to do what they think their mothers want. In Chapter Six, you will:

- learn to identify the rules set forth by your family concerning love, work, sex, money, appearance, marriage, and parenting
- explore how you feel when you break a rule
- examine which rules your mother broke—and why
- consider which rules influence your decision making
- discover that your mother's dreams and wishes don't have to be yours

Chapter Six will help you distinguish between your needs and your mother's, and identify what keeps those needs from being met. When we obey family rules, we feel like we are in familiar territory. But "familiar" is not always comfortable. We need to understand that these rules are not infallible; rather, they represent behavioral habits kept in place by family traditions. Breaking those rules that do not work for you allows you to create healthier parameters within which to live your life.

Chapter Seven will focus on the concept of separation, a troubling subject for both mothers and daughters. A daughter's struggle to separate from her mother and to metaphorically "leave home" is a crucial part of her growth and development. Yet this process of separation is often riddled with anxiety for both mother and daughter. During her teenage years a daughter begins to see herself not as a dependent child, but as a young adult, with all of adulthood's pleasures and responsibilities before her. For a mother, watching her daughter grow and move away can trigger memories and feelings not only of her own process of separation, but of her lost youth and opportunities.

Separation is a unique process in every mother-daughter relationship. But regardless of the way she goes about the process of separating, every daughter needs ongoing maternal support and acceptance to feel successful in her efforts. Without this support, her sense of inadequacy can fracture the development of a positive self-image. Chapter Seven will help mothers learn that supporting their daughters throughout the process of separation can lead to a closer and more positive relationship for the rest of their lives.

Chapter Eight will deal with the "stumbling blocks" and "immovable objects" that are part of the unhappy, everyday reality of some mothers and daughters. When you are confronted by events that feel insurmountable, your feelings may range from helplessness to apathy, and sometimes even to hatred and murderous rage. Also, no matter how strong your desire to create a different kind of relationship, if childhood abuse (sexual, emotional, or mental), substance abuse, or abandonment have been issues in your life, they cannot simply be talked away. This is true in the following examples:

- a daughter of an alcoholic mother who has to grapple with the reality that her mother has chosen alcohol over her
- a mother whose husband had abused her daughter, and who has to confront the reality of her daughter's rage, not only at her husband but at her
- a daughter whose mother has literally abandoned her in order to be with a new husband
- a mother whose daughter chooses a lifestyle that violates her religious beliefs

When dealing with these and other painful issues—circumstances that they were unable to change—many mothers and daughters have had no choice but to learn to adjust and to cope. Others have had to walk away from their mother or their daughter in order to save themselves. Chapter Eight will help you deal with the painful reality that sometimes the most important kind of mending takes place in an individual and not in a relationship.

In *Chapter Nine,* we will look at learning to accept and reconcile our differences. The need to see one another on common ground is the essence of creating a new kind of relationship. A cornerstone of this book, including Chapter Nine, is the understanding that your past history with your mother or daughter is part of your present-day reality. This allows you to take a look at your past interactions in terms of what has worked and what hasn't.

To create a new kind of mother-daughter relationship, you have to move beyond "finger-pointing" and blaming. To do this, you must replace these kinds of destructive actions with the only behavior that works in a relationship—taking responsibility for yourself.

Learning to let go of the fantasy of a perfect relationship eliminates the feelings of anger and depression that are aroused by unrealistic expectations. As each mother and daughter accepts one another, they can approach their relationship from a reflective, realistic, and healthier perspective. This is the path we will lead you toward in the following pages.

1 The Power and Legacy of the Mother/Daughter Relationship

My mother has expectations of me that I can't meet. I want her to value me like the other people in my life do. I am a different person around my mother because I think that I am disappointing her. I will never be the daughter she wants me to be. I am me, not her, and I want her to understand that.   —Hope, age 28

My daughter and I just can't seem to get along. Every time we are together, our conversations deteriorate into painful battles over nothing and everything. She seems so unhappy and discontented with herself and with her life. She takes all of her unhappiness out on me. I see other mothers with their daughters and they seem happy and close. My daughter makes me feel like a failure.   —Anne, age 52

Anne and Hope—a mother and a daughter—are caught up in the quandary of a relationship that is not working, a relationship that hurts. Each of them is struggling to understand her own painful and confused feelings, and puzzling over her inability to connect authentically with the other. They feel irreparably divided, as if they were standing across from one another on opposite sides of a deep chasm; they don't know how to bridge the gap between them, and they long for help so that they can somehow make it better.

What happened between this mother and daughter that changed the joyful promise that began with the daughter's birth? Where do they go from here? And why is their problem so common among so many women today?

What Do I Do Now?

This is a question that we hear constantly from women seeking our help in dealing with their mother or daughter. Perhaps it's a question you have asked yourself. In our work, we hear people describe many kinds of relationship pain. Sadly, some of the most profound and entrenched pain we see is that between mothers and daughters. We know that every daughter needs a healthy relationship with her mother in order to develop a sense of value and become an independent, involved member of society. At the same time a mother needs a viable and active relationship with her daughter to provide her with a sense that she has done her best—and hopefully succeeded—in managing the formidable task of mothering a daughter. No mother wants to think that she has failed at this important job.

In your own life, if this relationship isn't working, it has the power to leave you feeling frustrated, depressed, and anxious. You might ask, "How can I fix something that feels irreparably broken?"

Our goal in writing this book is to help you understand what is causing the pain in your relationship with your mother or daughter—to help you make sense out of something that feels overwhelming and confusing. From there, we will point you in the direction of concrete steps that you can take to mend your relationship.

Our First Relationship

Why does the mother-daughter relationship have the power to create so much distress between the people involved? For the daughter, this is her first intimate relationship. For the mother, the birth of her daughter arouses memories of her connection with her own mother. As you move through this book, you will see how the power of this "first relationship" impacts women's personal and professional lives—sometimes for the good, but not always for the better.

You would think that the one thing that both mothers and daughters have in common—the fact that they are both daughters—would help to create a positive bond between them. Unfortunately, it doesn't always work that way. The shared experience of being a daughter creates ripples, and sometimes tidal waves, that are felt by each mother and daughter pair throughout their lives.

For instance, a mother may experience feelings of disappointment when her daughter doesn't behave the way she did when she was a child or even like the things that she liked. A daughter may feel let down when her mother doesn't approve of her interests, activities, or choices. She may wonder, "Didn't my mother feel this way when she was my age?"

In this book, we will offer solutions to some of the common stumbling blocks that arise during a lifetime of this relationship. For example, here are some questions and issues that women frequently raise with us, and that we'll address in the following chapters:

- Why does my girlfriend get along fabulously with her mother and I can hardly bear to be in the same room with mine?
- Why does my daughter seem to resent the sacrifices I've made for her?
- Why is it impossible for me to talk to my mother about how I really feel?
- Why does my daughter avoid calling me or visiting me?
- Why don't I trust my mother to be there for me?
- Why isn't my daughter more like me?
- Every time I talk to my mother, why does the discussion always center around her?

- I made the effort to maintain a relationship with *my* mother; why can't my daughter do that with me?
- Why do I feel trapped in a family script that was written before I was born?
- Doesn't she know how much I love her?

The dynamics that underlie these "stumbling blocks" will be discussed in the stories of women you will meet in this book. We think that reading about their struggles to create different kinds of relationships with their mothers or daughters can be helpful to you in your quest to improve your own relationship.

Questions, Questions, and More Questions

Women themselves are not alone in being puzzled by aspects of the mother-daughter relationship. As therapists, in the process of talking with many women about their relationships and their lives in general, we initially found ourselves with more questions than answers. After many hours of discussions with daughters, both in groups and individually, we began asking ourselves the following questions:

- Why are so many bright and seemingly capable women beset by feelings of depression, low self-esteem, hopelessness, and helplessness?
- Why are these women underfunctioning in so many areas of their lives?
- Why are women with so much potential not taking full advantage of their intellect, education, talents, and capabilities?
- Why are they struggling so intensely with their work-related and intimate relationships?

What, we asked ourselves, is wrong with this overall picture?

At the same time, as we talked with groups of mothers, we came up with additional questions, based on their perspective of their relationships with their daughters:

- Why do so many women feel that they have been failures as mothers?
- Why do some mothers fear the process of separation from their daughters?
- Why is listening to what their daughters have to say problematic for some mothers?
- Why do mothers have difficulty expressing their own needs in conversations with their daughters?
- Why do many mothers have problems talking about their relationship with their own mothers?
- How does a woman's relationship with her husband influence her relationship with her daughter?

What's the Common Thread?

We began our attempt to answer these questions by looking at what these mothers and daughters appeared to have in common. The daughters who had come to us for help were, for the most part, well educated, articulate, and attractive. They all had talents and capabilities. However, the majority of them admitted that they felt "stuck" in their attempts to actualize their potential and move forward in their personal or professional lives, or both. And their awareness of lost or unmet opportunities only added to their depression and anxiety.

For example, our client Lindsey told us, *I'm thirty-three years old, but most of the time I feel like I'm fourteen. I don't know how to "do" my life now any better than I did then. I'm always second-guessing myself: Do I need a haircut? Should I go back to school? Is it better to stay in a boring relationship rather than have no relationship at all? It's so weird, but I keep thinking, "I need my mother to tell me what to do. . . . I want her to tell me what to do." Why can't I tell me what to do?*

The mothers we talked with were also bright and articulate. They ranged from housewives to professionals and corporate executives. All of them were frustrated, and many were downright angry. They felt misunderstood by their daughters and shut out of their daughters' lives. Feeling superfluous made them either anxious or depressed, and aroused questions about themselves as mothers: If they had really been "good" mothers, wouldn't their adult daughters welcome their advice and assistance? Why weren't their daughters interested in hearing about the life lessons that they had learned? How had they gone from being the central figure in their daughters' lives to being insignificant?

A tearful and frustrated Melinda, age fifty-three, a professor at a nearby university, told us:

I want my daughter to be healthy and happy. I am concerned and worried about her. Even though she is very bright, I think her impulsiveness and lack of organization are going to cause her problems down the road. I want to help her avoid them.

I realize that we don't listen to each other very well; most of the time we are busy defending ourselves. We need to work on listening to one another. I really have a problem when she questions my values. I am perfectly willing to listen to her point of view and I realize that she doesn't think the way I do. But if she wants me to respect her opinions and her boundaries, then I need for her to respect mine.

Part of the problem is that Lindsey and her mother and Melinda and her daughter are caught up in a relationship dilemma that is not entirely of their making.

The Core of the Problem

In our experience as therapists, the issues that cause people pain and that feel the most insurmountable to them have roots in their families of origin. This is certainly true for the mothers and daughters we have worked with. Each mother-and-daughter pair is part of a family system (see Chapter

Five), and each family system is unique in the way it operates and trains its members to behave in the world (see Chapter Six). The uniqueness of each family system provides us with clues as to what is happening in the lives of both mothers and daughters today.

When we decided to explore more deeply the impact of families on mothers and daughters, we began asking our clients some of the following questions:

- How would you characterize your immediate family relationships? Are they close? Distant? Overinvolved? Indifferent?
- To what degree are you overly concerned with your mother's well-being, opinions, and behavior?
- Were you required to take care of your mother emotionally while you were growing up?
- If you were a "caretaker," what did you have to do to care for your mother?
- Do your mother's unmet needs influence the problems you are experiencing in love and work today?
- How do your own unmet needs impact your daughter?
- How did your mother, if she was not appropriately mothered herself, provide emotional nourishment for you?
- If you were not appropriately mothered, how did this affect the way you mothered your own daughter?
- If you are currently dealing with the loss of a relationship (a spouse, a lover, a close friend), how do you think your experience of this loss is related to your relationship with your mother?

Some of the above questions may strike a responsive chord with you. Throughout this book, we will help you find answers to them. Our goal is to help you look at the impact of your family, and especially your relationship with your mother, on your present life. With the daughters we have worked with, we began this process by asking them to think about another set of questions:

- What do you think is keeping you from actualizing your potential?
- Why do you feel like a failure much of the time?
- What do you think has kept you from forming a successful relationship with a man?
- Why have you engaged in self-defeating activities at work?
- Do you see yourself repeating patterns of behavior that you learned in your family?

As these daughters thought about the questions, many admitted that they often felt inferior, or "less than." Inferior to what? When we asked them, the majority replied that they had an internal standard for what a woman should be—a standard that they compared themselves with, but could never quite achieve. They told us that not only could they not get around the major stumbling blocks in their lives, but in their attempts to overcome them, they seemed to create greater impasses. They all yearned for love, success, and fulfillment. They told us how they wanted to change their lives, but they were afraid of taking risks. The prospect of change was just too scary. This fear of change kept them behaving in the same old familiar, nonproductive ways.

And what about their mothers? These older women had a myriad of responses after hearing the same questions we asked their daughters. Some told us that the questions themselves made them feel defensive, as if we were blaming them for their daughters' failure to be happy or successful. Some felt a strong sense of identification with their daughters' struggle. One mother told us, *Sometimes I think my daughter would like to be me. She borrows my clothes, she wants to live near me, and she resents the fact that I have a better lifestyle than she has. The fact that I have worked very hard to create that lifestyle seems to go right over her head.*

I know this sounds strange, but sometimes I feel that, if she could, she would climb right inside my skin. I know it's a tough world out there, but trying to make herself into me isn't going to help her. It's only going to put her further behind.

These mothers, in fact, also expressed a great deal of sadness. All they wanted, they told us, was for their daughters to feel good about themselves. Instead, they saw their daughters reliving the same problems and patterns that they themselves had struggled with. To compound their distress, many of the mothers felt blamed by their daughters for their lack of success, in both their intimate relationships and at work. No wonder they felt frustrated.

Depression and Anxiety As a Common Denominator

As our experience and research continued, we began to ask ourselves, Is there anything that the mothers and daughters have in common? We found that almost all of the daughters and mothers we talked to, when asked to describe themselves and their feelings, replied that they felt either depressed or anxious. Some felt both.

Since we will be using the terms *anxiety* and *depression* throughout this book to describe some very important moods and feelings, let's pause briefly to define them.

> *Anxiety* is an uncomfortable awareness where a person experiences feelings of apprehension, along with physical sensations (headache, pounding heart, shallow breathing, empty feeling in the pit of the stomach). Very often, there is the urge to "fight or flee" in response to a situation that triggers fear and arouses strong emotions.

Depression, in its milder forms, can be experienced as feelings of worthlessness, sadness, and hopelessness. There may be a loss of interest in activities that previously were a source of pleasure. When it is more severe, it can be accompanied by periodic thoughts of death and/or suicide. Depression is often manifested physically by agitation, sleep disturbances, loss of appetite, low energy, and loss of sexual desire.

In questioning these mothers and daughters further, we often found that their feelings of depression were triggered by what they perceived to be the loss of a significant relationship. For example, daughters experienced the following as significant losses: a breakup with a boyfriend or partner, loss of a job, or a fight with a friend. The mother's losses were similar to those of the daughters, with one important exception: Mothers expressed an additional loss. They felt "out of sync" with their daughters. This feeling was recurring and very powerful—powerful enough to trigger feelings of loss.

As we listened to these women, we asked ourselves: What are they experiencing internally as a result of their losses? Is their pain a direct result of losing their present relationship, or are they reexperiencing a previous emotional injury, with their mother, for example? We also wondered, Why aren't they able to learn from their past losses, and grow from those experiences?

As we listened to our clients' stories, we discovered that their experience of loss also triggered feelings of fear and/or anxiety. They were afraid of failing in future relationships, and this fear was often accompanied by a downward spiral of sadness and depression. When they became anxious, they felt paralyzed and incapable of taking charge of their lives. In fact, many of them admitted that even the thought of making changes in their lives and moving forward caused them enormous anxiety.

For these women, the idea that they might learn from their experiences was inconceivable to them; they simply didn't believe they had the capacity to do anything differently. This sense of being "stuck" left them feeling more nervous and apprehensive. It also made them unable to calm or soothe themselves, and this inability to allay their fears made them even more anxious.

The Meaning of Loss

Many of the women we have spoken with have very specific beliefs about the nature of relationship loss and what it has meant to them. They told us about their expectations. For example, they expressed that if they "gave everything they had," if they "became everything their daughter or mother (or partner/spouse/boss/friend/lover) wanted them to be," they would then have a perfect relationship and that person "would love them or be there for them forever." In reality, by turning their expectations into a blueprint to live by, these women were giving up their own needs in service of someone else and, in the end, still found themselves painfully alone.

In *Women in Therapy*, Harriet Lerner eloquently writes that many "women betray or sacrifice the self in order to preserve relationship harmony." We see women do this on a daily basis: They give away their power, their potential, and their point of view. Whom do they give it to? Not only to their daughters or their mothers, but to anyone and everyone: their husbands, their lovers, their bosses, their family, their friends. In observing this recurring behavior, we asked ourselves, Where did these women learn to do this? How did they learn to give themselves away? And how is the process of giving themselves away related to the mother-daughter relationship?

We think that a troubled relationship between a mother and a daughter, rather than being the heart of the problem of failed relationships and feelings of inadequacy, only represents one facet of the problem. During the course of this book, we will explore with you the major components that make up the dense tapestry of your relationship with your mother or your daughter, and how this relationship relates to your life on a daily basis.

Mother Is Crucial

For both mothers and daughters, the concept of MOTHER is a critical one. Among most women, the picture of MOTHER that they carry in their minds colors much of how they experience themselves and the world they live in. A three-year-old girl, racing past her mother on her way to play, will pat her mother on the arm and say to herself, "My mommy." This verbal communication to herself about who she is in relation to her mother is repeated throughout their history together.

The stories told to us by our clients continue to confirm our belief in the significance of a mother's role in her daughter's progression from child to woman. Mother is not only the cornerstone of the family, she is the daughter's point of reference for how to be a woman, how to function in the context of a relationship, and how to interact with the "outside world."

The way a mother walks, speaks, dresses, relates to her husband, forms friendships, and deals with her problems and dreams creates the paradigm for her daughter's life. Fifty-one year-old Deborah, shared a memory with us. *I remember, as a little girl, loving to look in my mother's drawers— silky nightgowns with satin ribbons, the lace-edged slips she always wore, linen handkerchiefs with her embroidered initials. And always, the scent of Yardley's English Lavender soap that she used to tuck in every drawer. Sometimes, if my hands were clean, I would gently touch the contents of those drawers. It felt wonderful, like I was touching a piece of my mother. You'll probably think this is silly, but I have lavender soap in all of my drawers, and every time I open one, I'm back and connected to my mother.*

We don't think Deborah's actions are a bit silly. A girl's observations of and her interactions with her mother, in all their most minute facets, influence the way she thinks about herself and how she makes choices when she becomes an adult.

In order to form a cohesive picture of our clients' relationships with their mothers, we began by having them take a closer look at their early family histories. Together, we explored their early childhood memories, their elementary-school experiences, their adolescence, and young adulthood. We wanted to know more about their perceptions of their mothers and themselves at these crucial stages of development.

Of course, memories stir up feelings. So we wanted to know just what kinds of feelings were aroused in our clients when they recalled their experiences with their mothers. By taking them back to important stages in their history, we hoped to create an atmosphere where we could explore their frame of mind at each phase.

To illustrate our process of discovery, let's look in-depth at the story of Claire. Her situation is representative of many of the women you will meet throughout this book, and their struggles with the mother-daughter relationship.

"I'm feeling so stuck and I don't know what to do." Claire is curled up in a ball, on the corner of the couch, her head practically on her knees. Her fingers are in her hair, tugging at it. She is crying, silently, and her voice trembles with pain and longing. *"I've felt this way* forever. *I'm getting older and it's not getting any better; I'm* not *getting any better!"* She looks up at us with the eyes of a child—an old child, a wary child, a child who has learned not to trust the grown-ups around her. There is a sense that if we attempt to soothe her, she will push us away. She projects a pervasive sense of wanting something, and it pulls at us.

Claire appears depressed. Her sense of hopelessness fills the room. But what does she really want? How can we help her? To begin with, we know that we need to find out how she arrived at this painful place. We start by investigating her day-to-day interactions with other people, both past and present.

Claire is thirty-eight years old. She is an attractive woman, with curly black hair and huge brown eyes. She is slender—almost too thin—and stylishly dressed. She speaks assertively, but there is an edge of brittleness to her voice. She begins to express an idea, and then loses her train of thought in the middle of a sentence. At this point she looks beseechingly at us as if crying out for help.

Sitting in the room with Claire, we have the feeling that we are talking with a little girl wearing grown-up clothes. There are moments when we have a glimpse of her as an adult woman, but they quickly vanish, and we are left with a very sad, anxious child.

Claire describes herself as depressed. She says she feels directionless and unfulfilled, spending her time watching old movies on television and never leaving the house. In the evening, after she has "wasted" another day, she lectures herself about her inability to "go out and make a life for yourself." This critical voice creates even more feelings of hopelessness and helplessness. She feels trapped and confused by her inability to do something, anything, with her life.

As Claire describes her existence as bare and colorless, we begin to experience her despair in the room with us, pulling at us. We are starting to get a sense of how helpless she feels. We are feeling some of it, too, sitting and listening to her. We know, however, that we need to help her mobilize her resources in order for her to move out of this "stuck" place. And she needs to access the adult that we had caught only a glimpse of.

Born and raised in Los Angeles, Claire had recently returned there from Denver, where she had lived for the past five years. She left Denver after ending what she called a "dead-end" relationship with a married man. She describes the job as a laboratory technician that she had there as another "dead-end" aspect of her life. She says that she wants to find work that makes her feel more "alive." She also desperately wants a family. Her frustration is palpable as she talks about her inability to "take charge of her life."

At this point we begin to muster our resources. We ask Claire to tell us about the people in her life that she feels closest to. Most important, we ask her to tell us about her family.

Claire says that both her immediate and extended families are very close. She quickly adds, however, that this closeness borders on intrusiveness at times. She believes her life is under the constant scrutiny of all her relatives, especially her mother. She feels closest to her older brother, but he, his wife, and three children live in Arizona, and Claire keenly feels the lack of contact and support from him.

Claire has given us the first clue about the genesis of her inertia: She has ambivalent feelings about her "close" family.

It has been Claire's lifelong belief that something inside of her is lacking. Her attempts to find that "missing ingredient" are a part of her struggle, but she senses that it is related to her painful relationship with her mother. She feels that she has never been able to please her mother, yet she is desperate for her mother's approval. While her father, at times, has attempted to build up her self-confidence, it is not enough to offset the messages of criticism and disapproval that Claire gets from her mother.

As Claire begins to tell us about her relationship with her mother, we realize that this is a key part of the dilemma that she lives with.

Claire is painfully aware that she wants a nurturing and supportive relationship with her mother. She admits that part of her feelings of "stuckness" and depression about her life and her future stem from her belief that her mother sees her as deficient.

As we continue to listen to Claire, several questions arise in our minds: How did her unhappy relationship with her mother evolve? And what were some of the turning points that contributed to her current problem? These questions stir our interest in taking a closer look at four defining stages in Claire's life.

Early Childhood

Claire's earliest childhood memories are of trying to get her mother's attention. She was a vibrant little girl who wanted only to make her mother smile, to engage her mother, and to bask in her mother's approval. As she describes these feelings, she looks at us and asks, "Do all little girls do this?"

Claire recalls how persistent she was and how much energy she had spent trying to connect with and please her mother. Her mother, Eleanor, however, was, for the most part, unresponsive to her. Claire remembers being left with the painful feeling that she was not cared for or loved.

As Claire describes her frustrated attempts to connect emotionally with her mother, we realize that she is telling us something important—that her unproductive attempts to engage her mother were the genesis of her powerful belief that "I can't do anything and that there is no point in trying." Her inability to impact her mother has left her feeling impotent and invisible.

The Elementary-School Years

Claire's sense of not being cared for or loved continued to be a part of her elementary-school experience. She went from being an energetic and tenacious little girl, to feeling insecure and unsure of herself in her attempts to relate to her classmates. While she had friends, she tells us that she never had a best friend, and this felt like a significant loss.

Claire's insecure self-image led to academic problems. She

*was considered bright and capable not only by her teachers,
but she herself knew that she was smart. But her tenacity
and drive to achieve had vanished. She thinks that her inability to perform was grounded in her belief that, no matter
what she did, in either school or outside activities, it wouldn't
be enough to win her mother's love and attention.*

From our vantage point, Claire's budding sense of self-
worth had been crushed by the time she was eight or nine.
More important, we have the feeling that we are sitting in
the room with a starving child, a child longing for love, affection, and attention. Her sense of deprivation affects us
profoundly. Because we are moved by her vulnerability,
however, we have to be careful not to act too protectively
toward her. Our job is to help her feel more sure of herself,
not to reinforce her sense of incompetence.

Adolescence

*For Claire, the growing pains of adolescence were com-
pounded by her profound sense that there was something
wrong with her. She blamed herself for her inability to connect with her mother. As the gap between the two of them
widened, her sense of failure deepened.*

*Claire recalls that she had truly believed that the reason
she didn't do well in school was because she was "lazy." Her
"laziness," however, was a reaction to the sense of hopelessness she felt about her inability to connect with her mother.
Claire states, "I realize now that I must have been depressed
when I was in high school." This was the point in time when
she developed her tendency to just "slide by," an attitude
that has followed her into adulthood.*

As we continue to listen to Claire's sad narrative, it is difficult not to say to ourselves: Why didn't her mother pay
attention to her daughter? Couldn't she see how unhappy
and depressed she was? We have learned, however, that to
indulge in this kind of blaming is a trap for any listener. We

know that every story has more than one side and more than one point of view. So as our sessions with Claire continue, we keep our concern for her balanced by our objectivity.

Young Adulthood

According to Claire, nothing seemed to flow easily for her. What might be considered normal adolescent rites of passage—selecting a college, leaving home, going to an out-of-state school—became sources of enormous self-doubt and anxiety. She says that she sought advice and opinions from everyone because she did not trust herself. When she finally made a decision about college, she second-guessed herself, forever doubting her ability to make the right choice.

Everything Claire did was an occasion for self-doubt. At school, at work, and in relationships with men, she was filled with uncertainty and a sense of failure. She knew she was intelligent. She knew she was attractive to men but had no idea how to create or maintain a relationship beyond the initial attraction. Above all, Claire was haunted by the feeling that she was letting her mother down. Mother's standards, like the brass ring on a merry-go-round, always seemed out of reach.

Claire sadly concedes that she feels like Cinderella, waiting for her life to start. She looks up at us and says: "I'm still waiting."

Claire's story is a paradox. On the one hand, she wants to move forward, to begin to feel that she is in command of her own life, and not under the control of a self-defeating internal agenda. On the other hand, there is a hunger for validation, permission, and acknowledgment from her mother.

We want to reemphasize that, even as we learned more about Claire, we could not begin to fully comprehend her past and her present quandaries without understanding something about her mother, Eleanor. We needed to know about Eleanor in order to analyze the nature of their relationship and its impact on Claire's current life situation. The way Eleanor feels about herself and her own life could provide valuable clues to understanding the way she has mothered Claire. This is also information that they both need in order to begin the process of really looking at and experiencing one another in a different way and creating a positive and more fulfilling connection.

Eleanor's Story

I'm not sure where to begin. I know you want me to talk about my relationship with Claire, but I think it's important to tell you first about my mother.

Claire's mother, Eleanor, is nervous. Talking to a therapist is a new experience for her, and she is concerned about whether we are going to be judgmental. We assure her that we are delighted that she wants to talk about her relationship with her own mother. We know that the seeds of Eleanor's mothering of Claire were planted in her relationship with her mother. So we encourage Eleanor to continue.

I can only describe my relationship with my mother as distant. She was always there on the periphery, but never really involved with me. When she died two years ago, I never shed a tear. What made me feel worse was that I didn't feel any grief.

My father was a loudmouth and a bully. He verbally abused everyone in the family, but mostly me. My mother never lifted a finger to help me. She never tried to stop him. As a little girl, I couldn't understand how my mother could abandon me like that. All my childhood memories are full of feelings of loneliness and pain.

We find this sad piece of Eleanor's history very enlightening. It's hard to give what you have never had.

I used to imagine what it would be like to have a warm

and loving relationship with my mother. When Claire was born, I was determined to be a good mother, the kind of mother I always wanted to have. My problem was that I couldn't seem to get close to her. She seemed to want so much from me. I felt overwhelmed by her needs most of the time. I wondered to myself, "Is this how my mother felt about me?" I took good care of Claire physically, but I guess I just didn't know how to love her in the right way.

Claire and Eleanor are struggling with issues that had their genesis long before Claire was born. Eleanor never had the opportunity to deal with her disappointment, her anger, her sense of loss before she herself became a mother. So much of her unfinished business with her own mother came into play in her attempts to parent Claire.

It is important to remember that Eleanor wanted to be a good mother. However, she intuitively knew there were gaps in the way she was mothered. Unfortunately, Claire, who was impacted by these gaps, blamed herself. There was no way she could know how the mother-daughter relationship between her mother and her grandmother would affect her life.

By understanding the importance of these issues to Claire's problems, you now have a starting place to begin your own quest for information and understanding of your mother-daughter relationship.

Hearing Mother's Voice

Is there a woman alive who has not, at one time or another, felt influenced by the voice of her mother that she hears in her head? We find ourselves continually amazed by the authority of the "motherly voice" residing within grown women. Usually heard as an internal dialogue between herself and her mother, a daughter can experience her mother's voice as soothing, comforting, and emotionally grounding. At other times, however, it can agitate, criticize, demean, or paralyze.

This is an important phenomenon to familiarize yourself with early in this book. After all, the internalized voice of your own mother can sustain or devastate you as an adult. This voice is resilient and resistant to change. As a daughter, you may hear your mother's words whispering in your ear at all the wrong times. Frustratingly, you may also discover that the voice has disappeared at a time when you need to hear it most. Where does this voice come from? And how does it affect your life?

Young children, because of their limited view of the world, often believe that they are the source of all the feelings that they sense coming from their mothers. And so their logic may sound something like this: "If Mommy is happy, then I must be good. . . . If Mommy is sad, then I must have done something wrong." When a mother, by her facial expressions, body language, or tone of voice, reinforces these beliefs, the child begins to create an internal picture of herself based on mother's responses to her.

As each little girl experiences her mother's style of mothering, she is going to have a particular kind of response to the messages she receives from her mother. The correlation between the way a mother sends a message and the way her daughter receives it is based on each mother's individual style. We will elaborate on how this process works in Chapter Three.

The wish to please her mother is part of every young girl's emotional makeup. The image that the daughter sees reflected in mother's eyes, or that she hears in her mother's tone of voice, is the genesis of the self-image she carries with her throughout life.

To further complicate matters, we have noticed that our clients' desire to please mother often comes into direct conflict with their need to satisfy themselves. When a daughter receives a message from her mother, through a look or tone of voice, that all is not well because *mother is not happy with her,* she experiences this upsetting information on both a visceral and emotional level. Naturally, this negative impression conflicts with her need to feel good about herself. Since a mother's messages are persuasive and directly influence her daughter's self-esteem, fears, and hopes, the negative messages have the potential to override any existing positive feelings the daughter has about herself.

Thus, a daughter's sense of well-being can be seriously compromised when her mother repeatedly signals or expresses criticism, disinterest, or ridicule. This process is often subtle yet powerful, and it becomes the foundation for the punitive "mother's voice" that a daughter hears in her head. At the same time it, unfortunately, can become part of the way a daughter thinks about and experiences herself in the world.

Here are three points that are crucial for every woman's healthy emotional development. And since every mother is also a daughter, these points are going to be vitally relevant not only to the way a mother feels about herself, but also to the way she mothers her daughter. They are important issues that will arise repeatedly in this book:

- In order to feel worthwhile, a daughter needs to feel accepted and valued by her mother.
- A daughter's emotional response to her mother's behavior toward her will be experienced as both the inner "mother's voice" she hears, and her own internalized self-image.
- If the messages a daughter receives from her mother are experienced as critical and/or judgmental, they will have the long-term effect of eroding a daughter's sense of well-being.

The following vignette about our client Betsy and her mother illustrates these points well. Betsy, who is forty-one years old, self-consciously shared a childhood memory with us. She admitted that, as an adult, she thinks of herself as overweight and unattractive, although in reality, she is a slender, good-looking woman. She remembered, however, an interaction that took place between herself and her mother when she was nine years old. Her mother, who carefully monitored Betsy's food and weight, walked into Betsy's room one day when she was changing to go to the beach. She looked at Betsy in her bathing suit and said, "Dear heavens, you look just like my friend Eve—and Eve is pregnant!"

Betsy still felt the pain of her nine-year-old self as she related this story. *I know, because I have looked at old pictures of myself, that I wasn't particularly overweight as a child. I have asked myself, over and over, what did my mother see when she looked at me? Maybe I was a little chubby, but certainly nothing out of the ordinary. The shame of that moment is with me still. I had disappointed my mother in a way that I couldn't fully grasp, and my visceral response to my mother's disapproval comes up for me every time I look in a mirror.*

Fortunately, we were able to talk to Betsy's eighty-two year-old mother, Elaine, to gain her perspective. Elaine is lively and articulate. Looking at her, you can see the beautiful woman she once was. She wasn't quite sure about this "therapy stuff," but she agreed to talk to us "for Betsy's sake."

Elaine told us that she grew up in a household where the only quality for which a woman was valued was physical attractiveness. Never mind that Elaine, an only daughter, was highly intelligent, with a quick wit and a spirited personality. She learned early on from her parents, and especially from her mother, that her ticket to success (i.e., marriage) was her "good looks." Everything else was secondary.

Elaine grew up with tremendous fear, believing that the only quality she had that anyone admired was her looks. What would happen to her if and when she lost them? Would she find herself alone and unloved? The idea was unthinkable.

Elaine told us that when Betsy was born, she was terrified that her daughter would not be pretty. She said, "Betsy's 'baby fat' horrified me. What would I do if Betsy became grossly overweight? I was so worried no one would want her or love her." Elaine's mother (Betsy's grandmother) also voiced concern about Betsy's weight, which made Elaine feel guilty and ashamed. She felt as if she were a bad mother.

The intergenerational nature of Betsy's story is not unusual. Values are handed down from mother to daughter, whether they are applicable to a daughter's present life circumstances or not. As you continue to read, you will see how we zero in on various subtle (and not so subtle) ways the behavior of mothers and grandmothers affects the lives, feelings, and behavior of their daughters today.

The Threads Leading Back to Mother

The majority of women who come to us for help are very clear about *what* is not working in their lives. However, when we ask them *why* they think they're having problems in their professional lives or personal relationships, most don't have a definitive answer.

In fact, we found that this kind of question sometimes created more confusion than clarity. As we began to discuss family histories with different groups of women, they told us about incidents that, to us, appeared to be "red flags"—examples of behavior that were directly related to their relationships with their mothers. Yet, when we pointed out these incidents to them, most expressed surprise. They had never thought about these particular behaviors as problematic, let alone hazardous to their emotional health.

For example, one woman we worked with had never questioned her pattern of repeatedly dating men who were emotionally unavailable to her, or whom she had to take care of. We suggested that there might be a connection between her poor choices in partners and her relationship with her emotionally unavailable mother, whom she had cared for since childhood. She was surprised by the suggestion that there might be a thread leading back to mother in what appeared to be a random selection of unsuccessful relationships with men.

The following chart may help you make better sense of this phenomenon. It lists, on the left, some behaviors and feelings women have reported to us. Then, on the right, you will find our theories about the connections to their relationships with their mothers.

DAUGHTER'S PROBLEMATIC BEHAVIORS	MOTHER-DAUGHTER ISSUES
Unconsciously choosing unavailable men	Mother's inability to show daughter unconditional love
Inability to commit to a love relationship	Mother's over-controlling or overprotective behavior
Sabotaging career goals	Mother's constant lack of approval of daughter's choices and behavior
Inability to be assertive	Mother's poor self-image
Inability to trust her own instincts	Mother telling daughter how to feel and what to believe
Inability to deal with volatile emotions	Mother's anxiety about expression of feelings
Difficulty in maintaining a sexual relationship	Mother's unresolved issues with her own sexuality

Keep in mind that the theories we have listed are not absolutes—they do not fit for all daughters and all mothers. They are simply examples of links we have found between the unproductive behavior of some daughters and the unresolved emotional issues of their mothers.

We believe there are certain givens in the relationship

between mothers and daughters. From the way an infant daughter first attaches to her mother (see Chapter Two), to the impact of her mother's particular "mothering style" (see Chapter Three), certain elements influence how each individual woman:

- views the world
- perceives her role and the role of women in our culture
- filters information about herself and her place in society
- forms connections with other people

We also think it is important to look at how mothers and daughters are affected by the processes that operate inside the family (see Chapter Four) and by the "family rules," both explicit and unspoken, that are passed down through the generations from mother to daughter (see Chapter Six). A daughter's efforts to become an individual separate from her mother can create enormous anxiety in both herself and her mother. Very often we see this struggle manifest itself as a daughter's "fear of success" (see Chapter Seven).

We know that sometimes a bone that has been broken is even stronger after it has healed. Since this is a book about learning to mend, our goal is to help you and your mother and/or daughter heal your broken relationship and feel stronger in the process. An integral part of this task will be learning to view both yourselves and each other with greater objectivity than you have in the past. Take the time to use your imagination and "walk around in the shoes" of your mother or your daughter. This easy introspective exercise can lead to a deeper understanding that can reap rewards for both of you.

Beginning with the next chapter, you will find sections of what we call "Mending Moves." These "moves" are questions and exercises that have been helpful and illuminating for our clients. We think they can be useful for you, too. The number of Mending Moves you use are limited only by your energy and imagination. Start with the ones we have given you, and then jump in and create your own.

Your ultimate reward will be a healthier and stronger relationship between you and your daughter and/or mother.

2 *A Girl's First Love—*
Her Mother

The first thing in my life that I remember is standing
in my crib and crying for my mother. There are really
no words that I can use to describe what I was feeling.
Whenever that picture comes to mind, however, I start
to feel frightened and then that fear turns into rage. I
was only a baby. How could she have left me alone?
Where was she? Even as an adult, I get those panicky
feelings when I have to be alone for a period of time.

—Lizabeth, age 42

I hated going back to work when Lizabeth was just a
baby. She was so sweet and vulnerable, it just about
killed me to leave her. I had to go, though. We needed
the money. I felt so guilty. I wanted to be with her
and I knew she needed me. I just didn't have a choice.

—Edith, age 67

People have asked us what we think is the most important
component of the mother-daughter relationship. In fact,
many crucial elements combine to form the essence of this
very special relationship. These elements are created by
events that take place over the course of the lives of both
mother and daughter. We firmly believe, however, that the
first important interplay to take place between mothers and
daughters is the process of attachment.

What do we mean when we speak about attachment? The

dictionary defines attachment as "a feeling that binds one to a person; devotion; regard." But how does this feeling develop? Are you born with it? Do mothers and babies automatically bond with one another, or is attachment part of a process that evolves over time?

If you ask twenty-five new mothers to describe their experience of "attaching" to their new babies, you will probably get twenty-five different answers. One might say, "I had a sense of instant connection as soon as I held her." But another might recall, "I was scared to death. I felt helpless and I didn't know what I was supposed to do."

Dr. John Bowlby, a British psychiatrist and the pioneer of attachment theory, wrote that no experiences "have more far-reaching effects on personality development than . . . a child's experiences within his family." The initial bonding experience with our mother is the first place where we begin to create a sense of who we are, especially in relationship to other people.

According to Bowlby, our very first relationship, the one with mother, has the power to create expectations about all of our subsequent relationships. Later in life we may experience our lover/partner as trustworthy or manipulative, our boss as demanding or assertive, or our friends as helpful or intrusive. What is really at work here is the influence of our first attachment relationship. Our significant early perceptions affect the way we experience our world for the rest of our lives.

For example, six-year-old Nancy comes into a roomful of adults. She has a big smile on her face and soon begins talking to anyone and everyone. We can make an assumption, based on her outgoing behavior, that Nancy *expects* to be welcomed and admired. Where did Nancy "learn" that she was an acceptable person and that she was valued by the adults in her life? It started with her initial relationship—a secure sense of attachment with her mother.

On the other hand, let's look at twenty-one-year-old Judy,

who is going for her first job interview. She was a good student in college and knows that she is a hard worker. But she feels panicky. What if she can't talk coherently? What if the interviewer doesn't like her? What if she just doesn't measure up?

During their meeting, Judy has difficulty making eye contact with the interviewer. Although she desperately wants to be liked, she appears withdrawn and almost aloof. What the interviewer is seeing is Judy's habitual way of behaving when she meets people for the first time. Judy finds it almost impossible to believe that others will find her likable.

What happened in Judy's life to make her feel so insecure around others? We know that Judy's mother had become severely depressed a few weeks after Judy was born, and was unable to do anything except take care of Judy's most basic physical needs. As a result, Judy's important emotional needs were only sporadically met until her mother recovered. For many years thereafter these early experiences severely impaired her ability to trust in other people and in herself.

So what Bowlby is saying is that, as you go through life, interacting with others, choosing friends and lovers and mates, your initial attachment to mother influences the way you connect to every other important person in your life. As the stories of Nancy and Judy illustrate, your early attachment experiences can strongly alter your perceptions of yourself and your relationships with others.

Here are some of the behaviors and historical elements that are the hallmark of a troubled attachment relationship.

HOW CAN YOU TELL IF YOU HAVE ISSUES WITH ATTACHMENT?

- difficulty trusting and connecting with other people
- tendency to act impulsively
- inability to form long-term relationships
- tendency to be either clingy and/or aggressive
- inability to be empathic with other people
- tendency to be easily distracted

- problems with authority figures
- a mother who was depressed or emotionally unavailable
- separated from mother at an early age

Many of these traits, when looked at separately, can be indicative of problems other than an incomplete attachment relationship. Taken together, however, they provide clues to a puzzle that may have been in place since infancy.

Just Mommy and Me

Ideally, the first few months of an infant's life are a blissful cocoon for both mother and baby. Thoughts of mothers and their newborns often conjure up feelings of warmth, safety, closeness, and caring. Just watch a mother and baby gaze at one another while the infant is nursing, and you'll see where the attachment process begins. As the satisfied baby drops off to sleep in her mother's arms, she is feeling a special sense of security and contentment, created in that moment. The ideal is not necessarily perfect harmony between mother and child, but rather a sense of trust that is activated at the very beginning of their relationship.

Just how crucial is this drive toward attachment? In fact, we *must* engage with other people in order to survive. Beginning with our mothers, this need must be met, and is as important as our need for air and water.

Naturally, a baby's first connection with her mother is a physical one. John Bowlby, when formulating his theory on the nature of attachment, wrote how the newborn's very survival is dependent on the physical closeness between mother and baby. This is a connection that must be made if this helpless little being is to grow and thrive. The vital acts of nursing, feeding, and caretaking of the infant are triggered by the genetic and hormonal components that are present in both mother and her newborn. These behaviors, behaviors that most people would call natural, serve evolutionary goals, allowing us to survive as a species.

Fortunately, all babies are innately "wired" to attach. Their "attachment" behaviors are part of their biological makeup. Just watch a new baby in action. She naturally attempts to make eye contact with mother; she snuggles closer to her mother's body. Her mother, in turn, gazes back at her infant. She adjusts her body to cuddle her baby, who is moving closer on her own. By both initiating and responding to her baby's cues and actions, mother reinforces and encourages her baby's biologically motivated moves to attach. These interactions create a climate of safety and security for the baby—and are the beginning of a trusting relationship.

Experts on the subject of attachment underscore the concept that a secure and trusting connection to mother is an absolute necessity for the development of a physically and emotionally healthy individual. And, as we have said, the ramifications of the attachment process with your mother are fundamental to the way you make friends and form relationships for the rest of your life. Studies have shown that, at a very early age, the way a child interacts, or attaches, with her mother has a powerful impact on her ability to develop "people skills" in later life.

By the way, our emphasis here on mother-child attachment is not meant to downgrade the important role of fathers in a child's development. But what we are discussing here is the importance of the attachment process, and during these essential developmental periods, mothers do play a more significant role.

The Need for Attachment: Do We Ever Outgrow It?

What happens if your own critical initial attachment was not secure or, even worse, didn't take place at all? How did this affect you as a growing child and as the woman you have become? And what role does attachment play in the attempts of both you and your mother to create a better relationship?

If, as a baby, your attempts to attach were ineffective, you formed a lingering internal picture of the world based on a sense of insecurity. Judy, for example, whose attachment process was disrupted by her mother's depression, feels unlovable most of the time. Her belief that people won't like her or want to get to know her affects her attempts to form close, personal relationships with both women and men. In the few instances where someone has persevered and tried to get close to her, Judy hasn't trusted that they would stay. She does not believe that she has what it takes to sustain a relationship. This skewed internal picture of herself, based on her early attachment experience, has influenced how she will approach relationships throughout her life.

The need to attach is an integral part of our humanness. Even in circumstances like Judy's, the longing for a close bond with someone we love—our "attachment object," if you will—does not go away, no matter how many years have passed since we left childhood and entered the world of adults. So while Judy tells herself that she doesn't believe that she will ever have an intimate, loving relationship, a part of her is consumed with yearning for what she believes herself incapable of having.

The primary attachment to our mother also influences the sense of emotional well-being and safety that we carry into adulthood. If that attachment was fragile or nonexistent, our separation from mother—and later in life, our separation from any person we love—is going to trigger feelings of stress and anxiety.

Imagine a heartbroken toddler, sobbing after being left with a baby-sitter, or a woman whose husband has left her after thirty years of marriage. Entirely different situations? Not at all. Both of these sad and frightened individuals are suffering from grief—the grief of separation. They strongly feel the loss of someone they love, an "attachment" figure. And the way they deal with their loss is directly related to the quality of the early attachment process that took place between themselves and their mothers.

Think back to the beginning of this chapter and the quotes from Lizabeth and from her mother, Edith. Lizabeth talks about her "panicky feelings when I have to be alone for a period of time." In this statement, she clearly articulates an early, poignant memory about what it felt like to be left by her mother. She recalled this memory while describing to us the circumstances that brought her into therapy—the recent breakup of her relationship with her boyfriend.

As Lizabeth continued to describe the feelings of sadness and despair caused by the loss of this relationship, she gradually realized that these were not new sensations that she was experiencing. She was perceiving echoes of emotions that had their roots in the sense of loss she felt as a child when her mother had to leave her. What began, for Lizabeth, as an insecure attachment with her mother, has evolved into a perception that the world is not a safe place and that she will, ultimately, be left alone.

To understand this situation in the light of the mother-daughter relationship, let's take another look at the words of Edith, Lizabeth's mother. "It just about killed me to leave her," she said. In this instance, we have a mother who did not want to be separate from her daughter, a mother who felt the pain of separation as keenly as her daughter did. The ramifications of this rupture on their present-day relationship have been profound.

Lizabeth, for example, expresses her resentment over her old unmet needs for nurturing and attention by consistently reacting angrily to her mother. This behavior, ironically, keeps her from having the close, warm relationship she craves. Edith, still driven by feelings of guilt and the fear that she has been a bad mother, reacts to Lizabeth's angry outbursts in two ways. First, she responds with silence and what on the surface looks like stoic calm. When that gets no response, she launches a barrage of intrusive commentary about how Lizabeth should be leading her life.

This mother and daughter have both suffered a loss. For Lizabeth, her loss is experienced as a sense of something missing, something just out of reach. She is longing for something but she can't quite articulate what it is—a yearning for closeness with her mother. As for Edith, her feeling of loss is imbued with guilt—guilt that she was not able to measure up to her own internal standards about how a "good mother" ought to be.

Unhappily, their respective feelings of loss color the way they relate to one another today. They both know that they are stuck in a circular, nonproductive way of relating to one another. Their angry words only serve to make both of them feel more isolated and misunderstood. Each is left with the sense that their relationship is cast in stone and there is no way to change it. When we discuss the process of reconciliation later in this book, however, we will see how Lizabeth and Edith can create a new kind of relationship

Is There More Than One Way to Attach?

In a word, yes. Researcher Mary Ainsworth used what she called the "strange situation," a managed series of separations between babies and their mothers, to study the attachments babies form with their mothers. During the first part of her observations, the babies were separated from their mothers and left with a stranger, one of Ainsworth's staff. After a period of time the babies and mothers were reunited. Most of the babies displayed distress when they were first separated from their mothers. Then, when their mothers returned, many of the infants actively sought to hold on to them. They cooed, they clung. They did whatever was necessary to keep their mothers from leaving again.

Even so, that wasn't the only reaction of the infants. While observing the responses of the babies to the leave-taking and then to the return of their mothers, Ainsworth noticed that the behavior of the children fell into three distinct types:

- One group of infants showed signs of being securely attached to mother. These babies were openly upset when mother left, and they actively sought to make contact with her when she returned. Then, a short time after being reunited, the babies were able to move their attention away from mother and play separately again.
- The second group seemed to avoid mother when she returned. They had not appeared particularly distressed when she left, and they made little or no effort to connect with her actively when she returned.
- The third group of children appeared more anxious and ambivalent when their mothers came back. They seemed to want contact with mother, and yet they appeared to resist connecting with her.

What would account for such differences in the responses of seemingly healthy, normal babies to the same situation? Ainsworth and her colleagues noticed that securely attached babies had mothers who were much more "in tune" with and responsive to the needs of their children. These mothers were open and available to the signals of their babies, and the babies responded in kind.

By contrast, the behavior of the mothers of the avoidant babies was much less accepting and more intrusive than that of the first group of mothers. These mothers did not seem to be emotionally available to meet their children's needs. In fact, they appeared to have an agenda based on their own needs and not those of their youngsters. As a result, their children developed a way of relating to their mothers by avoiding them.

The third group of anxious and ambivalent babies had mothers who were highly inconsistent in their responses to their children. Sometimes they were attentive to their children's needs; other times they appeared to be oblivious of them.

So how does the information gleaned from this study and other research on attachment affect the mother-daughter relationship? Here is a summary of what we know:

- Babies make efforts to attach.
- The babies in Ainsworth's study were profoundly impacted by their mother's style of interacting with them.
- Each style of relating had been in place long before the researchers made their observations.
- Each baby's behavior when her mother left the room and when she returned was a microcosm of the way that the mother and child interacted on a daily basis.

To help you further understand the relevance of this study to the dynamics of the mother-daughter relationship, here are three stories, as well as points or lessons that can be drawn from the vignettes:

Maddy, age fourteen months, is playing with her mother in the yard of her mother's friend. Maddy's mother has to go into the house to make a phone call and leaves Maddy to continue her game with the friend. Maddy looks distressed. She looks beseechingly at her mother's friend, points in the direction that her mother has gone and says "Er?" (Maddy's way of asking, "Where did she go?"). Her mother's friend reassures her, "Mommy will be right back." She then asks Maddy if she would like to blow some bubbles. Maddy breaks out in a big smile and reaches for the container of bubble liquid. When her mother returns, she runs and hugs her leg and then goes back to blowing bubbles.

The lesson:

- A mother who is "in tune" with her child is a mother who has laid the groundwork for future trusting relationships. Even babies have expectations. The expectation that mother will return is learned from the baby's previous experience with her mother. The momentary sadness felt by the baby when her mother leaves is eased by an internalized sense of trust that she will return.

Cindy, seventeen months old, is sitting quietly at a table, coloring. Her mother looks over at her paper, hands her a blue crayon, and says, "The sky is blue. Color it blue." Cindy starts to use the blue crayon, but then proceeds to drop it on the floor. She gets up from her table and goes across the room to play with her dolls. Her mother says, "Don't you want to finish your picture for Mommy?" Cindy glances at her and then resumes playing with the dolls.

The lesson:

- If a child feels that her mother's needs take precedence over hers, this child will be resistant to her mother's agenda. She will, therefore, develop behaviors that may appear to rebuff her mother. This response is likely to express itself throughout the daughter's life.

Hannah, age nineteen months, and her mother are at the birthday party of a neighborhood child. Hannah is holding on to her mother's skirt, sucking her thumb, and watching the other children. She makes no move to join them. Hannah's mother seems almost unaware of Hannah's clinging, limpetlike, to her dress. She moves around the room, talking with the other mothers, ignoring Hannah. One of the mothers makes a comment to Hannah and suddenly her mother swoops her up in a huge bear hug, startling the child. Hannah starts to hug her mother back, and just as suddenly her mother puts her down and resumes her conversation with the other mothers. Hannah looks unsettled and confused. Her thumb goes back in her mouth and she, once again, clutches her mother's skirt.

The lesson:

- A mother whose interactions with her child are sporadic—sometimes attentive and sometimes not—is going to have a youngster who is anxious and ambivalent about interacting with her and other people. The lack of reliable responses from her mother leads the child to develop a sense of insecurity.

Understanding Why Certain Things Affect Us

To explore further the lasting influence of the mother-daughter relationship, let's look at an incident from the life of our client Tina. Her story is an example of how a woman's early attachment experiences have the power to affect her interactions with others later in life.

Tina's mother, Wendy, was very young—nineteen years old—when she had Tina. Wendy was a sophomore in college and dropped out of school when she became pregnant. Tina's father was also a student, and even though he and Wendy married, they were emotionally still college kids. Neither one of them was ready for the rigors of marriage or parenting.

After Tina was born, Wendy treated her more like a plaything than a child. She would take the baby to her sorority house, where her girlfriends would play with Tina as if she were a toy, cuddling her and passing her from person to person. When Tina became overstimulated and fussy, Wendy would then drop her off at her mother's house. Tina's grandmother would soothe the baby and take care of her for a while, and then bring her home to Wendy.

This pattern of behavior continued until Tina was two and her father graduated from college. He had a job opportunity in another city and they moved away from their hometown. Wendy became very depressed. She missed her mother and her friends. Most important, she was overwhelmed with the responsibility of taking care of Tina without her mother's support.

Now, many years later, how has Tina's early upbringing affected her as an adult? Since childhood, Tina has had tremendous difficulties trusting other women. She has friends and appears to lead a normal social life—but on the inside, she feels wary. She is always waiting for someone to "drop" her. She never allows herself to get very close to other people. Intimate relationships feel threatening and beyond her reach. She feels as though she is constantly guarding herself against being hurt or rejected.

Our physical and emotional dependence on our mothers begins with our first breath. But Tina's tenuous relationship with her very young and unprepared mother felt precarious to her from the beginning. No wonder the ramifications of this type of scenario extend far beyond childhood.

For a child's emotional well-being, she must be able to have and maintain a secure attachment with her mother. She needs to feel a sense of security in order to move forward with the vital developmental task of creating new attachments or relationships. If her attachment to mother feels precarious, the child is going to feel stressed and vulnerable. Even the smallest uncertainty in the nature of her emotional attachment to her mother will profoundly affect her sense of well-being.

The Source of Childlike Behavior

As we have suggested, lingering feelings of vulnerability from childhood often manifest themselves in stressful situations in a woman's adult relationships. In tension-filled moments the ghost of precarious attachment can come back to haunt us. It is at these times that we see behavior that we often label "childlike."

For example, Carla, age thirty-eight, told us about a recent incident in which she and her husband were discussing where they wanted to take their upcoming vacation. Carla had her heart set on going to a resort in Hawaii. Her husband of five years wanted to do something more action-oriented, like backpacking in the Colorado Rockies. When he suggested his plan, Carla immediately began to feel afraid and insecure. She was flooded by thoughts that he didn't really love her and, therefore, didn't want to spend time with her at a romantic place.

Instead of attempting to understand her own feelings, or to determine whether she was correct in assessing the reasons for her husband's vacation choice, she began to pout. She went into the kitchen and started banging the doors of the cabinets and slamming drawers. In essence, she had a tantrum. Later, as she reported her behavior to us, she sheepishly admitted that she had behaved exactly as she had as a child when she thought her mother wasn't listening to her. "Why couldn't I just sit down and talk to him calmly about what I was feeling?" she asked sadly. "What am I afraid of?"

We asked her for some information about her early history, and learned that her mother had had various illnesses, some going back to before her pregnancy with Carla. When Carla was a toddler, her mother spent a lot of time in her room, behind a closed door, sleeping. Her mother had also had several long hospital stays. These interruptions in her relationship with her mother left Carla feeling sad and lonely. This is the genesis of her feelings of being abandoned and unloved. The residual effect has stayed with her and is influencing the way she relates to her husband today.

Carla's story is an example of how the patterns formed during an early inadequate maternal relationship are replayed over a lifetime. Carla's deepest fears, that her husband will leave her, that he doesn't want to spend time with her, and that he really doesn't listen to her, all have their roots in her first love relationship—the one with her mother.

Carla's perception of the potential loss of her "attachment" relationship with her husband triggered a primitive sense of fear. When he made a vacation choice that was different from hers, her sense of security was rocked and she once again felt powerful feelings of abandonment. But as she looked back with us at the dynamics of her early relationship with her mother, Carla began to understand why she consistently felt "misunderstood" by her husband, and why it was so difficult for her to trust him.

Why Is It So Hard for Me to Trust?

If you can identify with much of what we've written here, you're not alone. After all, *everyone* has had an experience of some degree of attachment. This process of attachment exists on a continuum that ranges from nearly nonexistent to secure. Between those two extremes there is an enormous variety of experience. Whether you believe your attachment experience to be at either end of the continuum or somewhere in between, it is the *quality* of that attachment that makes the difference between having grown up believing that the world is a safe place, and fearing connections with others.

We all know that when we suffer a loss, we experience it on many levels. The sense that we have been deprived of something, that something has been taken away, strikes us at a rudimentary level of our being, and we grieve. This grief may take many forms, and one of them is the inability to trust.

To better understand trust, let's go back to Ainsworth's "strange situation" study, in which babies had such varied responses to their mothers' leave-takings and returns. Based on her findings, we can make the assumption that the babies who demonstrated a secure attachment with their mothers had internalized the beginnings of a trusting relationship. The availability of a compassionate, reliable, and empathic parent in those crucial early months of development provided the foundation for the capacity to trust.

We can also assume that this process stays in place and is

built upon as the child grows into adulthood. Securely attached babies can move out into the world and form relationships, first as children and then adults, based on an inner feeling that "I'm okay." These children grow up believing that relationships are part of what they need and want in their lives. They feel comfortable reaching out to others. It feels safe for them to get close.

Your own ability to trust is dependent on your sense of "okayness," which allows you to form secure relationships with others. But what happens when, as with the other two groups of babies in the strange-situation study, attachment is not so securely in place? In the following vignette, a thirty-four-year-old woman named Louise reveals the impact of a problematic attachment process on her ability to form intimate, trusting relationships.

My dad was killed in an automobile accident two weeks before I was born. My mother was overwhelmed with grief, so I was told later. When I was born, she felt incapable of taking care of me. She left me in the care of my aunt and uncle (her sister and her husband). I lived with them until I was almost three. They were good people. I know that they did their best to take care of me. But I always felt like I was too much for them.

Right before my third birthday, my mother came to take me to live with her. I guess I felt happy, but I don't really remember. I think that most of all I was confused. I was going to live with my mom, but she was someone I didn't know. I had always wanted a mother, but I think that I was afraid that I might be too much for her to handle. I remember thinking that I would be as good as I could be so that I would always have a mom.

I'm still not one hundred percent clear about how being separated from my mother at such a young age affected me. All I know is that I have always had difficulty making and keeping relationships. I can't seem to get close, no matter how much I care about someone. My ex-husband told me that I have a wall around me. I felt as if I was going to die when he left. But I had no words to ask him to stay.

As we talked to Louise about the problems she has had with relationships, she kept going back to her early years with her mother. We asked her why that time period felt so important to her.

I keep thinking about my ex-husband's description of me as "walled off." I remember not being able to really approach my mother when I went to live with her. I remember watching her every move, her every attempt to get close to me. I guess I didn't really believe that she was going to stay. So although I longed to be close to her, I still couldn't let her in.

The Legacy of the Attachment Process

Louise understood and was worried about how her precarious beginnings with her mother were affecting her present-day relationships with both men and women. She had a failed marriage and was reluctant to become vulnerable enough to allow another person into her life. She also had deep concerns about what kind of a mother she would be if she ever had children.

Louise entered therapy with the goal of improving the quality of her relationships and her ability to trust others. As she explored her feelings and her early history, she began to think more and more about how her childhood experience with her mother would someday affect her ability to parent.

In the book *Motherless Daughters*, Hope Edelman notes that when a woman, because of the early loss of her own mother, still yearns to be mothered herself, her own parenting may well become self-parenting. Rather than meeting her child's expressed needs, she may give the child what she, the mother, longed for but did not receive, thus putting her youngster at risk.

Louise knew that she did not want to contribute to the

continuation of a cycle where her child would not get his or her needs met. She did not know much about her mother's early history, and with much prompting and support she attempted to fill in the gaps by talking to her mother, Judith, and her aunts (Judith's sisters). She discovered that her grandmother (Judith's mother) had died when Judith was an infant. Louise learned that the family had been split up, and like Louise, Judith had been taken to live with an elderly aunt. Her older sisters stayed with their father. Judith was not reunited with her father and sisters until she was five years old, when her aunt died.

This is a tragic portrait of a family where scarcity of maternal warmth and connection appears to be the norm. John Bowlby wrote that the death of a mother can have a powerful effect on a young child's ability to function successfully as an adult. Such a loss leaves an infant or a toddler vulnerable to the development of depression later in childhood and in adult life.

Women like Judith, who have experienced the loss of their mother in early childhood, often develop a sense of unresolved grief that can remain with them for the rest of their lives. In fact, according to Louise, Judith battled bouts of depression for most of her life. Louise recognized that her own encounters with depression were sparked by incidents that triggered in her a sense of loss. At one point she asked us, *Is it possible that I'm not only experiencing the loss of my own mother, who was unable to care for me when I was born, but in some way I'm feeling her loss, too? Is this something that was passed on to me from her?*

Louise's theory about the legacy of grief from her mother may be close to the mark. From what we know of Judith's history, she was not in a situation as a child where she could resolve the loss of her own mother. Loss, especially the loss of a parent, can be worked through only in an atmosphere of warmth and family support. A young child who has suffered such a loss needs to feel secure among close and loving adults and siblings. In this loving and supportive atmosphere, a child can mourn appropriately and then move on.

And what happens to a child who does not have this kind of support? A significant childhood trauma, like the death of a parent, where the child never has the opportunity to mourn, can lead to the development, as an adult, of depression and/or anxiety symptoms. Sadly, this is what happened to Judith.

Researcher Mary Ainsworth studied the interactions of a group of mothers and babies, where the mothers had each suffered the loss of their primary attachment figure in childhood. She found that when mothers failed to resolve their mourning for their lost attachment figure, they had babies whose behavior was insecure and disorganized.

Judith's inability to parent Louise after her husband was killed was, in all probability, a cumulative response to the tragic loss of her partner, her "attachment figure." This loss had an intense impact because she had never been able to articulate her grief for the mother she never knew. Judith's losses became part of the legacy that she passed on to Louise.

In light of her history, how can Louise begin to mend her life situation?

MENDING MOVES FOR LOUISE:

As part of her ongoing work on herself, we suggested that she do the following:

- Continue her ongoing dialogue with her mother and use this as an opportunity to learn more about her mother's experiences as a child—what it felt like to grow up without a mother. Interacting in this way gives Louise the opportunity to experience Judith as a separate person, outside of the role of "mother."
- Use the new openness between them as an opportunity

to share, without guilt, some of her own feelings about what life was like for her while she was growing up.

• Express her interest and concern about her mother's childhood losses and their impact on the choices that Judith made for herself as an adult.

MENDING MOVES FOR JUDITH:

As a way of creating a new type of interaction with her daughter, we suggested that Judith do the following:

• Give herself permission to look at the way her early history has affected both Louise and herself.
• Allow herself to experience Louise as a warm and compassionate woman, and not just as her child.
• Gradually allow herself to get in touch with the vulnerable areas of emotion that she "walled off" years ago to protect herself from feelings of despair.

These steps have the potential to create an atmosphere of healing and a new kind of dialogue for both Judith and Louise.

When a Daughter Becomes Her Mother's Mother

Let's discuss further what happens when, as in Judith's case, a mother's attachment process was nonexistent or insecure. How else will her daughter be affected by the mother's limited attachment experience?

A mother whose own attachment experience has been lacking may look to her daughter to compensate for some of the emotional emptiness she feels. While this daughter is growing up, the imbalance in their relationship may not be apparent. In fact, they may appear to have a perfect relationship. For example, Ellen, age twenty-three, described her childhood to us this way:

My mom and I had the most wonderful relationship while I was growing up. We loved doing things together. She always made my friends feel welcome in our home. She volunteered for the Girl Scouts and to go on field trips with my class so that she could share in my experiences. When I started dating, she would listen to my concerns about boys without interfering or offering advice.

Sounds pretty terrific, huh? Well, it was until I went away to college and, eventually, met Bill, my fiancé. Mom went through a kind of blue period when I left for college, but then she seemed to perk up. Of course, I called her all the time to tell her what I was doing and who I was doing it with. I came home a lot on weekends and would bring half of my dormitory with me. Mom loved it! She was in her glory, sitting around the table with me and my friends, listening to our silly stories and escapades.

Then, in my junior year, I met Bill. We became inseparable. I brought him home to meet Mom. She was polite, but I sensed a feeling of distance in her. I was so in love, however, that I simply brushed it off. When I would talk to her on the phone, as soon as I started to talk about Bill, she would attempt to change the subject. The next time Bill and I came home together, she was very cool. I began to feel confused and anxious. What was going on? My mother, who had always been my confidante and ally, was bailing out on me when I felt I needed her most.

Well, it got worse. Six months after we met, Bill and I became engaged. All of a sudden my mother was creating all sorts of reasons why we shouldn't get married: "You're too young . . . he's too young . . . his parents aren't our type . . . he doesn't have enough money." I was devastated.

Then I got angry. I told her I was sorry that she didn't agree with our decision to marry, but we were going to go ahead with our plans anyway. My mother became depressed. She was hospitalized several times over the next few months with vague complaints that required a lot of tests, but there never seemed to be anything definitively wrong with her. She just felt sick.

Bill and I started fighting for the first time. I was going back and forth from school to see my mother. My grades started to slip and my relationship with the man I loved was unraveling.

At this point Ellen decided to seek professional help. We suggested that she bring her mother, Jane, in so that the four of us could talk about what was happening between them. This is Jane's story:

I was the youngest of six children. My parents were good, hardworking people. We didn't have much but we were always told that we were lucky to have each other. I guess that must have been true, but I always felt like I never got enough attention from my mother. My earliest memory is of following her around, hoping that she would notice me, or pick me up, or talk just to me, not to me and all of my brothers and sisters.

My mother made my oldest sister take care of me a lot. I didn't want my sister—I wanted my mother. I must have made a big fuss about that. I don't really remember, but I was told I was a handful.

When I found out I was pregnant with Ellen, I knew exactly the kind of mother I wanted to be. And so I was. I was there for her all the time. I was determined that she would never lack for attention. I loved every minute of her childhood. She was so loving and responsive to everything I did. She was the most wonderful daughter anyone could ever have.

When she became a teenager, I didn't worry about her like some mothers did about their daughters. I always knew where she was—right here with me. I made our house avail-

able for her and her friends. She was so grateful to me for being such an understanding mother. I thought our relationship was perfect and that it would never change.

I wanted her to go to college. Although it hurt to leave her in her dormitory that first day, I knew that separating from me was hard for her, too, so I did my best to put a good face on. We talked on the phone every day and I never felt left out of her life.

But everything changed when she met Bill. He was a nice boy, but I thought she was too young to be in a steady relationship. All of a sudden she didn't share things with me the way she always had. She was sharing now with Bill. She wanted his opinion, not mine. I felt terrible, empty and abandoned. My perfect relationship with my perfect daughter was disintegrating.

Then I got sick. I have always been a strong person and I don't think I'd been ill since I was a child. The doctors couldn't find anything really wrong with me. It was very frustrating. Ellen was wonderful, though. She came home from school and would just sit with me in the hospital. Even though I was sick, it felt wonderful to have my daughter back.

The case of Ellen and Jane is an example of what happens when the attachment deficits of the mother are so severe that the mother turns to her daughter to fill her unmet emotional needs. When this happens, it becomes very difficult for the daughter to initiate the basic developmental shift of moving beyond the structure of her immediate family.

Ellen had become her mother's attachment figure. On an unconscious level, Jane looked to her daughter to provide the nurturing and support that she herself had never received as a child. Jane's unspoken expectations were communicated to her daughter in all sorts of ways—most prominently in Jane's rejection of the man who Ellen loved.

By seeking professional help to aid her in redefining her relationship with her mother, Ellen began the process by which she and her mother could relate in a more productive way. Here is what we suggested that Ellen and Jane do:

MENDING MOVES FOR ELLEN:

- Tell her mother that while their relationship means a great deal to her, there is also room in her life for a relationship with Bill. Loving Bill does not mean that she loves her mother less.
- Honestly assess how much time she would feel comfortable spending with her mother.
- Give herself permission to set boundaries for that time frame. These boundaries, far from being punitive, would allow her to spend more time with her mother, freely and by choice, not from a sense of guilt and obligation.

MENDING MOVES FOR JANE:

- See Ellen's moves to form a relationship with a man not as a rejection, but as an appropriate part of Ellen's development as a woman.
- Understand that Ellen's boundary setting is an act of love, aimed at enhancing their relationship.
- Find out how her husband views her relationship with Ellen and what his role has been in this equation.
- Explore how she could get more of her relationship needs met in the context of her own marriage. It is possible that her husband has felt displaced by Jane's attachment to Ellen, and does not know what to do about it.

We will elaborate more on the topic of daughters who mother their mothers in Chapter Seven.

Is It Possible to Promote Better Attachments?

Is there a way to undo or redo the process of insecure attachment? If you are a mother and the information we have presented in this chapter strikes a chord, what can you do? If you are a daughter, especially a daughter who is thinking of becoming a mother, how can you break the cycle? Here are some thoughts to keep in mind:

- A great deal of data shows that good communication between parents and children is a part of all the relationships that we recognize as "secure attachments." Communication takes many forms, depending on the age of the child. The eye contact and body language of an infant is as important as the eager expression of a five-year-old. A parent who is aware of the impact of her ability to focus on and listen to her child is a parent who can make the difference between a successful and unsuccessful attachment.

- The process of reworking an insecure attachment already in place can take several forms. All of them require interaction with other people. Talking with your mother, talking with your daughter, and really *listening* to one another provides the opportunity for an exchange of viewpoints and creates an opportunity for change.

- And what about seeking professional help? In both individual and family therapy, we strive to create an atmosphere in which people can become more "tuned in" to one another. There is a great capacity for healing in a situation where people feel they are really being heard. Learning to understand how your attachment behavior affects you and the people in your life allows you to make different and, perhaps, better choices about your behavior.

To further your efforts at reworking your attachment, here is what we recommend:

MENDING MOVES FOR YOU AS A DAUGHTER:

- Begin a dialogue with your mother. Start with a noncontroversial subject that is of interest to both of you. The idea is to create a nonthreatening atmosphere where you can both feel safe. Pick a time and a place where you can talk without feeling rushed. Don't sabotage your effort by trying to squeeze it in between activities. Give yourself the luxury of a set amount of time that feels comfortable to you.

- Ask your mother to tell you about her childhood memories of her mother. This might be a very productive place to start; it gives you an opportunity to learn more about your mother's history and allows your mother to talk about herself as a child, which is much less intimidating than talking about herself in the here and now.

- Try to really listen to her, without judgment and without criticism. If you believe that your mother never listens to you, this task may feel daunting. But don't despair! This is worth it. You might want to imagine that you are listening to another woman—a very interesting woman whom you have just met—tell her story. It may not be easy at first, but you might be surprised to find yourself experiencing your mother in a very different light.

MENDING MOVES FOR YOU AS A MOTHER:

- Before you begin a different kind of dialogue with your daughter, you might find it useful to write some notes to yourself—notes about what you would like to be different about your relationship with her. Read your notes over carefully. Are the things you want realistic? If they are, how would you like to begin to implement them? If they are not realistic, can you change them to make them more doable?

- Make another page of notes about some of the events in your early history that may be affecting your relationship with your daughter today. At some point in time you might want to share your thoughts about these events with her. The sharing of this piece of your emotional history can be a valuable step in building a connection between the two of you.

- Listen to your daughter; try to really hear what she has to say. It is so easy to slip into that old habit of listening to her as if she were a child, because she *is* your child. But try to experience her as a woman—a woman who would like for you to see her as she sees herself. Allow yourself the experience of listening to her as an adult and not just as a little girl. You may hear things you've never heard before.

3 Mothering Styles

My mommy takes me to dancing class every week. I love to dance and I want my mommy to watch me. She always talks to the other mommies or sometimes she goes out to get some coffee. I feel bad when she doesn't watch me dance. —Rebecca, age 6

I like to help my mom in the garden. Every Sunday morning is our time to be together in the backyard. We have been doing this since I was really little. She shows me how to do everything and she never gets mad when I mess up. When I grow up, I want to be like my mom. —Jessie, age 9

Maddie, a fourteen-month-old girl attempts to negotiate the step from the walkway of her house to the backyard. It is a high step for her, almost half the length of her little legs. But she is determined to do it and wants no help. Repeatedly, she crawls up the step, stands at the edge, and steps off into space. She tumbles onto the grass, and each time her knees and hands accumulate another layer of mud from the damp ground. Again and again, she stands up, checks the faces of the surrounding adults, and goes back for another try.

Maddie's mother is nearby, closely attending to her daughter's efforts. Yet at no time does she attempt to help, rescue, or interfere with her daughter's desires to master the step. She smiles at her encouragingly and, when the toddler lands on the grass, tells her that she is a "big girl" and is doing fine. Six, seven, eight times, this routine is repeated. Some of the other adults present attempt to distract Maddie with another activity, but she will have none of it.

All at once it happens. Maddie negotiates the step safely and lands on her feet. Ecstatic, she races to do it again, to repeat her triumph, all the while looking at the adults around her, and grinning from ear to ear. Most of all, she looks for validation from her mother, who is laughing and clapping her hands, completely in tune with her child. You would think that Maddie had just received an Olympic gold medal and a Nobel Prize, all at once.

Maddie's joy in her own accomplishment is not just an isolated incident involving one little girl. All baby girls, as long as they are healthy and physically able, can achieve a sense of mastery. When such experiences are repeated throughout their childhood and teen years, little girls grow into women with self-esteem and confidence to face the world. They know that they have the capacity to work toward and accomplish particular goals. They possess a sense of competence that is reflected in their relationships with others and the choices they make.

So why doesn't this happen with the majority of girls? What goes wrong? Why do so many girls get the message and believe that:

- I can't do it.
- It is not okay to try.
- Something bad will happen if I try.
- If I do accomplish something, no one will care.
- I do not feel I have support from my mother.

Perhaps we can shed more light on these questions by changing one variable in the above scenario—the mother's role. How would Maddie have developed if:

- her mother frowned and made disapproving noises as she was attempting to master the step?
- her mother responded to her efforts by saying, "You've

gotten your hands and knees all dirty. We have to go inside and clean you up, and then you'll have to stop doing this"?

- her mother picked her up after her first attempt, and said, "Oh, my poor little girl. Are you okay? Let Mommy give you a big kiss and everything will be all right"?
- her mother was preoccupied with talking to the adults in the yard and never noticed what her daughter was doing?

Whether or not she is aware of it, a mother sends crucial messages each time she responds in a particular way to her daughter's behavior. From infancy, children have a tremendous capacity to absorb all types of emotion and action in their environment. They are very sensitive to being cared for and held, to being told to try—and not to try—to do something. They are stimulated, influenced, and shaped by their parents' behavior, body language, facial expressions, and words. Each mother and each daughter evolve within a particular style of relating to one another. Each of us has experienced some type or blend of these "styles of mothering."

In this chapter, we'll look at six common styles of mothering, each of which has a profound effect on the developing/growing daughter. They are:

- the "Me First" style of mothering
- the "Supermom" style of mothering
- the "Always Look Good" style of mothering
- the "Distracted" style of mothering
- the "Empathic" style of mothering
- the "Responsive" style of mothering

Much of a daughter's personality and core sense of herself comes directly from the way her mother related—and continues to relate—to her. Of course, we know that each woman's style of mothering began long before she had children. Her mothering style started in infancy, in the context of her relationship with her own mother. Patterns of relating, beliefs, and feelings developed not only within the relationship with her mother, but also through her other life experiences.

Ultimately, her mothering style is also shaped and influenced by her own daughter's first steps away from her and out into the world. The emotions stirred by watching her daughter's first interactions with the world may reactivate a mother's old fears and feelings of anxiety. These feelings may have their roots in the mother's own early exploratory experiences and how she perceived them to affect *her* mother. All of this is integrated into her style of mothering.

Let's take a close look at each of the six styles of mothering:

The "Me First" Style of Mothering

Some mothers need to be priority number one, even in their relationship with their own daughters. For example, Emily, age thirty-eight, called her mother to tell her some exciting news. She told her she was moving to London to create a European office for her company. Her mother, Virginia, reacted with stony silence. Virginia then told Emily that she was very distressed that was going so far away. "What will I do if you are not here? What will happen to me if I get sick? Who will take care of me?" To Emily, this conversation was all too familiar. She thinks to herself, "Why can't my mother just be happy for me? Why does it always have to be about her?" This Me-First style of mothering may meet the mother's own needs, but it can create conflict and confusion in her daughter, and barriers in the attempts to form a strong mother-daughter bond.

Problems with the Me-First style of mothering can surface in a number of areas, including interfering with a daughter's need to win maternal approval. A mother's approval is a sought-after prize, and all children try multiple ways to acquire it. No amount of effort and determination seems excessive in these attempts to win mother's approval. Often, as a daughter focuses all of her efforts on satisfying and pleasing her mother, she minimizes her own feelings in the equation—a sacrifice worth making, she believes, in order to be loved. In the process, however, this type of behavior begins to lay the groundwork for a lifelong pattern of endless and painful efforts to please others at the expense of herself. Does this sound familiar?

For instance, if a daughter believes that her mother is not happy with her school art project or her dance recital performance, she has two choices: She can give up or try harder. In our work, we have repeatedly found that daughters of all ages do not give up easily on the idea of winning their mother's approval; if giving up happens at all, it will occur much later in life. The driving force to strive for and believe in their mother's approval attests to the tremendous need for a strong mother-daughter bond, even in the face of a Me-First mothering style, in which the mother makes her own needs her top priority.

As futile as it sometimes appears, you might try many ways to win your mother's approval. For example, you may stop doing any or all activities that are perceived to be displeasing to her. Temporarily, this may have the effect of pleasing her. However, if these activities give *you* pleasure or satisfaction, then the price of your mother's approval becomes very costly. There is always an emotional debt to pay.

When the daughter learns to put aside or ignore her own passions in hopes of attaining her mother's unconditional approval, parts of her life are left undeveloped and undervalued. A daughter in this position is always struggling with low self-esteem. She also tends to devaluate her own thoughts and feelings about what's right for her. Whether she's choosing a dress or a marital partner, there are always elements of self-doubt in her decision making. This can lead to a sense of loss that she cannot identify or articulate.

For women in this situation, there are two processes going on concurrently. The first is the daughter's external responses to the perception that her mother is not happy with her; these are the behaviors that are seen and noticed by mother. In Emily's situation, she might decline the job promotion in order to soothe her mother's anxiety. What is not noticed, however, is the second process: the daughter's internal awareness that something is not right and does not feel good. On the inside, she may be feeling a sense of anxiety, a sense that somehow something has gone awry. For Emily, this would mean giving up an important career move to maintain the status quo with her mother.

The anxiety she feels, of course, is the result of her interactions with her mother. These kinds of discussions—where the daughter's needs remain largely unnoticed—may continue over time, and can generate an enormous amount of confusion throughout her life. Emily's ability to make choices is compromised by her mother's disapproval. When she becomes engaged in an activity that she enjoys, she will initially feel good about herself and her attempts to master her world. But this good internal experience will not last if it is in direct conflict with her mother's negative reactions to her behavior.

Emily may ask herself, "Why doesn't my mother feel good about what I am doing or notice my efforts? Have I done something bad?" With no answers forthcoming, Emily may conclude, based on her limited view of herself, that she is flawed or defective in some way. Her belief is that she must be inadequate; otherwise, her mother would be happy with her decisions. Again, these kinds of internalized conclusions about herself are often carried from childhood into adult life with little or no conscious awareness. Emily's story shows us how her ongoing experience with her mother's genuine lack of interest has become the seedbed for the development of her feelings of shame, guilt, and depression.

Women with this kind of mother—that is, one with a Me-First style of mothering—learn at an early age that everything in their lives is centered around how it makes their mother feel, think, or act. Women of all ages have told us that they still feel enraged that every conversation with their mother, no matter what the topic, somehow always comes back to her. This anger develops in response to the constant need of her mother for the spotlight and for attention.

This type of mother has little ability to participate in any dialogue that is less than positive. If she hears or feels the conversation as blaming or critical toward her, the daughter will lose any opportunity to be heard. In nearly all cases, this type of mother-daughter relationship becomes very strained, with frequent shouting matches, followed by long periods of no communication. Finally, when contact is reestablished, there is usually no mention of the blowup or the underlying issues surrounding it. Both women feel stuck and do not know how to change this ineffective style of relating. Many of these mothers were raised by Me-First mothers themselves, and are devastated when their own daughters insinuate that they relate in the same way that grandmother did.

Let's look at an example of this type of Me-First relationship: Alice, a forty-eight-year-old African-American physician, came to us to discuss her seventy-four-year-old mother, Clara. Alice started her story about her reasons for moving from Alabama to California in a defensive tone of voice. She stated, *I moved to Los Angeles out of spite because I was enraged at my mother. She missed my graduation from medical school because I would not drive her to the ceremony. Twenty years later she is still complaining about it to all the relatives. I had asked her to go with my uncle, but she wanted to go with me. I still cannot believe that she pulled that "helpless victim" stuff on one of the most important days of my life.*

Alice began to lower her voice as she recalled more about this painful experience with her mother: *I still feel guilty about moving out here, and once a year I have my mom come visit for a week. When she came last year, I felt like I was fourteen years old again. We argued about why I do not call her every Sunday. I tried to explain that every conversation we have always ends up focused on her and her problems. It seems as if there is never any concern or interest in my personal life.*

I feel that no matter what I do, she does not understand me, nor can she see past her own self. I hate it when I get this angry. I always decide not to speak with her until she apologizes. Of course, that never happens, and I usually give in and call her. Then we go through this same thing all over again. If I could tolerate the pain and guilt, I would never speak to her again. I mean it!

Alice paused for a moment. Then, with a very sad expression on her face, she continued, *I feel that no matter what I do, she will always take the credit for herself. My mother tells all the cousins back home about her doctor daughter, but I never hear a word of praise from her. This conflict between the two of us has been going on for forty years. She will never be the mother I need.*

What would you say to Alice after hearing her painful and frustrating story? Does this relationship between Alice and Clara seem beyond repair? Can you relate to any of Alice's frustration and anger? If so, what seems familiar in your own relationship with your mother (or your daughter)?

The "Supermom" Style of Mothering

When a little girl attempts a new behavior and her mother reacts anxiously and protectively, what does the child conclude? Ashley, age five, is getting ready for her first day of kindergarten. Her mother is nervously fussing with Ashley's dress and hair. This is a familiar scenario to Ashley. Even at age five, she knows that new experiences upset her mother. While Ashley is feeling some appropriate first-day jitters of her own, her mother's feelings take precedence. She takes her mother's hand as they walk out the door and says, "Don't worry, Mommy, I'll be fine."

But seeing the apprehensive look on her mother's face,

Ashley may think, "If Mom is worried, then maybe there's something to be afraid of." Another internal thought could be, "Maybe I'm not as okay as I think I am." On a much deeper emotional level, she could reason, "Maybe the world is not a safe place. I need someone to take care of me. *I can't depend on myself.*"

These thoughts and inner dialogues clearly illustrate how a young girl might begin to create an emotional picture of a dangerous world and her inability to cope with it. This ineffectiveness in mastering her life is fueled by her mother's narrow point of view. Mother's concept of the world as a hazardous and unsafe place is contagious and difficult to combat. Each of her spoken or visual messages of concern and anxiety undercuts her child's innate potential for spontaneous and creative interaction with her environment. As that happens, her budding self-confidence will become suffocated in the fearful atmosphere created by a Supermom's refusal to let her daughter take necessary risks and make mistakes.

This maternal unwillingness feels like appropriate parenting to the mother. When questioned about her beliefs or behaviors, she will become highly defensive and perplexed that anyone would feel differently. In reality, her rigidity serves as a powerful lid to cover up her own issues with safety. There may be some very valid historical events in her past that explain her overprotectiveness—but there is no room for discussion or change in her outlook.

This kind of mother tends to function with a high level of efficiency in the areas that she has deemed "safe." She can be the Girl Scout leader, PTA president, and manage a household. However, she won't permit or tolerate anything outside of her realm of "safe and secure."

For example, Kim, age ten, is one of the best players on her soccer team. Her mother, Colleen, is very proud of her and tries to attend every one of Kim's games. However, if for some reason, Colleen can't attend, Kim is not allowed to play. Colleen is afraid that something will happen. She can't articulate what she is afraid of, but her fear for Kim's well-being is a constant concern. Colleen has a certain box that she functions within, and she's not capable of moving beyond it or allowing anyone else in the family to do so.

You can see one of the problems with this Supermom style of mothering: It may teach a daughter that the world is a perilous place before she is able to find out for herself. She thus loses the chance to relate to her environment on her own terms, left only with the option of dealing with it in the ways that her mother has modeled for her. This overly cautious lifestyle becomes a cage in which risk-taking behavior and feelings are severely curtailed and discouraged. Unless her fearful beliefs and behaviors are challenged, any or all unknowns will permanently become off-limits. As an adult, she may find her life experience to be very "small."

The adult daughter may have no idea how to go beyond certain preestablished boundaries—and she often may not want to. She might view potentially dangerous situations outside the cage with both longing and terror—longing for the opportunity to experience and master what is feared, yet terrified that if she takes the risk, she will be destroyed. Ultimately, however, the cage becomes a refuge that feels safe—a place where longing and terror are no longer part of her conscious awareness. She can mistakenly believe that she will always be protected and secure. And as she matures and is constantly faced with the issues of risk versus safety, the cage may become even smaller.

Occasionally, as she grows up, the daughter in this scenario may make life choices based only on the fact that they are not what her mother would do. The results, however, may not be to her benefit. For example, a daughter may marry the "wrong" man even though she knows, deep inside, that she is not making the best choice for herself. But her "wrong" choice is sending a message to her mother: "I'm in control of my life and you're not." Or a daughter may cut herself off from any kind of uncomfortable feelings. The suppression and inability to acknowledge any degree of anxiety, fear, or panic on the part of the daughter can lead to the development of numerous phobias.

The persistent message from Supermom continues to be, "Anything new must be viewed as threatening, and all unfamiliar behaviors, situations, feelings, people, and opportunities are to be avoided." If this is a message that you received, then you are ultimately left with a very small window in which to experience and view life. You run the risk of becoming a woman who has tremendous potential but never taps into it for fear of doing the unimaginable. For instance, you would never consider:

- going to school in another state
- starting a challenging career
- moving away from your mother
- taking up a personal hobby
- feeling all the things that you really feel
- not asking for your mother's approval before doing something that you want

You can add to this list the things that you would like to do that have not been sanctioned by your mother—and then begin to expand your own limits. The Supermom style does teach you how to take responsibility for your own desires or wishes, but you have to go beyond the invisible limits that you observed at your mother's apron strings and tap into your deepest desires, dreams, and goals. It is never too late, nor is it "stupid," to do the things you dream about and want.

We would like to introduce you to Denise and Terry, a mother and daughter who came to us to learn some conflict resolution and communication skills. Their story demonstrates the Supermom style of mothering.

Denise is a fifty-eight-year-old homemaker and the mother of a son and daughter. Denise married Hank, the children's father, when she was nineteen years old and is still married to him. Terry, at the age of thirty-four, is the oldest child. She is not married and blames her mother for it. Denise's son, Lou, age thirty-one, still lives at home.

Sitting on the couch in our office, Denise looked at Terry and said, *I get blamed for everything that goes wrong in Terry's life, no matter what it is. I know that when Terry was younger I would not let her do much without . . . well, I was a little overprotective. Now she says that I did everything "right" and she was not allowed to make any mistakes or be herself. The reason Terry is not married is because she has dated the wrong kind of guys. She says this too is all my fault. The list of things I have done wrong, according to Terry, is endless. I just keep trying to keep the family together and do things right. I am scared something might happen to my daughter, and I do make a point to tell her whether I think that what she is doing is smart. All I want is for Terry to be safe.*

At this point Terry appeared ready to jump up from the couch and run out of room. Leaning toward her mother, she said, *You are a control freak. No matter what I do, you think there is some hidden danger or risk in it. I couldn't go away to college, but had to go to school locally so you wouldn't feel anxious. No matter what career choice I make, you have a better idea. I feel that my life is not my own and I cannot make a decision without my mother second- and third-guessing me. I know that you care about me, but you have raised me to always depend on you. You do everything that seems safe and acceptable to you, but if I do not do it your way, it's a battle.*

Did the Supermom style of mothering allow either of these women to be separate and yet still emotionally connected? Apparently not. At this point Denise sat back on the couch and Terry took a deep breath. Both women stared at each other, waiting for the other to break their impasse. Before the session ended, they both agreed that therapy would help them learn to hear and make the individual changes necessary for their relationship.

The "Always Look Good" Style of Mothering

For some mothers, appearance is everything. They may see and respond only to their daughter's dirty knees and dress, for example. But how does this affect a child's newfound joy in her accomplishments, or in exploring the world?

A mother's need to look good, and to have control of how things look, leaves a strong imprint upon her daughter's developing self-image. When a youngster recognizes that her mother's value system places top priority on appearance and looking good in the eyes of the world, this will be passed along to her in many subtle—and not-so-subtle—ways. The child will begin to feel pressure to conform to her mother's style of behavior and criteria for acceptance. She will start to place importance on what others think of her rather than on what she thinks of herself.

For example, on the evening of her high-school senior prom, Jody comes out of her bedroom, in a cloud of perfume, her hair swept up, wearing her prom dress. Her mother, Margaret, looks at her with a worried expression, and blurts out, "Oh, honey, that dress makes you look fat." How can Jody possibly feel good about herself when her mother is so obviously displeased with her appearance?

If your own mother emphasized physical attractiveness and acting in a way that "looks good," you got the message that what you look like on the outside is more important than what you feel on the inside. You might have then begun to develop the pattern of ignoring your inner feelings when they conflicted with the imperative to be attractive. This became the template for future behavior, which was constantly reinforced by mother's expectations that you look good at whatever you do.

In these circumstances, you may have started to feel that

the opinions of others were more important than anything you felt or thought about yourself. As an adult, a deep sense of who you were was not given room to grow, thanks to this constant emphasis on appearance. The inner person, what you feel, think, and desire, wasn't nurtured. Along the way, you and your mother probably had many arguments and disagreements about "what the neighbors will think" of your behavior. These conflicted interactions can start at a very early age and persist well into adulthood.

For a daughter to flourish throughout childhood and early adulthood, she must develop her potential. To do this, she has to feel that what she does is approved of and valued by her mother, whether it is her first finger-painting project or the profession she chooses. If she receives spoken and unspoken support to take risks and make mistakes, this becomes a key ingredient in her sense of well-being in the world. A mother cannot ignore this developmental requirement if her daughter's sense of self-worth is going to grow.

Not surprisingly, then, a mother whose top priority is looking good will render her daughter's attempts to define herself through accomplishment as of secondary importance, at best. The overarching message that the daughter receives is that it is more important to look good than to take risks and to excel. Thus, the daughter loses touch with her own ability to interact with the world in a way that feels comfortable and exciting to her. She may develop an intense fear that she does not really know who she is or what she wants. With the threat of mother's disapproval looming, she will avoid the process of developing a separate self, one that is different from her mother.

Yes, daughters may feel some degree of nurturing as a result of looking and carrying themselves in accordance with their mothers' wishes. But they are missing a sense of inner security, safety, and self-acceptance. They feel a "hole" or emptiness in their heart and are insecure about their place in the world.

As these daughters mature, they may develop a pattern of failed romantic relationships that can be traced back to the Always-Look-Good style of mothering. They may not be fully aware that they are looking to their partner, supervisors, or other authority figures, male or female, for approval. This need for acceptance has come from years of internal neglect, overshadowed by having the "proper" appearance. As adults, they lack a sense of self-importance necessary to feel good about themselves, and thus they feel that something about them is wrong or damaged. This becomes painfully clear in intimate relationships—relationships that go below the surface of appearance and looks.

Fearing that someone might see what feel like shameful flaws, they may terminate any close relationship. Or they might overattach themselves—emotionally, mentally, or sexually—to someone as a way to cover up their self-doubts. This partner or mate becomes the loving, nurturing "mother" these women never had. The daughter's craving for unconditional acceptance from her mother thus becomes the driving force in her adult relationships. She can make her relationships work, but only up to the point where she realizes that this person (husband, lover, friend, or perhaps boss, or older woman) cannot be the endless source of reassurance that she desperately needs. (In Chapter Nine, we will discuss at great length the practical ways in which a daughter and her mother can develop a vital inner sense of self—a self that feels safe and productive in the world and in personal relationships.)

We would like to introduce Carmen, age fifty-four, and Christina, age twenty-seven, to expand on the theme of a daughter's struggle with appearance and self-image. Carmen is from a Central American country and came to the United States to get away from her own mother, Rose, when she was twenty-one years old. Christina is the youngest of three daughters; the older daughters, according to Christina, have moved out of state and have no contact with Carmen.

Christina and Carmen came to our office for the first time

to discuss the problems that they were having with each other. Carmen started the session by saying, *I have done it all for my daughters. I have a good job, own my own home, and give Christina plenty of money. Yet Christina is overweight, cannot stay in college, and has never done the things that I want or taken pride in her appearance. I want to get Christina some help so she can make a life for herself. I cannot take care of her forever.*

Christina was listening very intently, and responded, *I have heard my mother say these things about me for years. I truly believe that if I were thin, my mother would be so happy that it would not really matter what I do. I am the only woman on my mother's side of the family to ever attempt to complete a college education. My two sisters left home because they could not take the pressure of conforming to my mother's demands.*

I feel that no matter what I do or accomplish, it is not recognized by my mother. I hate that I am so concerned about what other people think or feel about me. The amount of time that I spend worrying about other people's opinions of me is tremendous. I feel very stuck in my life. I want to be successful, but I do not feel that I have my mother's support for my efforts. And I don't trust that I can accomplish what I want without her help.

Carmen, hearing what Christina said, replied, *I do not need to come here to hear her complain about me! So I am not going to come back. You people [pointing at us—Barbara and Steve] help her. I cannot do it anymore!*

Christina began to cry and pleaded with her mother not to be defensive. But her mother left anyway. Christina continued in therapy without her mother. Over the ensuing months she began to develop a sense of herself that was not based on her physical appearance and her mother's approval.

The "Distracted" Style of Mothering

Some mothers simply do not pay attention to what their daughters are doing. As a result, it becomes very difficult for these girls to feel lovable or valuable. No matter what their fathers or other family members may do to compensate, these daughters feel inadequate because they keenly experience their mother's lack of response to them. These are feelings that will continue into adulthood.

For instance, Heidi, age seven, always has to borrow lunch money from the school office because her mother consistently forgets to send her to school with a lunch. Even when Heidi reminds her, inevitably her mother still "forgets." Heidi wishes that her mother was like the other moms— they never forget.

As we've already written, when toddlers move away from their mother's side and begin to interact with the world, they need to have their attempts to master and comprehend the world reinforced and validated. A little girl needs her mother to recognize her efforts and to cheer her on. This maternal encouragement becomes internalized and translated into messages such as: "It's all right to do this," "I'm okay," and "I can do it."

When a child says, "Hey, Mom, look at me," she is really seeking affirmation that her efforts to learn and to prevail in whatever task she has undertaken will receive her mother's approval. After all, mother is the main audience, and her applause and delight in her child's performance provide the spark for further ventures. A child is continually forming an internal picture of herself, which evolves not only from her own interactions with the world around her but also from the way she sees these interactions reflected in her mother's eyes. Without this type of validation, a daughter is at risk of developing a sense of rejection, or even self-hatred, or chronic depression.

The ability to internalize and own the sweet feeling of accomplishment does not just happen. As adults, we have the ability to learn and intellectually understand the virtues and rewards of perseverance. For a child, however, whose sense of self and identity is in the formative stages, the crucial validation from her mother becomes a large part of her internalized self-image. Without it, the daughter feels unlovable and defective.

So when a mother is consistently inattentive, distracted with other things, too busy with her own life, or perhaps depressed, her daughter is going to have to look elsewhere for the validation she needs. By age five or six, she learns that she needs to find support outside of the home. Feeling emotionally neglected, she knows that she needs to make friends and begin to build an emotional support network. Like other daughters raised in this Distracted style of mothering, she learns to make significant connections with girlfriends and others who begin to take care of her needs.

To repeat, a mother who remains indifferent to her daughter's endeavors creates an emotional climate that will produce varying degrees of self-doubt throughout her child's life. The long-term effect of this unsatisfactory and meager connection can be devastating to the daughter's future. She may develop deep-seated fears about her competency to perform and excel. Or she may become an overachiever who feels that in spite of her accomplishments, no one likes her— most of all, her mother.

A good example of this dynamic is our client Gayle, who is twenty-nine years old. Commenting on her childhood relationship with her mother, she said, *My mother was there physically, fixing meals, brushing my hair, doing laundry, checking my spelling papers. But she was also* not *there. I could feel her lack of attention. It wasn't that she didn't care. I'm sure she cared. I just couldn't gauge if anything I did had any impact on her.* As a result of this absence of meaningful attention, this very successful woman still struggles with the sense that there is something defective about her.

What can a daughter in this kind of situation do to compensate for her mother's inattentiveness? Like the young girl Maddie at the beginning of this chapter, she can double or triple her efforts to get mom to pay attention. That is the route that Gayle took. She made a special effort to be at the top of her class throughout high school and college and to excel in extracurricular activities. Her goal was to be so good, so outstanding, that she could see her competence mirrored in her mother's eyes. Unfortunately, when that validation was not forthcoming, Gayle believed that her achievements were meaningless. She continues to struggle with a nagging inner fear that she is worthless and a phony. When we challenged Gayle about this unrealistic way of viewing herself, she said, *I know, in my head, that I am not a phony and that people truly care about me—but I do not feel it. On the inside, I always feel that there is something wrong with me. This emptiness, in spite of all my work on myself, is the primary feeling that I carry with me every day. This nagging pain in my heart never seems to go away. It doesn't matter how busy I am or how many friends I have. The pain is always with me.*

I have a hard time truly believing people care about me, even though I am aware of it on some level. I know my friends don't hate me. I just don't let anyone get very close to me. Although I am a grown woman now, my mother's lack of attention still triggers feelings of anger, hopelessness, and fear in me.

Because the ultimate goal of her hard work was to gain approval and acceptance from her mother—which never did occur—Gayle could not experience for herself the pleasure of her hard-won academic and professional successes or the friendships she developed. This is not uncommon. For many women we have worked with, this is "business as usual."

The "Empathic" Style of Mothering

This style of mothering is centered around the mother's intuitive nature and awareness of how to support her daughter in day-to-day life. This type of understanding allows her daughter to develop feelings of love, self-worth, and competence. The young girl's feeling of *being* loved is more important than *how* she is actually loved. For example, there is the mother who takes the time to really listen to how badly her daughter feels about not being picked for a solo in the ballet recital. Or how about the mother who has to leave her daughter for long hours in day care? This mother makes sure that she schedules some special time with her daughter every day.

The empathic mother knows these parental truths and communicates warmth and acceptance to her daughter. No, this mother is not perfect, but rather she is alert to her daughter's emotional states and acts accordingly. The cornerstone of this and other styles of effective mothering is the ability to focus on the daughter as a person, rather than on a particular behavior. By focusing and connecting with the child, the empathetic mother communicates with her daughter and consistently sends messages of love and support.

For instance, Maddie, the toddler described earlier in the chapter, is thrilled when she successfully climbs the step and jumps off of it. Her mother, Sarah, empathetic to Maddie's feelings, is able to "join" her daughter in the exciting moment she was experiencing, and communicate her pleasure to Maddie. Even if Sarah is feeling upset by a phone call that she had just received, she is able to refocus on her daughter and share her emotions. This type of empathic attunement fosters a young girl's sense of self-worth. This self-worth, in turn, becomes the internal confidence that allows her to face challenges and further her ability to trust that people care about her.

When a mother repeatedly connects on the same level as her daughter, she communicates feelings of safety and love. We all know the disappointment when someone important (mother or daughter) does not intuit our excitement about a particular task, event, or feeling. These empathic misses lead to many incorrect messages that get formed in our heads and buried in the back of our minds. We may forget about this loss of support or disappointment—until it happens again. Then, like an old wound that never healed fully, the pain surfaces all over again. A past that is replete with these emotional injuries can leave us feeling as though our feet are in cement. Whenever we make an emotional connection and cannot move forward from this place of disappointment or pain, the old issues get replayed.

Sarah connected with her daughter by smiling and clapping her hands. Maddie, even at fourteen months, had already developed the ability to read her mother's tone of voice and body language. This nonverbal but highly attuned communication became one of the building blocks for Maddie's self-esteem.

Every mother and daughter experiences some type of nonverbal communication. You need to know what cues you react to from your own mother or daughter. For instance, what kind of look sets you off? What look makes you feel good? The empathic mother knows the importance of not only nonverbal communication, but that her words and the tone in which they are said have tremendous power to shape her daughter's self-image. There is no question about it: *Words have power*. But words must match feelings. If Sarah told Maddie with a frown that she was pleased with her, it would pose a conflict. Daughters know when there is a discrepancy between what is said and the intended meaning. It is nearly impossible to convince a young child that you're not mad when all you feel is anger. Children know the truth about what their parents feel, and their interaction becomes the foundation for a youngster's trust or mistrust. Maddie sees the joy in her mother's eyes and tone of voice, and trusts it. The feelings she has match the excitement that her mother shares. This type of relationship allows Maddie not only to trust her mother but to feel the security of being understood.

As you are reading about this particular style of mothering, you may wish that your own mother had been more empathic with you. This is completely understandable, considering how much anger or sadness can be generated when you feel like no one—especially your mother—understands you or cares. We hear repeatedly from mothers that they never got the kind of nurturing that they needed in order to give to their daughters. But it is never too late or too early to give and receive this kind of empathic understanding and support. (In Chapter nine, we will further discuss how to develop an empathic attitude in your own life and mend the wounds within your mother-daughter relationship.)

Keep in mind that the empathic mother is not without failure, or moments of temperamental outbursts or negative feelings. But at an early age, her daughter learns that mother does care, even if she completely misunderstands her daughter's moods at times. The daughter knows that she has her mother's support and love to carry her through periods of great difficulty. That unspoken support allows the daughter to feel like she is always emotionally held by her mother. This support creates safety, which allows the daughter to take risks and pursue her dreams. It is very difficult to take venturesome steps if there is not a foundation of empathy to build on.

Let's look at the importance of emotional support through the experiences of Trudy and her mother, Margie. Trudy is a forty-year-old woman with two daughters (ages three years and eight months old). Trudy described her relationship with her mother as follows: *My mother had me when she was twenty-one years old. She did a great job as a mom. I hear my girlfriends say that they felt like their mothers didn't like them or didn't like being a mother. That is something I've never thought about. There has never been a question in my mind, when I was a young girl, or now as a mother of two daughters, about my mother's enjoyment of being a mother.*

I knew that my mom wanted to be a mother. It showed in her enthusiasm when she was doing things with me and my two younger sisters. My mom was young, but that didn't affect her ability to care for and love us. When I think back on my childhood, my mom never held me back or appeared jealous. Rather, from my earliest days, she encouraged me to pursue my goals and dreams. The support that I felt from her was like the air I breathed—it was always there.

Trudy paused, looked out the window, and said, *I cannot imagine what my life would have been like without my mother's belief that I could do whatever I chose to do. I remember being in junior high school and starting a mail-order business for teen clothes. You have to remember, we lived in a small town outside of Denver and there were no malls then. Hard to picture—no malls for teenage girls to hang out in.*

At the time, my girlfriends and their mothers thought that my mother was nuts to let her fourteen-year-old daughter start a mail-order business. My mother gave me the money to start. She called it a loan and the business took off. The business got so big that my two sisters joined it a few years later. I made enough money to pay my own way through college.

Now I own my own import-export business and it all started when I was fourteen years old. I feel lucky that my mother was not passive or scared of me becoming a businesswoman. She gave me emotional support when I really needed it. Probably the most important thing I received from my mother is the support and unspoken permission to do the things that I wanted. My mother has been the one constant force in my life. I was raised to believe that whatever I wanted was possible and worth trying. I want to pass on that positive support to my daughters.

This vignette about Trudy and Margie, and Maddie and Sarah's story, point out that the emotional support from a mother to her daughter creates a foundation from which both women can grow and develop. These two daughters, Maddie and Trudy, have the internal belief that they are competent and capable of going out into the world. They have a sense of security about doing things that others might dismiss or would never consider trying.

The empathic mother's strongest message to her daughter is that she is lovable and worthy of positive and good things in her life. The daughter develops the capacity to trust and accept good things, and believe that they can happen for her. There is an absence of shame and self-doubt in both daughter and mother; they can give each other support throughout their lives.

The "Responsive" Style of Mothering

We have discussed a variety of mothering styles that impact a daughter's development. But one particular way of mothering encapsulates the positive side of all those mentioned— specifically Responsive mothering. This type of mother goes beyond empathic atunement to what we call the unlimited capacity for self-worth development. Her daughter is given the tools to develop and draw from her mother's and grandmother's rich life experiences. The daughter can call upon a background of unconditional female (not male-dependent) support in order to move out into the world.

When she was a young girl, the mother in this scenario was given permission, by her own mother, to separate and make a life for herself. Because of the quality of her own life experiences, this mother has developed the understanding to give her young daughter room to grow. She has created an emotional environment that fosters the full blossoming of her daughter's inner self. The daughter is properly prepared to deal with the cultural distortions of whom and what she should be. The mother functions, for her daughter, as a reality check and support system for how to be a successful and competent woman at any age. The safe haven of maternal love allows the daughter to use her own power to create her life's path.

In this family, the mother's own mother (the girl's grandmother) further nurtures the daughter. In order to do this, the grandmother does not have to live in the same community or even be alive. Rather, she is a positive image residing inside the mother (her daughter). This mother has successfully created her own life apart from her mother, and is now in the position to assist her daughter with hers. There is no age requirement for benefiting from this type of unspoken and spoken permission for growth and expansion; the daughter breathes in this acceptance and nurturing for her entire life, day in and day out.

This mother has been able to model herself after her own mother and/or other strong women. The sense of competence and courage of both herself and her daughter is a foundation that allows them to be independent and interdependent simultaneously; they have the capacity to be separate and yet deeply connected. The daughter does not feel the pull of her mother's unfulfilled dreams or unresolved fears, so her own struggle for independence, beginning at about five years of age and continuing through her life, is not fueled by her mother's unresolved issues from the past.

Thus, this daughter has the unspoken freedom to create her own life with the safety net of her mother's love and support. This does not mean that mother and daughter do not disagree, but rather permission exists for their differences. This agreement to disagree creates room for the daughter's self-worth to tolerate rejections and disappointments. Her life does not become a series of letdowns or doubts about her ability to perform in the workplace or to be lovable in relationships. At the same time mother and daughter can discuss hot issues—such as sexuality, parenting, career, money, and men—without having to fight for their opinions to be heard. They have learned to listen to and support one another, even when it is not to their personal liking.

Let's illustrate this style of mothering with Sally, a thirty-seven-year-old, first-generation immigrant from Seoul, Korea. The family—Sally's mother, Lee; her father, Leo; and two sisters, Jessie and Tammy—arrived in the United States in 1967, and moved into a small, two-bedroom apartment in

West Los Angeles. Sally recalled, *I wasn't afraid of moving to Los Angeles. I knew my mom and dad had everything under control, and my sisters and I trusted them. My mother wanted to come to this country because she felt there was more opportunity in this culture for women. I remember my parents agreeing on this issue, and telling me when I was four years old that we were moving to the United States. We moved here when I was six years old, and I still cannot believe that we all learned English after we got here.*

Sally is now a civil-case attorney and is unmarried. We asked her how she got from being a new immigrant to becoming a practicing attorney. What happened along the way to help her pursue her lifelong dream? Sally said, *I always felt my mother's support and direction in my life. She wanted me to do what I wanted to do and not let my nationality or race get in the way. It was painful when I first started school here. I had no language skills and was the only Korean in the class. My mother always comforted me and told me not to be discouraged or give up after a hard day at school.*

Within six months of moving here, my mother's parents also came to Los Angeles. They were in their fifties at the time, and knew no English. Inside of one year, my mother and grandmother had found financial supporters to open up a bakery. My father got a job in the aerospace business and Grandfather was our full-time baby-sitter after school, when he was not working in the bakery. I learned that if you put your mind to something, it will happen.

My mother and grandmother got along very well. They had a style of support that they both could depend on at critical times. My grandmother would always tell my mother and me to be the kind of women who had no regrets. I guess I have lived my life with no regrets. I learned from my mother that no matter what I chose to do as a woman, she would support and love me. I have always felt her support and cannot imagine my life without it.

Sally was emotionally moved as she verbalized the powerful influence that her grandmother and mother have had in her life. Sally's grandmother died in 1994, at the age of eighty-four. Her grandfather is still living and walks three miles every day to keep in shape. Sally is close to her family and has recently bought a house. Sally said, *It's hard for me to believe that I am a home owner and not married. I want to get married and I know it will happen at some point in my life. I am frustrated with not having a long-term relationship. Sometimes I wonder if my sense of independence and drive gives the appearance that I do not want a relationship. I hope that my personality is not overpowering to men. I would like to have children so they can enjoy their grandmother like I did and have the kind of family support I experienced growing up. My mother reminded me the other day that marriage is an addition to my life, not the whole picture. Being single, I sometimes forget that idea.*

We hope it has become clearer in this chapter, particularly through the vignettes about six very different mother-daughter relationships, that what happened years ago—or is still happening today—between you and your mother or your daughter affects every aspect of your life. Even so, many women do not factor their relationship with their mother into how their life is unfolding on a daily, yearly, and lifetime basis.

Beginning to explore the many facets of your relationship with your mother or daughter can evoke stressful and painful memories. It is completely understandable that most women who have had a disappointing or even a turbulent relationship with their daughter or mother might tend to avoid any discussion of it. The goal in this chapter is to encourage you to begin a responsive discussion with your mother or daughter to create new insights and dialogue.

Also remember that no daughter is neutral about her mother or how she was raised. But we do not want you to get stuck in a circular mother-bashing cycle; it is a negative rut that yields no growth or change in the relationship, and in fact, it leaves the blamer in poor emotional condition. Nevertheless, it is easy to fall into a cycle of blaming with no insight into one's own role in the problem. Instead, as you seek to discover how and why your mother related to you, try to recall the part you played in the relationship, and look forward to how you can benefit from understanding this dynamic.

MENDING MOVES:

We want you to explore the areas in your mother-daughter relationship that could have worked better. Take a few minutes to carefully complete the following four Mending Moves:

- List ten things you would have liked to have done with your mother when you were living at home. If you are still living at home, list the things you would like to do now.
- List five things that you would have liked from your mother while you were growing up.
- List five things that you would like to give or have given your daughter in the past, present, or future (even if you are not married or have five sons).
- List five things that you can do to nurture yourself.

These are very powerful Mending Moves designed to open up the discussion between you and the mother *in your hearts*. You might be surprised that many of the things that you want and/or wanted from your mother can now be accomplished by you, the daughter. By looking at these types of questions and issues, you can begin to mend your very important mother-daughter relationship.

In the next chapter, we are going to explore how your extended family impacted your relationship with your mother or your daughter.

4 Understanding the Family You Came from and the Family You Are Creating

I went to visit my mother the other day. It was the first time I had seen her since I moved out six weeks ago. She immediately started yelling at me and accusing me of not loving her. She believes that if I loved her, I would never have left her or moved on with my life. I asked her if she was happy that things were going well for me. My question only made her start to cry.   —Christina, age 27

Does this statement sound familiar? Does the impasse that Christina finds herself in with her mother, Carmen, seem like a normal mother-daughter exchange to you?

We first met Christina and Carmen in Chapter Three in our discussion of the Always-Look-Good style of mothering. Their relationship is characteristic of a particular style of family functioning and relating. Christina is a daughter who is struggling to be recognized as an adult woman and who wants her mother's approval and support for her steps toward independence. The problem for both women is that their family system does not encourage this type of growth.

Christina and Carmen are trying to find a balance between feeling abandoned and enmeshed. Christina wants to have more personal space, which is totally appropriate for a woman of twenty-seven. She wants it, however, without having an emotional confrontation with her mother. Carmen takes Christina's normal and appropriate shifts toward independence very personally—almost as if they were an indictment of her and her performance as a mother. Carmen says, *Is there any other reason Christina would not want to spend time with me? I have been a good mother, so why doesn't she call me or still live in my house?*

Carmen is not only deeply troubled by Christina's behavior, but she told us emphatically that she was not going to tolerate it. Christina wants to move away, both emotionally and physically, from her mother. Unfortunately, she doesn't know how to implement her decision without experiencing enormous guilt. These two women are clearly stuck in a developmental gridlock, where each of them feels terribly misunderstood by the other.

In this chapter, we will discuss the issues faced by Christina and Carmen and what to do when they arise in your own life. But first, let's meet another mother and daughter.

Maggie, age fifty-five, told us, *My daughter, Joyce, and I don't talk very often. We have never been very close, and since she has moved to Hong Kong, we have very little in common. I call her every month or so, and we talk for a few minutes. I think about her, and I think she thinks about me. Our personal lives are very private and we don't share a lot of personal thoughts or feelings. We really see each other only on special occasions. I guess you could say we are like friendly strangers.*

Maggie is describing a family style of relating that is the polar opposite of Christina and Carmen's. The emotional distance between Maggie and her daughter, Joyce, makes them almost strangers. Their only real connection seems to be that they lived in the same house for twenty-two years.

Maggie and Joyce's relationship is the product of the Me-First style of mothering. Maggie is at a loss to explain why her daughter is so distant. But Joyce has her own opinion:

My mother only calls me or wants to talk to me after she hears her friends bragging about their daughters. My mother doesn't call to talk to me, but rather to bolster her public image of being a wonderful mother. She can go six months at a time and not call me. That's because her life is so complete that it has not required any contact with me. We have been distant for as long as I can remember—at least since I was five years old.

Joyce makes it very clear that she does not want to spend large amounts of time with her mother or invest emotional energy into their relationship. One thing is obvious about both of these woman—neither knows how to close the gap between them.

These two very different mother-daughter histories point out, among other things, that every family has its own style of relating. The particular styles do not imply whether a family functions well or not. They simply indicate where the family, or in this case, the mother-daughter relationship, fits on the continuum of family intimacy and functioning. Does it fall more on the side of *enmeshment* or *disengagement*?

Very few mother-daughter relationships fall at either extreme of this continuum. Rather, most fall someplace in between. In this chapter, we will discuss enmeshment and disengagement—two very different styles of relating and intimacy—and where you and your family fit. But first, as a starting point, let's look at the influence of the overall family system on the mother-daughter relationship.

The Influence of Your Family

No woman is neutral about her mother or her family. When a client tells us that she has no feelings about her family, positive or otherwise, our antennae go up. It is simply not true. As a daughter or mother begins to talk with us about her family, we can see the vast sense of power and control with which she has imbued her family. Our birth family, our first family, is the place where we origin... about life, relationships, and ourselves, y... to downplay the importance of our fan... they are so much a part of our existence...

In this book, we never underestimate... fluence that your family has on your... woman, daughter, and mother. By exploring the dynamics of your first family, you will gain insights that you can use as a foundation on which to build your own family. Whether your daughter is grown and living on her own, or your mother is no longer living, we still believe it is valuable to deepen your understanding of your family roots.

The first question that begs to be asked—and the one that women usually fear when beginning a discussion about their family of origin—is: Was your family a functional masterpiece or a dysfunctional mess? As you explore the answer to this question, you may find yourself asking another one: Can a family be functional *and* dysfunctional at the same time? These questions are important to examine because, since you first learned about trust, intimacy, and yourself from your family, it stands to reason that understanding the environment in which you were raised is critical.

What is a functional family? If daughters are raised in an atmosphere where there are no arguments or disagreements with their mothers, does this necessarily imply that this family is a model for good mental health? The answer is an unequivocal no; it just means that no one in that family discussed emotional issues openly. Here are some vital characteristics of a functional family:

- There is emotional space for the daughter to develop into her own person—from childhood, to adolescence, and on to adulthood.
- The family is flexible enough to allow for individual needs and changes over time.
- The family is able to allow a daughter to move from a

place of emotional closeness in childhood to appropriate emotional boundaries in later years.

- The family is able to cope appropriately with the stress of life changes and losses.
- There is an absence of any type of personal abuse or exploitation on the part of the parents toward their children.
- A competent emotional support system exists within the family that allows each member to be nurtured and cared for. Emotional connections lead to safety, not instability.
- The daughter has been able to internalize the love and concern of her mother, and integrate that into a personal sense of self-worth.
- The daughter is able to develop a sense of self, without the interference of her mother's own dreams and desires.
- The family has an internal structure of support, with rules that encourage individual expression and permit differences of opinion.

This list of competent behaviors associated with a functional family is by no means exhaustive. In fact, we would like you to expand upon it, adding any other qualities and characteristics you think are important. It is simply a reference point to start our discussion.

Several of the elements listed above are fundamental in a functional family. First, the mother needs to be flexible and feel at ease with her daughter, as the daughter moves through her normal stages of development. In a functional family, the mother gives her daughter the room to grow and the opportunity to create a sense of herself as an individual. The rest of the family is also supportive of her growth. At the same time the mother's ability to be flexible and accepting of differences extends to her intimate relationship with her husband. A daughter learns important lessons about love and intimacy by watching her mother work at and solve the everyday demands of a marriage. The bond that holds the family together is a pattern of flexibility and respect for each individual's opinion.

Another vital element of a functional family is the mother's ability to handle stress and change. The way she deals with the strains of daily living provides the model on which her daughter will unconsciously pattern herself. In this type of family, a daughter learns that stressful encounters can teach her something about herself and her ability to meet the challenges of life. Very few families function at this level consistently, but it is a starting point for our understanding of how far awry a family system can go.

We have found that when families relate to one another in nonproductive ways—yelling, blaming, ignoring one another, threatening to leave—this behavior can be traced back to the emotional maturity level of the parents. A mother's tendency to get angry or upset is not the issue. What is important is her ability to hear feedback from her daughter about the way her daughter feels and thinks. This feedback may not be what the mother wants to hear. Yet she is willing to hear it.

Families become dysfunctional when they relate in ways that do not allow for individual differences. A mother's resistance to her daughter's attempts to change may cause her to become more inflexible over time, until the needs of her daughter are no longer recognized at all.

In this kind of family environment, the lack of emotional nurturing creates an atmosphere that makes it difficult for the daughter to develop essential emotional connections with either herself or the outside world. If a daughter feels neglected at home, she will expect the same treatment from the outside world. As a result, she learns that she can't implement her dreams or fulfill her desires. This, in turn, has a profoundly adverse effect on her sense of self-worth, and she develops into a woman who, as an adult, does not know who she is or what she wants.

Is My Family a "Basket Case"?

After reading the list of characteristics of functional families, you might feel like your family is truly a "basket case." However, we caution you against making any quick assessments of your family or, particularly, your mother. There is so much negative attention in the popular press and media about dysfunctional families that the term *dysfunctional family* has now become a common designation for *any* type of family history or conflict. No family nowadays, it seems, is considered functional. But we find that the opposite is true—very few families are totally dysfunctional and incapable of providing some degree of emotional and mental stability.

There may be issues that create a great deal of pain and anger between you and your mother. This does not imply that your family is a basket case. This only means that there are people in the family with differing sets of needs, perceptions, and desires. In a functional family, there is room for discussion about different points of view. The ability to be open to the opinions of others can be learned, and is part of the process of creating your own functional family.

We know that you would not be reading this book if you had not received some degree of emotional nurturance in your life. While there may have been lapses in your relationship with your mother, those "emotional misses" have fueled your desire for a better kind of relationship.

Before we go any further, we want to discuss a specific issue that affects families at every level of functioning. Because every mother-daughter relationship is influenced by the presence or absence of a father, we think it is important at this point to address the topic of fatherless families.

The Fatherless Family

Sadly, we know many women who wonder why their fathers were never around while they were growing up. Society does not have many answers, nor do we, as to why men leave their families physically, emotionally, and mentally. But when a father leaves his family at any stage or time, it is traumatic for everyone.

In this book, we have focused on the power that a mother has in relation to her daughter. But we do not want to overlook the impact of a father on his daughter's life, especially when he is unavailable. The loss of a father—whether from death, divorce, immaturity, career, or simply the decision not to participate actively in his youngsters' lives—is particularly life altering for children. It also leaves a mother with the responsibility of raising her family alone.

While the loss of a father to unavoidable circumstances, like illness or accident, is significant, it does not carry the additional sense of rejection that occurs when he consciously abandons his family. A daughter's need for her father's emotional involvement with her does not end just because he is no longer living at the same address as she. It can be just as devastating for her if he leaves her *emotionally* even while living in the same house.

This emotional disconnection and rejection by her father creates a wound that goes to the very core of a daughter's being. The loss of the primary male figure in her young life, regardless of the circumstances, will to some degree leave her emotionally bereft and longing for male attention. Her sense of deprivation may develop into an inability to trust men and form meaningful relationships with them.

A daughter's anxiety can intensify if her father has had an extramarital affair or, perhaps, numerous affairs. His behavior sends her mixed messages about her own sexuality. She is often left wondering whether she has the ability to maintain a man's interest. If she has watched her mother struggle with the agony of the "other woman," she may fear that if she lets a man get close, she won't have what it takes to keep him.

Daughters depend on their fathers to reflect back to them that they are wonderful and capable of dealing with men. By their supportive actions and admiration, dads give them the message that they are desirable women. But the loss of a father to another woman creates a situation that a daughter finds almost incomprehensible. After all, one of the pillars of her self-esteem is the presence of a consistent man in her life.

In a divorce, a father may not have the emotional capacity to see beyond his desire to get out of the marriage. But the real victims in many of these breakups are the children, who get lost in their parents' marital disillusionment. The father's unfinished business with his ex-wife often has a way of spilling onto his daughter, who is vulnerable to the anger that is really meant for her mother.

When daughters are constantly exposed to their fathers' resentment toward their mothers, they may assume his anger is directed at *all* females. As a result, they often feel that dad is angry at them, or that they are in some way responsible for his leaving. When confronted with a situation like this, a daughter may begin to behave in a way designed to keep peace with her father. Thus, she may become the father's "younger mother," assuming the job of watching over him. For example, a young girl won't invite her friends over to her house because she is afraid her father will feel left out; or she won't accept invitations or make weekend plans because she doesn't want her father to be left alone.

If this "fatherless daughter" issue feels familiar to you, take a few moments to think about the following questions:

1. What were the messages, both unspoken or spoken, that you got from your mother about men?

2. What were the messages, both unspoken or spoken, that you got from your father about men?
3. What did you learn from your father about relationships?
4. What did you learn from your father about female sexuality?
5. Do you blame yourself for your father leaving? Do you feel in some way responsible for it?
6. What type of man makes you feel unsafe when you meet, work with, date, or marry him?
7. If you are married and a mother, what kind of man would you *not* want your daughter to be with?
8. How do you cope with anger, depression, and fear? Are you more like your father or your mother?
9. What is the one thing you have always wanted from your father?
10. What are three things that you would like your father to know about you?
11. As an adult woman, what is the most important thing that you want from your father now?

These questions are important and, we hope, will create some new insights into how your father has influenced and shaped your life as a woman. As an example, let's talk about thirty-seven-year-old Kathy, a bright, attractive woman who has tremendous difficulty trusting men and overcoming her feelings of abandonment. Kathy told us, *I never get emotionally close or allow myself to be vulnerable with men. I have never had a significant relationship with a man, and always stop short of developing one each time I have the opportunity. I know this pattern of safety is related to my parents' divorce. I was in the sixth grade when my dad left.*

My mother fell apart. She had always believed that my dad put his career ahead of us. I remember that she used to make me call him at the office at night to get him to come home for dinner. He always said he would be home soon, but then he'd come two or three hours later. Since he left, I've felt that I could never get or keep a man's attention. My mother could not do it, so how was I going to? Now I don't believe any man wants to be close to me, other than for sex.

After he left us, my dad still worked long hours and seldom came to see me. He would always apologize for being late or for forgetting to come at all. I never told him how badly I felt because I didn't want him to leave my life for good. Now I act just like my dad, and I use my work to keep men away.

Kathy longs to form a significant relationship with a man, and possibly get married someday. Yet she is terrified of reexperiencing the same kind of neglect that she experienced with her father. She doesn't doubt that her father loved her, but she has suffered emotionally from his neglect.

Kathy is not alone in wondering if she can keep a man's attention. If you've watched your own mother go through a painful divorce, you, too, might be left with an incomplete picture of relationships and men.

In all five levels of family functioning, you can find examples of fatherless systems. But the difference at each level is how the entire family, including dad, deals with his leaving.

Five Levels of Family Functioning

At this point we want to present the five levels of emotional competence and functioning in families. This index will be the foundation for our discussion of how families live together and communicate. It will help you gain a deeper understanding of the direct influence your family has had on your relationship with your mother and/or daughter. Robert Beavers, M.D., has developed this theory of five major levels of family development. They are:

- Level 1: *Optimal families* are defined as the most functional. These families have the capacity to foster deep, meaningful connections among their members.

- Level 2: *Adequate families* are open to and can handle the changes that each member needs to make in order to develop his or her own identity.
- Level 3: *Mid-range families* are at the level within which most families fall. They make up about 60 percent of the families studied. They are flexible up to a point, and are able to avoid the rigid behavior of less functional families.
- Level 4: *Borderline families* have a very rigid structure, with no tolerance for differences or change. Their hallmark is strong adherence to rules and a literal application of the "family laws."
- Level 5: *Chaotic or severely disturbed families* are the most confused and least functional. They are found at the lowest point of the functioning continuum. The hallmark of these families is turmoil and chronic confusion.

Each of these levels represents a different way that families handle their key difficulties. The process of dealing with and solving problems is what separates the more functional families from the less functional ones.

According to Dr. Beavers, only 20 percent of all families are at levels four and five. Only one in ten families would be diagnosed as clinically dysfunctional, at level five. Looking at this research in another, more positive way, nine of ten families fall within the range of functional to extremely competent. This vantage point should help you break out of the current cultural trend of bashing families, choosing instead to concentrate on the 90 percent of families who are stronger than we've been led to believe. This statistical reality reflects directly on the mother-daughter dynamic, and the state of these relationships.

In looking more closely at these five levels, let's begin by describing the most disordered family system, and then proceed up the ladder of family functioning. Each level has certain developmental tasks that must be achieved in order for the family to improve its relationships and heal.

Level 5—the Chaotic or Severely Disturbed Family

A family at level five is in a constant state of confusion and chaos. There are complete lapses of attention between family members that keep them at extreme emotional distance from one another. A teenage daughter in this type of family might leave and go live with her boyfriend, who is ten years older than she, and not be missed or questioned. There is no connection, acknowledgment, or hope that the problems that exist within the family will ever be resolved.

Their problems can range from child abuse—sexual, physical, or emotional—to a sixteen-year-old daughter having an abortion without any parental knowledge. No one wants to be the authority or parent. There are no responsible adults in the family.

Denial is rampant, which serves to maintain the instability among family members. Anyone manifesting any form of stability or consistency will be undermined by other members. Normal developmental steps, such as a daughter beginning to date, will be ignored. There is no emotional connection or discussion about commonplace life happenings, such as graduation, the onset of menstruation for the daughter, or even a death in the family. Members can actually go for years and never speak to one another in order to preserve their chaotic patterns.

To an outsider, this family's dynamics appear to make no sense at all; there is a sense of constant craziness and confusion among the members. Members of this type of family, when a certain level of anxiety is reached, pull in people from the outside, which contributes to the craziness. An outsider—teacher, social worker, therapist, law-enforcement official—who becomes involved with this system will become part of the instability.

When new spouses or other partners enter the family structure, they will initially be disliked and feel unconnected with other family members. But, ultimately, they will become part of the unpredictability of the family's emotional system. They will add to the existing chaos, and keep it going, even if their relationship fails.

The emotional pain generated by this family is extreme. Members strongly avoid talking about or dealing with the pain they are experiencing, nor do they foster any hope or ability of reducing the behaviors that cause their suffering. This is a family whose members can have multiple marriages and divorces without giving any thought to the impact of these changes on other family members. The family really has no ties to one another, other than their biology.

A daughter in a level-five family would need a strong outside support network to extricate herself emotionally and mentally. Even if her mother is supportive of her moves toward independence, her father or other family members have the power to undermine any action that her mother might take on her behalf. In other words, a daughter in this type of family soon learns *not* to depend on her mother's support. At a very young age she recognizes that her mother will "cave in" at the first sign of a challenge from another family member.

This maternal instability only fuels the air of confusion that dominates the level-five family. The daughter is left feeling abandoned by her mother, and the mother has no insight or understanding into why her daughter feels betrayed by her. Their relationship, if it is going to heal and grow, needs to do so outside of the immediate family. In their Mending Moves, mother and daughter have to make an emotional break from their chaotic system in order to develop a meaningful, stable relationship. But that may not be easy. Members of this family cannot function without some sort of chaos in their lives because, to them, chaos is the norm. There is a strong emotional pull, almost like an addiction, toward creating situations that become explosive and crazy.

Dana, twenty-six years old and her mother, Paige, forty-six years old, are an example of this type of chaotic mother-and-daughter relationship. Dana told us: *My mother had me when she was twenty years old. My father was sixty years old at the time of my birth, or at least that's what I've been told. He died before my second birthday, and my uncle Hal moved in with us and told everyone that he was my father. My mother went right along with the story. Hal was not really my uncle, but rather my mother's boyfriend who had worked for my father. I grew up believing that my father was not my father, and that Hal was. Then, when I was five years old, Hal left my mother and Uncle Mike moved in. My mother told me at the time that Hal had to go work in California, and Uncle Mike was going to stay awhile. Mike stayed ten years. He forced me to call him "Daddy," and my mother punished me when I didn't.*

I grew up with everyone in town knowing that my mother was dishonest and not a respectable woman. I remember people talking and pointing at us when we would go into a store. I heard them joke about who was my real father.

I finally left home at sixteen, when my mother brought home Uncle Paul. I have struggled for the last ten years to find some level of sanity and stability in my life. I raised myself and continue to do so. At home, I had always lived with two adults—but I never had any parents. My mother never stood up for me. She only listened to whatever man she was with at the time about how to treat me. It was awful!

Dana's story is a devastating one. She readily admits to repressing much of her childhood memories in order to keep going forward. She has not spoken to her mother in two years, and is relieved not to have to deal with her. Dana's ability to form a sense of self outside of her family is remarkable, given her chaotic background. She is aware that she may never know the truth about her father and who he really was. And she has accepted the fact that she has to create her own family, and not depend on her first family for any type of support or love.

Level 4—the Borderline Family

On level four, the family situation is improved somewhat, compared with the previous level, but only to a limited degree. At level five, the family has no rules, no direction, and no authority. At level four, this chaos is replaced by the cementlike rigidity of black-and-white rules. There is no room for gray, or for allowing someone the opportunity to have her own opinions. There is an atmosphere of inflexibility, and a need to control all family members. Each member's thoughts, feelings, and actions have to be within acceptable limits as set down by the "dictator"—a mother, father, or grandparent.

The level-four family is controlled by this dictator whose sole purpose is to hold the family together. Over time the dictator becomes a tyrant by means of the continued, excessive use of fear and intimidation. Fear of the tyrant's rage and impulsive behavior allows him or her to control the family. No one in this system wants to provoke the explosive nature of the tyrant.

On level four, problems arise as children grow up and begin to have their own thoughts and feelings. The "no tolerance" stance for individuality flies in the face of a child's normal developmental needs and personal growth. This family expends a tremendous amount of energy to ensure that everyone continues to follow the rules—"or else." There is a looming fear that something cataclysmic might happen if a daughter, for instance, does not follow a certain family rule (i.e., about dating, drinking, arguing with her parents); thus, she becomes the object of the tyrant's rage.

Everyone knows the family code of behavior without ever

having to be told. The daughter who openly disobeys the tyrant, with any type of developmental move, risks being punished. Early on, she learns that any self-expression is grounds for the tyrant's wrath, so that, after a while, she won't even try.

Even so, this family system can become the perfect breeding ground for the most actively rebellious teens and adults. The only personal space that they can achieve is through direct confrontation with the tyrant and his or her rules, even as other family members remain openly compliant and internally paralyzed with fear. Although the label *rebellious daughter* may be used by the family, it is an inaccurate description of what the young woman is truly attempting to accomplish.

As we've already discussed, a daughter wants to grow and find out what life has in store for her. It is appropriate and desirable for her to want to be free to think her own thoughts and feel her own feelings. However, because of her age and maturity level, or because her resources are limited—financial dependence, limited job opportunities—her moves toward independence may take the form of extreme behavior. For example, her attempts to express herself may evolve into excessive drug use, an unwanted pregnancy, academic failure, or an eating disorder. As a result, her goal of personal autonomy is sometimes lost in the wake of her self-defeating behavior.

In this family system, a daughter may also find it very difficult to make a personal statement that is not loaded with anger or revenge toward the tyrant. And that animosity may build as she experiences no emotional support or encouragement to express her own thoughts. The harder she tries, the greater the family's efforts to suppress anything and everything that falls outside of the group's rules.

In this type of family, the mother-daughter relationship has no means of conflict resolution or compromise. Control is the central issue in the family, which lends itself to brutal power struggles. Any moves a daughter makes away from the family control base can leave her feeling terribly abandoned by her mother, because the level-four mother doesn't have the emotional capacity to give approval or support for such independent moves. Mother and daughter are caught in a dead-end cycle of control that is never ending. This struggle for control keeps both of them from developing personal intimacy with one another.

Not long ago we met a bright, energetic woman in her early forties at one of our mother-daughter workshops. She introduced herself as Jackie, and said she wanted to come to see us in our office to discuss her marriage. Shortly thereafter, we met with her; she walked into the office, beautifully dressed, sat on the couch, and without a moment's pause, said, *I got married to Charles, a minister, when I was twenty years old. At the time I was attending a large midwestern Bible college. My mother forced me to go to Bible college because I had been so rebellious in high school. I got pregnant when I was seventeen, and had an abortion behind my mother's back. It was a crazy time in my life. The guy I was dating had long hair and was the total opposite of the boys at church.*

Jackie continued to tell her story with a tremendous amount of energy, as if she had only a few minutes to talk. When we shared this observation of her apparent urgency, she nodded and said, *If you only knew my mother. I could only speak when spoken to—and it had better be good news or keep my mouth shut. My mother always told me that a good Christian girl never gossips or talks too much. I was raised in a strict fundamentalist Christian home, where we went to church twice a week. My mother used guilt to control me when I became a teenager. We fought like cats and dogs about everything. No matter what I did, it was never right or it was a sin.*

I used drugs from the age of fourteen, and at that time taking them was unusual. I married Charles, who is still my husband, to please my mother. He wanted to be a minister and that was the only type of man my mother would ever approve of. Well, twenty-five years and three adult children later, I am still rebelling in my heart against my mother and her rules. Now both my mother and husband believe that I am a bad person. They talk on the phone weekly about how much I drink and where I am after work. My husband had a major panic attack when I bought a Harley-Davidson motorcycle.

No matter how much I do or accomplish, I am still looking over my shoulder for my mother's approval. I tell myself it doesn't matter, but all of my life decisions always include her opinion. I am weighed down by the feeling that I am guilty for not doing what she wants, and now those feelings have been transferred to my husband. Both my husband and mother are tyrants!

Jackie is the typical product of the level-four style of family relating. Like most women, she craves a more fulfilling relationship with her mother. Jackie is attempting to find a way to relate to both her mother and husband without having to continue her rebellious behavior. She chafes under the burden of family rules while longing for her mother and husband's approval to break them. The immovable object in Jackie's first family and current marriage are rules that forbid any type of genuine, intimate connection and feeling.

Level 3—Mid-Range Family System

This family system represents another move up the family developmental continuum. As you will see, the primary issue that the level-three family struggles with is intimacy.

These families are guided by a basic belief that "if you love me you will do the things that I approve of...." Although the level-three family does not operate under martial law or barbaric decrees from a dictator, each family member feels the need to always do the "right thing" for themselves, or for a partner or others. The tyrant or dictator is no longer needed in this family. The tyrant has been internalized by each family member and is experienced as the *shoulds* and *oughts* that direct their behavior. Each person generates strict adherence to the rules internally. The motivation: to be a good family member.

For example, let's say that the wife in a family is invited to go on a weekend reunion trip with some of her old college sorority sisters. Although she really wants to participate in this once-a-year trip, she lives by the following internalized family rule: A good wife/mother never leaves her family on the weekend. With that rule in control of her choice making, she is in a no-win position. If she goes away for the weekend, she feels guilty about leaving her family; if she stays home, she feels disappointed about the lost opportunity to have fun with her old friends. So she ends up feeling resentful and, before the weekend is over, provokes an argument with her husband about an unrelated issue. Neither of them has any insight into the underlying tension that is generated by this system of rules.

Here is another example of level-three functioning: A wife may feel she ought to have sex with her husband three times a week, even though she has no desire for it. But she is controlled by *oughts, shoulds, have-to's*. In this situation, she has no conscious awareness of what her sexual desires are. She either conforms to the "policy" and feels resentful—or doesn't conform and feels guilty. In either scenario, she does not have the freedom to rewrite the internalized policy for her own fulfillment. There is no emotional permission to discuss or question the rules. As a result, the level of intimacy in the family never goes very deep. The obligatory duties of each family member removes any opportunity for genuine emotional connection.

Dr. Beavers has created the term the *Invisible Referee*, which refers to an internal judge residing inside each family member's conscious mind. This Invisible Referee is an unspoken, unseen force that permeates all levels of behavior and feeling in this type of family. It is difficult to identify who the "good people" or "bad people" are, because it is the internal rule structure of the family that keeps all of them functioning this way. But no one in these families would argue about the power of these rules, or about the sense of guilt that is generated when certain rules are not followed.

Thus, the members of the level-three family act out the "invisible duty" they feel. Members do not know if they are doing or thinking something because they want to—or because they "should." For instance, an adult daughter, age thirty-one, living in Boston, three thousand miles away from her family in Los Angeles, plans to come home for Thanksgiving dinner because she "should be with her family." But she has no conscious awareness as to whether this trip is something she really wants to make. A similar situation may occur with a daughter who calls her mother every week; is it because she wants to, or out of a sense of obligation?

There is a fundamental underpinning of a level-three family—namely, that people are not capable of behaving spontaneously in responsible and loving ways. There must be rules to govern any and all loving acts of kindness and genuine concern. Their basic belief about human nature is that people are not trustworthy or caring. People do not know how to behave properly toward one another without clear-cut guidelines. Thus, the thrust behind all the rules and obligatory behavior is the inability to trust that a family member will unexpectedly behave in an authentic or loving manner. No deep, heartfelt emotional connections can be made with this invisible barrier in place against close, unstructured relating. The coldness and rigidity of the rules guarantee proper family and individual behavior, but the chance for individual expression—and real intimacy—is not possible for this family.

Thus, in level-three families, mothers and daughters become involved in struggles around the issues of self-expression and individuality. Any behavior that violates the family's sanctioned rules will not be tolerated. The rules serve to regulate behavior, but at the same time they prohibit any chance of personal connection between the two women, and interfere with any age-appropriate closeness and heartfelt feelings.

For example, there is no room for a daughter to proclaim, "This is who I am and what I want to do." Statements like this are met with admonitions from the mother, such as, "You know what people will think if you do that." What would ideally be a typical developmental discussion between a mother and daughter can, in this type of family, become a source of conflict and resentment.

Of course, you learn to develop your inner self as a woman by saying what you feel and think, even if it is considered "politically incorrect" by your family. But again, the development of a sense of oneself outside of the family rule structure is certainly not encouraged or fostered in the level-three family system. A daughter who begins to voice her inner thoughts and feelings will find her words met with criticism from her mother. Their chance at intimacy will be traded for *shoulds* and *oughts*. In this family, the legacy for a daughter is a deep sense of deprivation.

Dana, age thirty-three, came to us to find a way to emotionally move past the compulsion she felt to fail. She would sabotage herself at the most critical times to minimize any chance of success. This behavior was deeply connected to her mother and the family rules that Dana grew up with. She told us: *Every time I feel ready to move to the next level in my life, I find a way to mess it up or at least make myself miserable in the process. I work at a large law firm, and this self-defeating behavior of mine is always in operation.*

I think I hold on to this habit because I have never really forgiven myself for moving away from my mother. I feel like I never should have left home or tried to become successful. My older sister got married at age eighteen, has three chil-

dren, and lives two miles away from my mother. But I went to college out of state, struggled through law school, and still have never passed the bar exam. During all this time I've been so scared because I've never really asked for my mother's permission.

I have accomplished a lot, but I always feel like I'm looking over my shoulder. I have a sense of guilt for doing things differently from my mother and sister. They are both very critical of me, even for not being married. No matter what I do, it always seems wrong. I have made some serious career errors, and I do find my mother's support when I bottom out. But I also can hear her voice in my head, telling me what a bad girl I am for not doing things the right way.

Dana is clearly struggling with the internal rules that have governed her mother and sister. The issue of becoming a practicing attorney is forcing her to look at how she becomes so self-defeating at critical times. She wants to move beyond her family rules and become a more fulfilled and contented woman. But she fears she won't have her mother's support for this step forward; instead Dana will have to make a commitment to herself in order to rewrite the family rules. In Chapter Seven, we will further examine how an inadequate relationship with her mother can contribute to a daughter's fear of success.

Level 2—the Adequate Family, and Level 1—the Optimal Family

We will discuss these last two levels together. That's because adequate and optimal families are more similar than they are different. These families are at the healthier end of the clinical ladder of family functioning. They share important characteristics such as the ability to be comfortable with feelings, whether they be loving, annoying, or frustrating. These families have an emotional aptitude that allows them to take responsibility for mixed feelings and thoughts, ranging from ambivalence to unconditional love. They know they have permission to experience and respond to the everyday ups and downs of life.

Level-one-and-two families also display a great capacity for flexible responses to the circumstances in which they find themselves. They can focus on the issues at hand and the tasks they need to accomplish. Yes, these families do have conflicts and arguments. But angry or depressed feelings are not merely allowed, they are expected to exist as part of each individual's expression of his or her humanity. Unlike families at the previous levels, however, those at levels one and two generally experience little or no conflict that they find unresolvable. When misunderstandings arise, there is a desire among family members to clear them up and to facilitate greater communication. They have the ability and patience to work out problems. No predicament cannot be discussed or is off-limits emotionally. Most importantly, family members can acknowledge their differences without the fear of losing one another's support and love. This safety net of approval allows each member to develop a positive sense of self-worth and competence.

What separates functional families from chaotic ones is a sense of trust that allows relevant maturational events to take place. The generation gap between children and adults, for example, is expected, and is considered an appropriate part of family living. Individual differences are not suppressed in these families but are encouraged by years of safe, unconditional emotional bonding and interactions. There is a foundation of stability, trust, and mutual respect among all members that remains intact regardless of the surface issues or problems. This makes intimacy safe, without fear of being swallowed up by the family unit. We think the following story told to us by Sandy, age forty-six, and her daughter, Caroline, age nineteen, illustrates this process.

There's something going on here that I'm not comfortable

with. I hope that you will be able to help us. Sandy sat on the edge of her seat in our office. She looked tense and her speech felt pressured. Caroline was sitting next to her on the couch. Sandy continued: *Caroline came home this week from college and told us that she was not going to go back to school next fall. Rather, she is going to take an internship in New York and spend the next year working on a project. She says that she has every intention of returning to school the following year, but I don't know. It doesn't feel right to me.*

Her daughter looked at her for a moment and said, *Look, Mom, we've been over this. I know it's sudden, but I've been presented with an incredible opportunity and I want to take advantage of it.* Caroline turned to us and explained: *My economics instructor is going to New York next year to do a project for a major firm. He has asked two of us to accompany him. He has arranged for the university to give us partial credit for our work and we're getting paid. What could be better?*

Biting her lip, Sandy said, *I think it's wonderful that you have been selected. But this has all happened so fast. I'm concerned that you are making a hasty decision.*

We asked Sandy if there was anything else she was concerned about. She replied, *I'm not sure. I've raised my kids to think for themselves and to be open to change. It's so strange, now that I'm confronted with the results of my parenting philosophy, I feel like I've created a Frankenstein!*

Caroline put her arm around her mother and said, *Look, Mom, I know how you're feeling and I don't want you to be upset or worried. I also know, because you've often told me, that your own mother never let you roam beyond the parameters of your hometown. You've said you wanted to do it differently with your kids. Now you have the chance to.*

Sandy replied, with tears in her eyes, *I feel like a hypocrite. You know I trust you and I trust your judgment and I've always supported the choices you've made. But somehow this feels different. Maybe I'm having a reaction to your growing up!*

Caroline laughed. *Don't look now, Mom, but I am grown up! But seriously, I want to do this but I also want your support. I don't want you and Dad to feel anxious. You gave me the tools. I just want you to tell me that you trust me to use them.*

Here we have a mother and a daughter who obviously love and respect one another. While they value each other's point of view, they are not willing to sacrifice their own needs for the sake of the other. Therefore, they have learned to express their feelings so each of them has a clear understanding of the other's position. This kind of interaction is typical of the level of give-and-take that level-one-and-two families are capable of.

Whatever the style of family functioning, the common issues that ALL families—including your own—deal with are:

- power/control
- intimacy
- structure
- flexibility
- emotion

What sets the Optimal Family apart from the Chaotic or Severely Disturbed Family is how those key issues are dealt with and resolved. The presence or absence of positive relationship and communication skills determines a family's level of functioning. At the same time the way in which a family lives significantly affects the mother-daughter relationship.

Kinds of Families

Now that we've introduced you to the levels of family functioning, let's look at the kinds of families that exist within each of these five levels. The *kind* of family you come from does not necessarily define your *level* of family functioning.

Rather your family level explains how the key family issues (power/control, intimacy, structure, flexibility, emotion) are handled.

Mothers and daughters frequently ask us, *What kind of family did I come from?* We divide the answer to that question into two parts—*kinds* of families and *levels* of family functioning.

> *Kind of family:* understanding your family relationships in terms of the amount of emotional closeness or distance between family members.
>
> *Level of family functioning:* the way your family deals with the essential issues of power/control, intimacy, structure, flexibility, and emotion.

Now let's examine the *enmeshed family* and the *disengaged family*.

The Enmeshed Family

The enmeshed family is a very tight family group that believes that no one should have secret thoughts, feelings, or behaviors. Any and all things a daughter might want to feel, do, or dream are considered public domain by this family. Their emotional glue is closeness that, at critical times of change, can become a form of suffocation. But conformity is always the ideal, and it is rewarded in the enmeshed family. Actions such as moving away from the family for a career promotion are neither encouraged nor supported. In fact, they are punished by the family's withdrawal of its approval.

Of course, this style of relating might be appropriate at certain stages in a daughter's development. But serious problems arise when a daughter begins to want her own private space outside of the home. In the teen years, it is a normal part of personal growth to have a close group of girl and boy friends apart from the family. In an enmeshed family, however, a mother may allow her daughter's friends to come to the house, but she will want to know what they are saying and doing. She allows no room for separateness.

This kind of mother, when challenged about being overly involved in her daughter's life, will say that a good relationship is all about closeness. She won't understand her daughter's need to be a separate individual. But this degree of enmeshment often contributes to a daughter's developing an addictive-behavior outlet. Frequently, it takes the form of an obsession with food, leading to eating disorders like anorexia nervosa and/or bulimia nervosa.

The daughter's need to control her food intake and her body are her direct reaction to being intruded upon and overcontrolled by her mother. She needs to feel in control of some part of her life, and her body becomes the battleground that she will not allow her mother, or any other family member, to usurp.

Daughters with intrusive mothers may choose other escape practices, such as drug abuse, alcohol abuse, and sexual acting out. These three addictions, like eating disorders, serve to create personal space for a daughter. Each of them, however, can impair her ability to mature. While a daughter might win the fight over her body, she may lose many years of life as a result.

As we mentioned earlier, the family needs to use some enmeshed behaviors at times—for instance, to ensure a baby's health and development. The key is to have the flexibility to change, and to know when to give a daughter the room she needs. In your own family, that may mean allowing your daughter to separate and begin to have her own thoughts, dreams, and goals, separate from yours. As a mother, you don't have to experience it as a personal assault or a sign of disrespect when your daughter wants to keep some of her own thoughts to herself. It's part of growing up.

Take a few minutes to think about the following questions

about enmeshment. Some of them are just for mothers and some for daughters:

1. List two areas of your life where you do not feel in complete control.

For Daughters:

2. How important is it for you to have separate space from your mother?
3. What role does guilt play in your interactions with your mother?
4. How scary is it for you to take an action, or make an important decision, without your mother's approval?
5. If you could have your way, how much emotional distance or closeness would you have between you and your mother?
6. How much emotional space do you need from your mother in order to feel comfortable?
7. How willing are you to let your mother do what she desires without your approval?

For Mothers:

8. How much emotional space would feel ideal between you and your daughter?
9. How scary is it for you to let your daughter do what she desires?
10. How scary is it to make a decision without your daughter's approval?

These questions are designed to create a new kind of thinking about the role that enmeshment has played in your relationship with your mother or daughter. Your Mending Move here is to remain connected to significant people in your life, but to maintain this connection without becoming enmeshed. You don't have to be enmeshed in order to feel safe and competent.

Your goal, ideally, is to develop the ability to remain close to your mother or daughter without losing yourself in the relationship. The challenge is to find a balance between emotional enmeshment and abandonment. Living life at either end of the continuum leaves family members emotionally starved. Mothers and daughters thrive with a balance between closeness and distance.

Susan is a full-time mother of two daughters—Christy, age nine and Karen, age fifteen. She came to us when her oldest daughter began to openly challenge her. She said, *I have allowed my daughters to sleep in my bed since they were little girls. But now Karen does not want to have individual time with me. I wish I didn't take her actions toward independence so personally, but I do. I have resorted to reading Karen's journal at night to find out what is going on in her life. She won't talk to me, and I need to know who her friends are and if she is having sex.*

I don't like the fact that people tell me to leave Karen alone. You see, she needs me right now. What kind of mother would I be if I just let Karen do what she wanted? I am doing everything I can to be the best possible mother and I won't let Karen "do her own thing" without my support.

Since this discussion, Susan has begun to learn that Karen's reaction to their emotionally enmeshed relationship is normal and part of becoming a young adult. Nevertheless, Susan has tremendous issues with separation that still cause her to overfocus on Karen's age-appropriate behavior. Susan is resistant to her daughter's need for autonomy and personal space. She experiences Karen's moves toward independence as a personal rejection, and thus still fights this natural process. As result, the relationship between Susan and Karen will continue to be strained until there is a shift in their emotional connection.

The Disengaged Family

This family system creates cement walls between family members. In the disengaged family, no one is noticed or acknowledged. Even major life events, like a graduation or a wedding, don't cause many ripples. Emotional distance is the rule, with family members showing no interest in developing close, intimate, loving relationships.

Members of disengaged families avoid overinvolvement or excessively close emotional ties. They discourage and avoid intimate connections that are part of normal family living. For them, there is safety in never being close to other family members, and so they ignore all intimate thoughts, feelings, or needs.

This family, from an outsider's point of view, appears cold and uncaring. But the truth is that their feelings are simply repressed and out of their conscious awareness. The family rules work to keep all important and meaningful things inside. They adhere to an unspoken family law to resist expressing emotion, feeling connected, or sharing.

In this type of family, a daughter might be tempted to share with her mother some insecure feelings. She will find, however, that nobody is listening, literally and symbolically. This style of relating teaches her that there is no point in paying attention to her own needs and wants. There is no one around to support her in her attempts to satisfy her longings.

Disengaged family members feel insecure, abandoned, and resentful. These feelings are often exhibited outside the home in the form of violence (directed either at oneself or others), gang membership, drug experimentation, and poor school performance. In adolescence, a daughter's acting out is really the lament: "Does anyone notice me?"

For the disengaged family, home is just the place where you sleep at night and leave every morning. In this situation, a daughter quickly learns to look outside the home to get her emotional needs met. Later, as an adult, her challenge will be to create and maintain an intimate relationship with a partner. But because consistent love and attention have never been available to her inside the home, she may end up involved in extramarital affairs.

As you can imagine, if you've grown up with a lack of nurturing, you will probably have an insecure self-image. After all, it is difficult to value yourself if you grew up believing that you or anything you did were not deserving. If you came from this type of family, you will tend to minimize the importance of a birthday, the loss of a friend, or the importance of personal achievements (educational, relational, and professional).

The following story describes a client of ours named Connie, who comes from a disengaged family. At age thirty-seven, she has grappled throughout her adult life with a sense of worthlessness. She told us: *I remember when I was about nine years old, and my mom forgot to pick me up after school one day. It was snowing, and I stood in the front of the school, in the snow, for three hours, waiting for her. Finally, one of my classmates' parents, who was driving by the school, gave me a ride home.*

When I got home, my mom was in the house. I asked her why she hadn't picked me up after school? She said, "I'm sorry, I forgot." I believed her. I know that she hadn't even noticed that I wasn't home, so how could she be concerned?

I also remember that during my senior year in high school, my mom promised to come to our class play. I was so excited because I had the lead role. She never showed up, and never mentioned it or apologized to me for not being there.

Connie continued talking with increasing sadness in her voice: *It's really hard for me to trust people now or to believe that anyone cares about me. I have developed the pattern of dating men, having sex with them, but never encouraging any type of emotional connection with them. I have a difficult time being close to people emotionally, even though I really enjoy it when it does happen. As for my mom, I have lived in California for fifteen years, and she has never come to see me. She rarely calls, and if we do speak, it's because I call her.*

Connie's story is a painful example of how a daughter from a disengaged family learns not to value herself or her life.

She is working with us on her inability to emotionally connect with people, with the goal of cultivating more meaningful relationships.

At this point we hope that you've begun to think about the descriptions of enmeshed and disengaged families, combined with the five levels of family functioning, and used this as a starting point to begin your own family exploration. This is crucial information for your own life today. After all, it is a challenge to create your own family when you are living with the emotional deficits caused by your past family injuries. Hopefully, a better understanding of old wounds, misunderstandings, and arguments will allow you to learn, as a daughter and/or a mother, how to proceed forward and avoid repeating the same mistakes. No particular type or style of family functioning is insurmountable, nor is it a reason to avoid having a family of your own.

The Importance of Safety

If you were raised in a chaotic or a rule-bound family, with a strong tendency toward enmeshment or disengagement, you might start this process by examining the issue of safety. Whether you are a young woman looking toward starting your own family, or woman in midlife with grown children of your own, it is never too late to address this issue of safety. Unless you set aside the emotional, physical, and psychological weapons of the past, and make a commitment to the creation of a safe family environment for yourself, it will be difficult to build a different kind of family experience.

The safety we are referring to is all-encompassing. For instance, if you are a survivor of incest, sexual and physical abuse, or neglect, the first step in creating your new family is to find emotional refuge. Your partner may not understand how crucial it is to you to feel emotionally, physically, and psychologically safe until you explain your history. Then, to create your new family, you can begin with the commitment to make your family atmosphere more flexible than the one you were raised in, with ongoing dialogues about the need for security.

As you begin this process, ask yourself the following question: What were some of the valuable things I learned from my family of origin? With a few exceptions, our original families do provide some meaningful tools and insights that you can use to build your own family. As an adult, you need to sort out what was meaningful and useful there, and discard the unproductive behaviors, beliefs, and inappropriate rules.

For some women, the idea that their original family provided a foundation for them to build on might seem to be an incomprehensible concept rather than a reassuring reality. If that's the case with you, ask yourself: What is the first constructive and valuable thing that you think of when you contemplate what you learned from your family about living? Something should come to mind. You can amend and add to it, but use it to enhance the quality of life that you want for yourself and the people you love.

Consider the experiences of Amy, who, at the age of forty-four, has overcome a very problematic family background and created her own family. Amy was born when her mother was sixteen years old. She grew up living with her mother and a series of stepfathers until she left home at the age of seventeen. Amy's father is a convicted felon, and she never spent time with him outside of prison. She has also survived sexual abuse and neglect. Amy told us: *I do not like to talk about my past because it scares people. I made a decision when I was eight years old that I would live my life differently. I knew that no one was going to help me, and I had to find a way to make things happen. I got myself into college with an academic scholarship. I knew that an education would help me overcome my problems. I got married when I was twenty-four years old to a wonderful man. My husband, Andy, still does not know all the things that have happened to me.*

I made a commitment that my children (Thomas, eighteen

*years old, and Carl, fourteen years old) would have a safe
and stable home. So I have worked very hard to make our
home emotionally, mentally, and physically safe. We do not
argue, but we discuss things in an open-minded manner.*

*I refuse to allow my mother or father to be a source of
conflict in my life. They could not get their lives together,
but I have. My growing up taught me how to survive. Now,
as an adult, I have learned to thrive, in spite of my past.*

Amy is a very strong woman who, at a young age, decided
to do something with her life. She has never lost sight of her
chaotic family of origin, but she has moved herself beyond
her early history. The twin values of safety and stability are
the hallmark of the family she has created for herself and
her children.

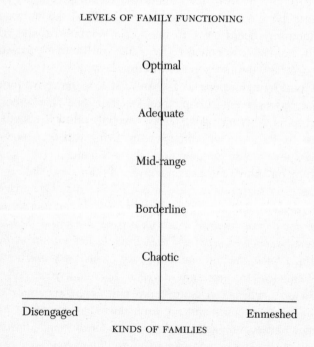

LEVELS OF FAMILY FUNCTIONING

Optimal

Adequate

Mid-range

Borderline

Chaotic

Disengaged   Enmeshed

KINDS OF FAMILIES

Scale of Family Functioning

Now try to identify where your own family of origin is located on the scale of family functioning. How did your family cope with intimate feelings, trust, differences of opinion, and independence? Was it a safe environment? Was your family leaning more toward the enmeshed or disengaged ends of the family continuum? Where would you put your family on this continuum?

Next, if you had to place your family into a category of functioning, where would you put it?

1. Chaotic, Severely Disturbed
2. Borderline
3. Mid-range
4. Adequate
5. Optimal

You can use this chart to create your own family blueprint. If your family falls on the enmeshed side of the continuum, how far up does it go on the perpendicular axis of levels of functioning? For instance, you can have an enmeshed family that is chaotic or an enmeshed family that is adequate. Or you can have a disengaged family on the mid-range axis. You can use this chart to expand your awareness of how your family operates.

Now think about the direction in which you would like your new family to move. You have enough information to begin the process of creating a more fulfilling family life. Yes, it is a tremendous undertaking to make personal changes, but it is extremely important to begin this mending process. And what if you believe that the issues before you are just too overwhelming? We suggest that you seek out professional support. Do not underestimate the power of an objective, supportive professional who can assist you in dealing with unresolved family issues.

5 Shaking the Family Tree: Three Generations of Mothers and Daughters

I am still supporting my fifty-two-year-old daughter financially. She couldn't have raised her own daughter without me. She still needs me to help her.

—Mary, age 76

My mother is still telling me what to do. Sometimes I just go along with it because she is old and has no one else but me and my daughter in her life.

—Marcia, age 52

I feel like the parent when I deal with my mother and my grandmother. All they do is fight and argue. The only time either one of them acknowledges me is when they want me to take sides. —Jennifer, age 24

I can't believe I just said that. I sound just like my mother! Marcia is sitting across from us, discussing her relationship with her daughter, Jennifer. She has been saying how difficult it has been for her to talk to Jennifer. *I feel that I have to walk on eggshells when I'm around her.* Then, at this point in our conversation, she made the remark about sounding like her mother.

This is a statement that we hear frequently. Sometimes a woman is horrified when all-too-familiar words come out of her mouth. Or when she recognizes similarities between herself and her mother, she may feel overwhelmed with sadness or regret. At one time or another, however, almost every woman has made this kind of statement to herself or someone else. It usually creates such an emotional jolt that, in this moment of awareness, her powerful feelings bring her life to a screeching halt.

History—Are We Doomed to Repeat It?

We are always curious to learn how women react when they realize that an active piece of their mother resides, alive and well, inside of them. If you have spent time and energy attempting to "do it differently" from your mother, it can be very disorienting to hear yourself echoing her words. Even if you have always admired your mother and patterned your behavior on hers, you may find yourself surprised and even unsettled by how very much like her you really are. No matter what your reaction, the reasons for the similarities among generations may lie deep within your family history.

If you were our client and you suddenly realized that you sounded like your mother, we would usually ask you to tell us more about your relationship with her: How do you feel about your mother (or felt, if she is no longer living)? What was your life like with your mother while you were growing up? What style of mothering did you experience? As therapists, we find that the answers to these questions allow us to help you begin to understand your own behavior and that of your mother.

We try to look at each mother-daughter relationship from an evolutionary point of view. Whatever is going on in this relationship did not start with just that one mother and her daughter. Each mother is also a daughter and her relationship with her own mother has the power to influence all the generations of women that will succeed them.

To look at what else impacts the mother-daughter relationship, for good or ill, we also need to look at the larger picture—specifically, the influence of factors outside of the family. The society and the culture we live in have always had a profound effect on the way women parent their daughters and the way daughters experience their mothers. Let's examine this issue more closely by looking at the specific case of our client Marcia.

If we were going to help Marcia improve her relationship with her daughter, we needed to find out more about Marcia's relationship with her own mother. After all, we know that the behaviors of families, like history and the culture we live in, tend to repeat themselves. And by reading about Marcia's mother, Mary, and her life experience, you may gain insights into your own mother-daughter relationship.

We started this chapter with quotations from Marcia, her mother, Mary, and her daughter, Jennifer. Their words are powerful and painful statements about where these three generations of women—grandmother, mother, and grand-daughter—feel that their relationships with one another stand today. Each quote can be evaluated in terms of what we have already talked about in previous chapters, as well as what you are about to read in the rest of this chapter.

To begin with, these statements might tell us something about the early attachment relationship that each of these women had with her own mother, and how that early attachment experience is affecting them today. For instance, Marcia grew up experiencing Mary as having her own agenda—an agenda that had nothing to do with Marcia's feelings. Mary still believes that she knows better than Marcia about almost everything, especially Marcia's life. When Marcia has to deal with her mother, like the avoidant babies we discussed in Chapter Two, she either gives in or takes an oppositional stance to anything her mother says.

We also may glean something from their comments about the style(s) of mothering that each of them experienced. For example, Jennifer grew up experiencing Marcia's Supermom style of mothering (*My mother is still telling me what to do.*).

Marcia's underlying fears about her own inadequacies were covered with a veneer of rigid *shoulds* and *oughts*. These strict limits on her behavior were direct legacies from her mother, Mary, who, in her own right, practiced the Supermom style of mothering (*She couldn't have raised her own daughter without me. She still needs me to help her.*). In this kind of atmosphere, there was no room for Jennifer's concerns or feelings.

As we try to understand the basic differences between these three generations of women, we need to consider another important dynamic. These women must be looked at in the historical context of the times in which they were born. We need to understand the influence of the culture that surrounded them, and the culture experienced by their parents, if we want to create a more complete and accurate picture of who they are and why they function as they do today. The dominant messages, attitudes, beliefs, and customs that influence parents at the time that their children are born are an important part of the belief system they pass on to their children.

For example, a recent survey revealed that 58 percent of "baby boomer" parents (parents who came of age in the 1960s) did not consider drug use by their own adolescent children to be a particularly serious problem. After all, this generation of parents did a lot of experimenting with drugs in their own adolescence and early twenties. Having survived their own youthful experimentation, they seem to assume that their children will somehow survive as well.

But if this same survey had been taken among parents who were born ten years earlier and, therefore, became parents earlier than the "boomers," the outcome would have been markedly different. The times we live in have a great deal of influence on how we think, feel, and act. They also affect how we were parented.

Mothers have always depended upon feedback from the culture around them to reflect on their performance as parents. This is especially true of women who do not have an extended family system to rely upon for support. Young parents, and especially young mothers, are always looking to "experts" to tell them what is best for their baby.

For example, in a interview with Mary, Marcia's mother, we learned that for her parents' generation, the experts on child rearing were the older women in their own families and the women in the neighborhood. Mary was raised in the era of "spare the rod and spoil the child," and this attitude was shared and reinforced by her family network and community. Mary became a mother during World War II, when the prevailing influences were still the family and the community. The war affected women in ways they could not have predicted as the winds of change regarding their roles began to blow for them.

Marcia told us that by the time she became a parent, the old rules had become new rules or "no rules." When she had Jennifer, she had no extended family or community network immediately available to help her. She and her husband had moved to another city, and like many others of her generation, she felt isolated and on her own. Dr. Spock was her bible, and her mother's protestations, during Mary's frequent visits, that she was spoiling Jennifer fell on deaf ears.

Meanwhile, when Jennifer was born, Marcia, along with many of her contemporaries, had become caught up in the currents of the women's movement. These women fervently believed that because of their newfound awareness of their own potential, their daughters could "have it all." Jennifer, however, as she approached young adulthood, found herself in what felt like a "no win" position. For Jennifer and her generation, the goal of "having it all," was not a realistic one. In order to take her own place in the adult world, she had to make choices and deal with realities that her mother and grandmother never dreamed of. Today, she feels frightened, shortchanged, and very unprepared.

Changing Times and Changing Values

In the lifetimes of Mary, Marcia, and Jennifer, three generations of women, there have been more advances in science and technology, and more changes in lifestyle than took place during any other time frame in history. One of these changes, however, is that the close-knit, extended families and communities that nurtured Mary and Marcia's generations are no longer an expected and predictable part of our social fabric.

At the beginning of this century there was a clear line of demarcation separating "men's work" and "women's work." The work of women, homemaking and child rearing, was intended to help and sustain the men in their lives. By supporting men, these women were maintaining the structure of the society they lived in. Without this kind of sustenance, men could not do what was expected and valued: be productive and maintain the way of life of their community.

Thus, society needed women to support men by taking care of the home front, and this particular tradition was handed down by generations of mothers to their daughters. Daughters were taught to meet the needs of men and, therefore, society as a whole, just as their mothers had. Questioning their role or their mother's role was not an option. The message from mother to daughter was "this is what we do." A potentially unruly daughter who challenged this way of life was brought back sharply into line by her parents or community.

These restless daughters learned quickly that it is hard to sustain a rebellion alone. A woman who doubted the relevance of her limited and limiting role would be threatening not only to society at large but, ironically, to her own mother. If a daughter questioned whether she wanted to replay her mother's role, this might make her mother take a closer look at her own life. And looking back at a life without choices, a life based on *shoulds* and *oughts,* can be devastating.

So we had generations of women who, with few exceptions, didn't question who they were or what they were doing. In turn, we had generations of daughters who learned from their mothers how society wanted them to be and, instead of challenging their culture, grew up either resenting or blaming their mothers.

During just the past thirty years there have been other major shifts in our society. Our perceptions of ourselves, our work, our relationships, and the world we live in have undergone major upheavals. Think about the impact of the following on women's lives today:

- The pill
- legalized abortion
- the increase in single-parent families
- families in which both parents work full-time
- babies born to mothers in their late thirties or forties
- lack of competent child care
- the need to choose between career and family
- juggling work, children, and the care of an elderly parent

Think about the power of each of these changes and the dramatic shifts they have created in women's roles—and the impact they have had on the mother-daughter relationship. Each mother and her daughter coming out of this crucible have had to alter their concepts of what they expect from themselves and from one another.

Here is what we hear from women in response to these changes.

Impact of Changes on the Mother's Point of View

- "I cannot relate to my daughter and the way she lives her life."

- "My daughter is more interested in her career and her friends than she is in her family."
- "Her work takes precedence over everything in her life. I'm afraid I'm never going to have a grandchild."
- "Did I do something wrong?"
- "Why is it so hard for us to talk to each other?"

Impact of Changes on the Daughter's Point of View

- "My mother doesn't *get* it!"
- "It was easier for her when she was my age. She had all those rules to go by."
- "My mother doesn't understand why I haven't married and had a family like she did."
- "If and when I do marry, I won't be 'taken care of' by my husband the way she was by my dad."
- "I have to be prepared to take care of myself and not depend upon a man. She doesn't understand that."

Statements like these have a "never the twain shall meet" feeling to them. We have learned, however, that even when it seems as if an insurmountable gulf exists between a mother and a daughter, a face-to-face discussion about something they have in common, like their shared family history, works wonders in helping them reconnect.

Emotional "Stuck-Togetherness"

Family theorist Murray Bowen studied the way family members relate to one another. Watching and listening to these family interactions, he discovered clear patterns of behavior that are passed down from one generation to the next. When we work with families like those of Mary, Marcia, and Jennifer, we begin the process by helping them examine their families through the lens of two important concepts formulated by Bowen: *the undifferentiated family ego mass* and *the multigenerational family transmission process.* These two complicated-sounding processes are very commonsense ways of describing what goes on in families. We will now illustrate what we mean by them and why we find them useful.

Bowen's observation of the various types of conduct that take place among family members led to his theory of the *undifferentiated family ego mass.* He used this very long (and to many, incomprehensible) term to describe the way families relate to one another at times of great stress and/or anxiety—a marriage, a birth, a move from one city to another. In fact, he found that in times of stress many families react by becoming "emotionally stuck-together." What this means is that, in a crisis, it may appear as if the members of a family are acting in total accord, each thinking and feeling in exactly the same way. When the family is in this mode of operating, they act like a thermostat on a furnace. Any family member with a differing opinion is going to be experienced by the rest of the family like a change in temperature in the house. The family responds by "turning up the heat" on the offending member—"you don't really want to do that," "you don't really believe that," "change back."

According to Bowen, anxiety often develops in families around issues of separation. Separation, in this instance, can take the form of behaving or even thinking differently than other family members. The anxiety surrounding separation issues can be a warning sign that old conflicts between family members that have never been sufficiently dealt with are being replayed in some way today.

The tension that results from this "unfinished business," in either an individual or a family, can lead to the kinds of behaviors we call symptoms, such as:

- a child with behavioral and emotional problems in school
- an acting-out teenager
- a husband or a wife with a psychosomatic illness
- the development of depression in a spouse

These symptoms usually bring people into counseling. By analyzing the patterns of a family's behavior, we can find the source of this anxiety and its ensuing symptoms.

Unresolved issues or unfinished business may also be the origin of specific types of behavior between family members. In other words, the way one family member relates to another may be profoundly affected by a piece of old business that could even date back to a previous generation. Bowen believed that directly addressing the persistent, underlying issues that produce tension is crucial. His goal was to help family members change their perspective about their ongoing relationships with one another. By altering their perspective, they could create an opportunity to change the way they relate to one another.

The following vignette about our client Annie graphically reveals the emotional "stuck-togetherness" found in her family and in many others.

Annie is thirty-two years old. A transplanted New Yorker, she has lived in California for five years with her husband and two children. She is attractive and articulate, with a very expressive face. According to Annie, her marriage is solid. She says that she has enjoyed her life in California and that it feels like home now. She hesitantly adds that she does have "down times" that seem to come out of the blue. These "down times" have led her to seek our help.

We asked Annie to tell us more about her "down times": What did they feel like? How frequently did they occur? Most important, what was going on in her life right before they struck?

Annie said that they rob her of all her energy—that she just can't do anything while they are going on. She said they make her feel "blue," "weepy," and isolated from her family. She added, almost as an afterthought, that they happen an average of once a week, usually on Sundays

Following her lead, we asked her what happens in her house on Sundays.

Annie told us that Sunday is family day. They go to church in the mornings and then out to lunch. The afternoons are devoted to an activity with the children—visits with friends, playing ball, going to the movies. They are always home by five o'clock so that they can call their families on the East Coast.

This last statement really got our attention. We asked Annie if her down times started before or after the phone calls to her family. We were operating, at this point, under the assumption that her "blues" were being triggered by someone or something connected to these calls.

Annie, looking very thoughtful and subdued, said, "You know, I just realized that I begin to feel strange, you know, different, on our way home in the late afternoons. It's almost like a cloud covering up the sun. I know that sounds foolish, but that's the way it feels. By the time I've finished talking to everyone on the phone, it's there—full-blown."

We asked her who she specifically talks to. We also wanted to know if she feels more down after talking to her family or her husband's family.

By this time Annie was looking more and more troubled. She said that they usually talk to her in-laws first and then to her family. Her voice was firm as she explained that she has no difficulty talking to her in-laws. But then she hesitated. Her voice became quieter and she slumped down in her chair as she told us that it was difficult for her to talk to her own father, mother, and grandmother. She pulled herself up a little straighter and added "No, that's not quite right. I don't really have a problem talking to my father. It's when I talk to my mother and my grandmother that I start to feel sad and blue."

We asked Annie to tell us about her relationship with both of these important women in her life.

Annie said that she had a wonderful relationship with her mother and her grandmother. Her grandmother had lived with Annie's parents since her husband died, when Annie was six years old. She said that her mother and grandmother did everything together. She described growing up feeling very loved and special, "like I had two mothers."

We asked if there had ever been any kind of disagreement between any of them. Was there anything that would have made Annie, as she was growing up, feel uncomfortable?

Annie vehemently denied the existence of any problems in the family. "All the women in our family are very close," she said.

Annie had just shared with us a very important family rule—"women in our family are close." We wondered about Annie's move to California and how it had affected her mother and her grandmother. If women in her family were supposed to be "close," then Annie had broken that rule by moving so far away. Was she being punished, in a very subtle way, for her actions? We asked her how her mother and grandmother felt about her move.

Annie reported that her whole family had been very upset by her decision to leave the East Coast. She had never had a conversation with her mother or her grandmother without one of them asking when she was going to move back "home," or when she was coming to visit. Both women bemoaned the fact that Annie's children were growing up so fast, and that they were missing out on a day-to-day relationship with them.

Annie said these conversations made her feel guilty and sad, the same way she had felt as a child when she had done something bad. She also was aware of some feelings of anger within her "This feels very new and very uncomfortable. I don't ever remember feeling angry at my mother or my grandmother. I realize that's impossible. I watch my own children. They have angry feelings. It's normal. Why can't I remember mine?"

At this point we explained to Annie about the emotional stuck-togetherness that happens in families, and the anxiety that surfaces when something creates tension (like breaking a family rule and moving to California). Annie's move had caused a strain among herself and her mother and grand-mother. We made an educated guess that it also activated some old issues between her mother and grandmother that might not have surfaced if Annie had never moved.

If our hypothesis about Annie's family was true, what was the best way for her to take care of herself and mend the breach with her mother and grandmother? Here is what we advised (these same guidelines may work for you in a similar situation).

MENDING MOVES FOR ANNIE

- Plan a series of visits, phone calls, or letters to her mother and grandmother, specifically for the purpose of information gathering about the relationships of the women in their family. While face-to-face dialogues are terrific, they are not essential for opening a discussion about family history.

- Talk or write to both her mother and grandmother, separately. Find out the following from each of them: (1) What was her relationship like with her own mother while she was growing up? (2) Was there anything in her life that she would have liked to have done differently?

- Give herself permission to accept that her decision to move to California was made in *her* best interest. It was not made to deliberately hurt or upset her mother and grandmother.

- Recognize that a close relationship with someone does not mean that you are glued at the hip. Give herself permission to see herself as a separate person.

If we had the opportunity to work with Annie's mother or grandmother, we would make the following suggestions.

MENDING MOVES FOR ANNIE'S MOTHER/GRANDMOTHER:

- Make a list of the ways that you and your mother are alike. Then make another list of the ways that you are different. Which items on these lists are affecting the choices that you are making in your life today?
- Take a look back at your relationship with your mother. How did it affect your own style of mothering? How is it affecting your relationship with Annie today?
- Write a letter to Annie (you do not have to mail it). Tell her how her moving away made you feel. As you write, allow yourself to experience all of your feelings fully. Some of them might be uncomfortable and some may be downright painful. In the long run, however, it is more painful to pretend they don't exist.
- Allow yourself to honestly acknowledge, perhaps for the first time, that there are differences between you and your daughter. Doing so can free you to appreciate her as a separate person.

During the next few months, Annie worked on her Mending Moves. In the process, she learned things about herself, and about the relationship between her mother and grandmother. Annie had turned a corner and they all will benefit.

The Genogram

Murray Bowen believed that the inability of family members to have any meaningful interaction with one another is the result of a breakdown in their patterns of relating over the course of several generations. If left to their own devices, without some kind of intervention, these families will become more and more dysfunctional with each succeeding generation. He called this concept of family functioning the *multigenerational family transmission process*.

We find this complicated-sounding concept useful in helping our women clients understand how the patterns of relationships in previous generations are still affecting their relationships with their mothers or daughters today. We use a device called a "genogram" to illustrate the way patterns of relating tend to repeat themselves from one generation to the next.

In appearance, a genogram resembles a family tree. In reality, it is a tool for gathering information about three generations of family members. Besides graphically illustrating the history of marriages, births, and deaths in a family, a genogram also provides information about the kinds of relationships that exist (or existed) between the members of a family.

When you examine a genogram, you can vividly see the transitions that have taken place in the life cycle of the family. And because so much of the behavior in families is repetitive, from one generation to the next, you can use a genogram to make tentative projections about future behavior trends.

A genogram provides many other kinds of information. Some is purely historical; one genogram showed how four generations of women on both sides of one family had married career military men. We have done others that trace patterns of alcoholism from grandparent to parent to child.

In other instances, genograms can reveal critical information relevant to a woman's present life circumstances. For example, a recent genogram showed that the women on both sides of a daughter's family had a tendency to marry men who were abusive or substance abusers, or both. In light of this information, we made a tentative assumption that the daughter herself might be at risk for marrying the same kind of man.

A genogram is a blank slate, waiting to be filled in with all of the historical and emotional data about a family. The beauty of the genogram is its simplicity. At the end of this chapter you will find a blank genogram and instructions on how you can use it with your mother or your daughter to explore your own family dynamics. It is an information-gathering tool, and everyone can use it.

The following is a brief explanation of each element of the genogram key.

- male ▢ All male figures on a genogram are represented by squares.

- female ◯ All female figures on a genogram are represented by circles.

- marriage ▰▰▰ A solid unbroken line denotes a marital relationship.

- Conflicted (relationship) ⋙⋙ A relationship where discord and antagonism are the norm. Arguing and fighting are the common form of communication (and sometimes a substitute for intimacy).

- Fused (relationship) ≡≡≡ A fused relationship occurs when the degree of closeness between two family members is so intense that they lose the sense of being individuals. This type of relationship is similar to the enmeshed relationships we wrote about in Chapter Four.

- Close (relationships) ▭▭▭ A warm and caring relationship, whose hallmarks are the ability to communicate openly and the capacity to tolerate differences.

- Distant (relationship) ▬ ▬ ▬ A distant relationship is defined by little connection, caring, or communication between individuals.

- Former (relationship) ▬▬·· Used to designate a former significant relationship with an old boyfriend or girlfriend.

- Divorced ▮▮▮▮▮▮▮ This symbol is used to show the relationship between former spouses.

- Dead ✗ This symbol is used to show that a family member is no longer living.

Opening Doors to the Past

As we have pointed out, emotional themes and sequences that are present in one generation tend to resurface in others. Most people, however, are unaware that elements of past family relationships recur in present-day relationships. They are usually surprised to see how an issue that has particular meaning and intensity for them can appear and reappear on their family genogram.

That was the case with Julie, one of our clients. Julie is forty-one years old. She has been married for five years to her husband, Chuck. She describes their relationship as "good, with the usual ups and downs." They have a three-year-old son, Robby, whom they both adore, and she is expecting another child.

Julie entered counseling after experiencing a series of recurring nightmares. These nightmares began after she had an ultrasound test, and learned that she was going to have a girl. She told us, *I think I'm losing my mind. In my dreams I'm surrounded by people and things I cannot see. I have this overwhelming sense of dread, and I wake up gasping for air.*

We explored the history of Julie's marriage, and how she felt about motherhood. She said she loved being a mother, but admitted that she was a little nervous about having a girl. *I don't know why, but I feel like I don't know how to be a good mother to a girl*, she told us.

We decided to do a genogram with Julie (the results of her genogram are on page 151). First, we asked her for the names, ages, and dates of death of all of her immediate family members. Then, at our request, she also gave us a list of adjectives that she would use to describe each family member and herself. We put these lists of adjectives next to the symbol representing the particular family member she was discussing. In other words, while Julie was telling us about her maternal grandmother, we put the list of adjectives that Julie used to describe her grandmother next to the symbol on the genogram that represented her grandmother (circle in upper right-hand corner).

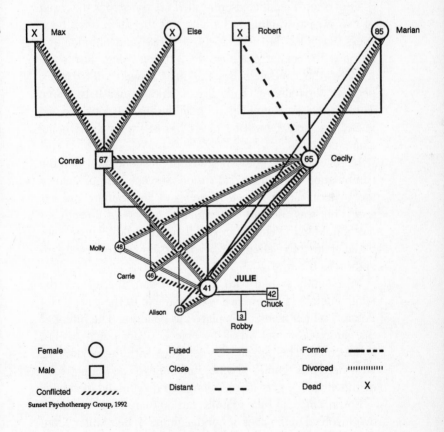

Julie's Genogram

Finally, we asked her to describe each of the relationships between the members of her family, using the key below the genogram as a guide.

We handed Julie a completed copy of her genogram and let her interpret what she observed for herself. She expressed amazement at what she saw. All of the major relationships between women in her genogram were a mixture of conflict and fusion. And when an enmeshed relationship is combined with conflict, all the individuals involved experience feelings of anxiety.

Very often a conflicted-enmeshed relationship is the result of two people wanting to be close. At the same time, however, they feel the need to be separate and autonomous, because too much closeness feels threatening. For some families, the concept of separation is fraught with danger, because separateness feels like a kind of death to them. Therefore, a push-pull type of relationship develops. No one is really separate, but one never has to worry about being alone, either.

In Julie's family, you can see from her genogram that the combination of conflict and fusion was not only present in the relationships between herself and her mother and her sisters but was also part of her mother's relationship with her mother, Marian. This is an excellent example of how emotional styles of relating can be passed down from one generation to the next.

In a family system with a lot of fusion, the anxiety the family members experience is comparable to the game "Hot Potato," which many of us played as children. The intent of the game was to get rid of the object, or hot potato, as fast as we could. The person who got stuck with the object lost. How does this "game" play out in families? The hot potato— or the anxiety—gets passed along to other family members.

For instance, in Julie's family, her mother, Cecily, was very overinvolved in the lives of her daughters. Julie's father, Conrad, felt left out because his wife's energy was focused on the girls. Because his need for attention was not being met by her, he would criticize his daughters as a way of releasing his unexpressed anger toward his wife. Julie and her sisters, in turn, would run to their mother to complain about how unfairly they were being treated by their father. Julie's mother would then berate her husband for being "too hard" on the girls, and attempt to make it up to them for their father's "inexplicable" behavior. Thus, the cycle would begin again.

When you pass the anxiety along to others in this way, you may feel a sense of relief (Julie's father felt relief when criticizing Julie and her sisters, and Julie and her sisters felt relief when they complained about their father to their mother). This respite, however, is short-lived. Another wave of anxiety is sure to appear, and as it gets passed along, the exhausting "game" goes on.

As Julie continued to look at her genogram with us, she said, *No wonder I'm scared of having a girl! Look at my relationships with my mother and my sisters!* We asked her specifically to tell us more about her maternal grandmother, and what their relationship was like.

Julie described her grandmother, Marian, as warm and loving. She had always been available for Julie while she was growing up. Julie believed that her grandmother provided her with the significant "maternal" figure she craved. She could experience her grandmother as a person separate from herself, which felt impossible to do with her mother.

We pointed out that in her new role as mother to a daughter, Julie needed to understand the importance of her special relationship with her grandmother. It was critical for her to see that she was capable of having a warm, loving relationship with a woman. Having her grandmother as a role model provided Julie with the balance that she longed for in her life. She could depend on her grandmother in ways that were impossible with her anxious mother. She felt gratified when she realized that her style of mothering her son was patterned on the way her grandmother had nurtured her.

Julie also needed to know that she had the capacity to form a loving relationship with her new daughter, even though she had not resolved all of her unfinished business with her own mother or her sisters. Not surprisingly, as all these insights fell into place, her nightmares stopped.

The Role of Grandmother

In light of Julie's positive experiences with her grandmother, let's take a closer look at the importance of a grandmother in the life of her granddaughter. We have already discussed patterns of behavior that run in families. Now, in focusing on grandmothers, we will begin by asking some interesting questions:

- If an outside observer were to look at the mothering styles of both a mother and a grandmother, would she/ he see more similarities than differences?
- How is a granddaughter affected by the inadequacies in the way her mother was mothered by her grandmother?
- Will a grandmother have the same kind of relationship with her granddaughter that she had with her daughter?

To answer the first question, we can turn to recent research into an *attachment theory* perspective (see Chapter Two) and a *family systems* approach. Together they support the idea that those behaviors that were part of a grandmother's experience with her own mother will influence the way she mothers her child. In particular, in a family where the grandmother's mother was experienced by her daughter as intrusive, there is a better-than-average chance that when this younger woman becomes a mother herself, she will be either overprotective or intrusive with her own daughter. So the answer to question one is yes.

Our second question is addressed in the following vignette, told to us by our client Peggy. The story of Peggy's niece is an excellent example of the way the influence of a grandmother can be felt throughout the family system, even by its littlest member.

My, She's a BIG Girl!

Peggy, was telling us of a recent visit with her family. Peggy is the oldest in a family of four daughters and a son. All of the daughters had suffered from eating disorders as adolescents and young adults.

Peggy told us how horrified she was when she heard her mother's comments about her sister Judy's two-year-old daughter: *My, she's really a BIG girl. What sturdy legs she has. She's quite a little chowhound, isn't she?* Every comment out of her mother's mouth, according to Peggy, was directed toward her niece's physical appearance and/or her eating habits.

Peggy recalled, with dismay, similar messages that were a part of her and her sisters' childhood. She told us that, as an adult, she realized that her mother's concerns with her own body image and with food had been passed along to herself and her sisters, and were as omnipresent as the air they breathed.

Before returning home to Los Angeles, Peggy had a long talk with her sister Judy about their mother. While talking to Peggy, Judy began to connect her own adolescent struggles with bulimia with the messages that she received from her mother. Judy, with Peggy's help, realized that she needed to intervene before her mother began a new round of comments about Judy's daughter. Peggy returned home, hopeful that she had helped to break the cycle of toxic messages to the next generation in her family.

Mother, Daughter, and Grandmother—Who Comes First?

Marnie, age twenty-seven, and her mother, Katie, age forty-nine, came to talk to us about their inability to get along. Marnie appeared very tense, and spent most of the session watching her mother. Katie just looked sad. She almost apologized for being there when she began to speak.

I don't know where to begin and I really don't know if this is going to be helpful. However, I am willing to do anything I can to improve my relationship with Marnie. This is so confusing and hurtful to me. I have a wonderful relationship with my mother. We talk every day, and we share so many interests. I was thrilled when Marnie was born. I had a daughter of my own and I was going to have the same kind of wonderful relationship with her that I had with my mother. I don't know what went wrong.

Marnie began to speak tentatively, but her voice got stronger as she warmed up: *I don't know where I fit into my mother's life. She goes at ten miles a minute—she has her own business, she's a volunteer at a women's shelter, she entertains a lot for my dad, and she spends a lot of time with my grandmother. It's always been this way, ever since I was a little girl. Now, all of a sudden, she's worried because we don't have a good relationship. Where has she been? I've always known there was a problem.* She began to get teary. *Maybe there's just not enough of her to go around.*

Katie, sat there, looking very upset. *I always felt that Marnie wanted more than I could give her. I've tried to create a balance in my life. The irony is, I also thought I was being a pretty good role model for Marnie; you know, a mom who could do it all. I guess I'm not so good after all, but I don't know what I could have done differently.*

By this time, Marnie was crying. *My life is a mess, both relationship and workwise. I'm not blaming you,* she said, looking at her mother. *But I know that I've spent most of my life trying to please both you and grandma so that maybe you would be as happy with me as you are with each other.*

We decided, at this point, that we needed to know more about their family history. As they spoke to us, we began to work on their genogram (See page 158).

Katie told us that her parents divorced when she was ten. Her father, Edward, had been unfaithful, and her mother, Dorothy, unlike many women of her generation, was not willing to turn a blind eye to his infidelities. She gave him an ultimatum and he left. Katie missed her father, but her mother made sure she had the opportunity to spend time with him. *My mother never made me feel that I had to choose between them, and I was grateful to her for that.*

Dorothy went to work in a local clothing store. She proved to be an innovative and energetic employee. As the management expanded its base of operations, Dorothy was promoted. She had recently retired from managing a chain of women's boutiques about the time that Marnie and Katie came to see us.

Katie told us that she and her mother developed a very special relationship while she was growing up. *I felt so supported and loved by her. She took pleasure in my achievements, both academic and social. She was always right there, encouraging me every step of the way.*

When Katie brought her future husband, David, home to meet her, Dorothy was thrilled. *He became the son she never had,* Katie reported. Having Marnie two years after they were married, according to Katie, made their circle complete.

Marnie interrupted her mother at this point. *I didn't make your circle complete. You and grandma were a circle all your own. Dad I were always on the outside.* Marnie turned to us and said, *You need to know that my grandmother is a wonderful person. I have just always felt that I had to compete with her for my mother's attention. Aren't mothers supposed to put their children first?*

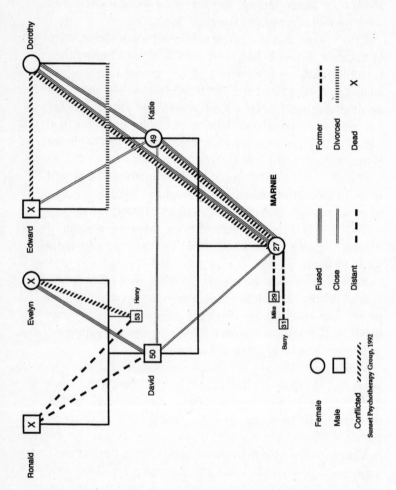

Marnie's Genogram

We, in turn, asked Katie if she had always felt that she came first with her mother. Katie thought about this for a moment. *I never had any doubt that I was the primary focus in my mother's life. I knew it from the time I could walk and talk. Maybe that's why my father had to go outside their marriage to get attention. I think that once I was born, my father got put away on the back burner by my mother.*

We asked Katie if she knew anything about Dorothy's relationship with her own mother. Katie told us, *I don't know much about my grandmother, only that she died when my mother was two. My mother was raised by her father's two unmarried sisters. My mother used to tell me how the only thing her aunts cared about was if her hands and clothes were clean. My mother was physically cared for and that was it—no hugs, no affection, period.*

Marnie looked at her mother and said, *Boy, no wonder she was happy to have you. She finally had something to hug!*

We asked both of them if they thought that the deficits in Dorothy's early history had an impact on their relationship.

Katie looked at Marnie. *I never thought about why my mother and I were so close. Why should I? It felt normal to me. That's probably why I feel such a sense of loss that you and I don't have that kind of relationship.*

How can we? Marnie replied. *There's no room for me between you and Grandma! I love my grandmother, but it doesn't seem fair that she gets all of my mother just because she never had a mother.*

The Past As a Mirror of the Present

Marnie, Katie, and Dorothy have their work cut out for them. As you can see, the emotional deficiencies in Dorothy's childhood have had a profound effect on both her daughter and her granddaughter. Marnie and Katie, however, have an opportunity, especially with their new insights into the influence of Dorothy's early history on their relationship, to make some important changes.

MENDING MOVES FOR MARNIE AND HER GRANDMOTHER, DOROTHY:

- Visit your grandmother and ask her about what her childhood was like, what she liked to do as a girl, and what her dreams were. Find out what it was like for her to grow up without a mother.
- Ask your grandmother how she felt when she became a new mother. Find out about who and what influenced her in her parenting of Katie.
- Even if your grandmother is no longer living, you can make a list of the questions you would like to ask her about her early history. If older family members or friends are available, you could contact them and see if they could answer some of the questions on your list. By talking with them and hearing their memories of your grandmother's life, you could gain some valuable insights into this important person in your life.

MENDING MOVES FOR MARNIE AND HER MOTHER, KATIE:

- Continue to fill in the details of your family genogram with your mother. This will give you an opportunity to explore parts of your shared family history from both of your perspectives.
- Tell your mother what you would like from your relationship, without anger and without blaming. Focusing on the here and now and not dwelling on past hurts will allow you to take responsibility for the changes you want to make in your life and in your relationship with your mother.
- Ask your mother what it was like being your mother while you were growing up. Try to look at your own childhood and adolescence from your mother's point of view. It can help you broaden your perspective on

yourself.

MENDING MOVES FOR KATIE AND HER DAUGHTER, MARNIE:

- Ask Marnie to talk about what has been missing for her in your relationship. As she talks, try to get a sense of what it has felt like for her to have to compete with her grandmother.
- Instead of telling Marnie how hard you've tried to be a good mother in the past, ask her what you can do now. By including Marnie in the circle with your mother, you may provide her with some of the support she needs to move forward with her life.

MENDING MOVES FOR KATIE AND HER MOTHER, DOROTHY:

- Ask your mother to tell you more about her early history and what it was like for her to grow up without a mother.
- Tell your mother that you want to include Marnie in more of your activities and conversations. If you get the feeling that the inclusion of Marnie is threatening to your mother, you can reassure her that you still want to be with her, but that including your daughter is important to you. This is an important stand for you to take, and by being firm in your resolve, you will help your mother adjust to the change.

MENDING MOVE FOR KATIE:

- Give yourself permission to think about what you want from these relationships. It's difficult when you feel pulled by two people who want you, even when they are people you love. By being clear with yourself about what your own needs are, you can do a better job of being both a good mother and daughter.

The Power of the Past

The stories of Annie, Julie, Katie, and Marnie in this chapter illustrate the power that past generations of mothers exert on younger women today. Each of these younger women, in order to move forward, needs to take a step backward and observe where she is in relation to the women who went before her.

The task that these women face today is to experience themselves as separate individuals, while still remaining part of a family. That may mean breaking old patterns of behavior and questioning the ways that the women in their families have always lived their lives. In the next chapter, we will explore the meaning of the rules that govern women's lives.

Constructing Your Family Genogram

In a genogram, women are designated by circles and men by squares.

1. Fill in your age inside the bottom circle and put your name next to it.
2. Add names, ages, dates of death, siblings, and divorces of other family members.
3. Make a list of adjectives for each grandparent. Remember, even if you did not personally know your grandparents, you know about them through family stories and myths.
4. Make a list of adjectives for your mother and another for your father.
5. Make a list of adjectives for yourself; underline those that appear in the above lists.
6. Enter the nature of the relationship between your parents, using the key below the genogram.
7. Enter the nature of the relationships between grandparents, and between grandparents and their children, using the key below the genogram.
8. Enter the nature of the relationships between parents, children, and siblings.

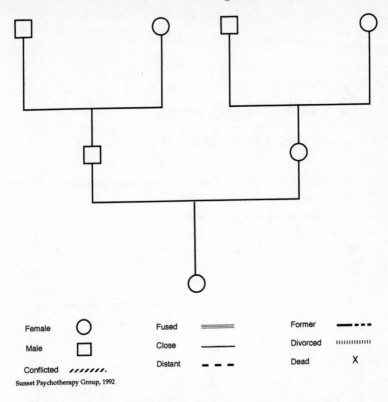

Female ○	Fused ═══	Former ▬ ▪ ▪ ▪
Male □	Close ────	Divorced ‖‖‖‖‖‖
	Distant ▬ ▬ ▬	Dead X
Conflicted ⁄⁄⁄⁄⁄.		

Sunset Psychotherapy Group, 1992

Sample Genogram

9. Enter the nature of the relationships between children and grandparents.
10. Check to see if anything appears to be missing.
11. How do you interpret your genogram?

6 Rules We Learn from Our Mothers

"Marry a man who loves you more than you love him."
"Do not express your anger."
"Be like me."
"Don't be like me."
"Love yourself."

Rules about being a woman
shared by participants in a
mother-daughter workshop

Let's fast-forward with Maddie, the toddler we met in Chapter Three. She is now almost three years old, and as she willingly tells everyone, "I'm a big girl!" Maddie is on the patio, painting pictures with her watercolors. She makes a sudden movement with her arm and knocks over the glass of water that contains her brushes. She immediately bursts into tears and runs into the house, crying, "Mommy, Mommy, help me!"

Maddie's mother rushes to her side to see what is wrong. Maddie is sobbing. Her mother attempts to comfort her, but Maddie doesn't want soothing. She wants her mother to "fix" it. Maddie keeps crying until her mother has mopped up all of the spilled water.

What just happened here? Maddie is a very bright little girl and an excellent observer, as are most children, of her mother's behavior. Maddie's mother is an intelligent, capable professional woman, and in order to juggle the demands of her career and motherhood, she runs a very well-organized household. Everything is in its place. So it is not surprising that Maddie learned, from a very young age, that it is very important for her to put her toys and crayons away when she is finished with them. If she forgets, her mother frowns and tells her to clean up her things *right now*.

Maddie is learning a set of rules, as most of us do, literally at her mother's knee: "Messes are bad. . . . Mommy doesn't like messes. . . . If I make a mess, maybe Mommy won't love me."

Does this sound exaggerated? Not at all. Young children think in very black-and-white terms. This kind of either/or thinking becomes part of how they view their world. It may seem simplistic, but it's powerful.

So, with this background in mind, Maddie's tearful response to spilled water makes sense. Her discomfort is grounded in her belief that she has broken a rule ("Don't make messes") and, as a result, Mommy won't love her.

Rules and the Family

As with Maddie, the family you grew up in—and the family you later create—are governed by rules. By definition, these family rules are behavioral habits that are kept in place by family traditions. Some are passed on from generation to generation; others originate within the present family unit. Family rules influence everything, from your day-to-day behavior to your choice of a life partner. They ultimately affect how you interact with members of the opposite sex and how you use money, and sometimes they keep you from seeing yourself as others see you. To truly understand yourself means understanding the rules that govern your life. Many of these rules are beyond conscious awareness. So the challenge is to become actively aware of what rules have contributed to your beliefs about yourself.

One of the most important roles that a mother plays in her family is that of "rule giver." Because a mother, for the most part, has the responsibility for the socialization of her young children, her job is to make sure that the rules that she learned, both consciously and unconsciously, from her own mother are passed on to her children.

The first set of rules you learned from your mother were age-appropriate ones: "Don't touch the stove," "Always hold my hand when you cross the street," "Share your toys," "Don't hit the baby," and so on. These rules were easy for your mother to implement and you to follow.

The concept of age-appropriate rules, for most of us, gets a little fuzzy and more confusing as we grow older. Both parents and children struggle with the idea of what rules are appropriate as a young girl becomes a young woman.

Children question rules that don't feel comfortable or that frustrate them: "I don't want to go to bed," "I hate the dentist," "I don't want to play with my cousin Sara—she's dumb," "*Why?*" This reaction to rules we don't like is part of the process we go through to learn the kind of behavior valued by our family. With time we discover how to live with these rules and, under our family's protection, how to be a functioning member of the family.

All families live by rules, regardless of their level of functioning. For instance, in a chaotic family, when a member is upset, the rule may be to blame someone else. A subsequent rule would be, "Never take responsibility for your own actions." In a disengaged family, a rule might be, "Never talk about strong feelings." Even though these rules may seem less than optimal, they are the rules these families live by and are dictated by the way they operate.

We will discuss later what happens when parents feel uncomfortable or are ambivalent about the rules they pass on to their children.

Operating under the Rules

How do you know when you are behaving under the influence of a family rule? A rule is probably coming into play when you find yourself acting in ways that are repetitive and that feel familiar. Whether you recognize it or not, there is a feeling of comfort in living in a system that is grounded in rules. It allows you to predict, with a fair degree of accuracy, who is going to do what, when, and with whom.

If you find yourself saying, "I *should* read more," ask yourself if there is a rule that members of your family should be well-read. Or if you are thinking, "I *ought* to call Aunt Jeanne," you might wonder if there is a rule in your family about how often children should call their older relatives. *Shoulds* and *oughts* are the hallmark of rules.

Here are some other examples of clearly visible family rules. These rules aren't talked about because everybody "knows" them:

- Mom always serves Dad first at the dinner table.
- Dad pays all the household bills.
- Children do not watch television on school nights.
- We always spend Thanksgiving with Mom's mother.
- On Sunday nights, we go out for Chinese food.
- Grandpa always sings his favorite song on everyone's birthday before we can eat cake.
- When Dad comes home, Mom only pays attention to him.
- Children don't go into Mom and Dad's bedroom if the door is closed.

There are other rules that everyone knows about, but they are open to discussion, and sometimes are fought over openly:

- "Why does Mom always sit in the front seat? I want to sit next to Dad!"
- "I'm tired of Chinese food. Can't we have pizza for a change?"
- "It's my turn to pick a television program. The boys always watch sports. It's not fair."

A Mother's Motivation

Mothers pass on rules to their daughters in many ways. First and foremost, mothers impart rules that were part of their own upbringing and life experience. The rules that they learned from their own mothers are going to be at the top of the list of rules they bequeath to their daughters. For most mothers, there is an unexpressed sense of "doing the right thing" in the act of conveying familiar rules to their daughters.

In Chapter Five, we discussed how the lives of each generation reflect the times in which they live. The prevailing culture can have an enormous impact on rules that are passed along from mother to daughter. Each generation of daughters has to struggle with the direct conflict between the rules they learned from their mothers and grandmothers, and the rapid changes in customs, habits, and mores of the world in which they live.

For example, twenty-one-year-old Heather told us: *Last Saturday I spent the night at my boyfriend's apartment after we had been to a party at his fraternity. I didn't want to drive after I'd been drinking, and he wouldn't have let me anyhow. Well, my mother called my apartment early Sunday morning and my roommate told her I was at Todd's apartment. She went ballistic! All she could say was, "I didn't raise you to be that kind of woman. We"*—meaning she and my grandmother and every generation in my family going back God knows how far!—*"don't do things like that." Even when I explained to her that all I did was sleep at Todd's, she couldn't hear it. I had broken a rule about how "nice girls" should behave.*

Her daughter's behavior was foreign to Heather's mother and it frightened her. These fears and anxieties, which affect each generation of mothers, create an ongoing dilemma for both their daughters and themselves. On a conscious level, mothers may be afraid that their daughters will be hurt, perceived as different, or won't "fit in"; on an unconscious level, mothers may be reexperiencing their own youthful fears as they pass on these "self-protective" or "defensive" rules to their growing daughters.

These anxieties can give rise to still another set of rules: rules reflecting the mother's fears. For example, a mother who is afraid of feeling vulnerable and unprotected will express her fear in rules like these:

- Don't make waves.
- Be gracious (no matter what).
- Don't tell everyone what you think.
- Be a peacemaker.
- Don't be different (from me or the rest of the women in our family).

The combination of a family legacy and a mother's fears can have a powerful impact on a daughter's behavior and her perception of herself.

Unspoken Rules

As much as highly visible, spoken rules influence individuals and families, their power pales in comparison to unspoken rules that exist within the hearts and minds of all family members. These unspoken rules are funny things. Even though they have enormous power over the way we live, they are not part of our everyday awareness. They are, however, an ingrained part of each of our belief systems. As a result, they influence how we relate to the rest of the world.

Mothers pass unspoken rules of behavior on to their daughters in myriad ways. For example, every time mothers interact with other people, they become role models and are providing rules to live by. Here are some unspoken rules and ways of behaving that daughters learn from their mothers:

- *How women are supposed to act around men:* Are they submissive or assertive? Do they ask for what they want, or do they ignore their own feelings and desires in order to maintain a relationship?
- *How women are supposed to act around other women:* Do women view themselves as more or less valuable than men? Are women given the same amount of respect as men? Do they regard other women as likable and trustworthy?
- *How women feel about their work:* Do they enjoy and value the work they do? Do they feel equal to or less than the men they work with? Are they fulfilled by what they do or are they just working for a paycheck?
- *How women feel about themselves:* Do they feel valued and lovable? Do they feel as if they have a voice, and if so, is that voice heard? How does their image of their body affect how they feel about themselves?
- *How women feel about themselves as sexual people:* Do they feel comfortable with and take pleasure in their sexuality? Do they feel confused and/or ambivalent about their sexuality? Are they able to communicate not only the enjoyment but a sense of responsibility about an adult sexual relationship to their children?

Whether or not a mother is aware of it, her daughter is watching her. And as a daughter observes her mother's behavior, it becomes the daughter's basic instruction manual for how to be a woman.

If you were an outsider observing the impact of unspoken

rules on the behavior of members of a family, you might think you were watching an elaborately choreographed dance, clearly orchestrated by an unseen director. These rules, silently communicated from parent to child, can unconsciously become part of that child's life. Here are a few more examples of common unspoken rules:

- We don't talk about the baby that died.
- We avoid spending holidays with Dad's family because he doesn't speak to his sister.
- We never mention that Mom was briefly married before she met Dad.
- We never talk about money.

The problem with unspoken rules is that everybody "knows" about them but no one speaks about them. One of our clients described them like this: *They are always there, in the air around us, like a cloud hanging over our heads.* When everyone knows that a subject is off-limits ("We don't talk about that!"), the topic takes on a life of its own. For instance, in your family, if you cannot talk about the fact that your dad doesn't talk to his parents, you can't freely acknowledge that you might have feelings about how Dad's behavior is impacting you. This, in turn, raises the following questions:

- If Dad doesn't talk to his parents, does that mean I can't talk to them?
- If his parents did something wrong, how will I know that I won't accidentally do the same thing?
- Does this happen in all families?

Unfortunately, the longer a rule goes unaddressed, the more powerful its impact on members of the family.

Rachel, age forty-six, told us, with a great deal of emotion, the following story about the impact of an unspoken rule on three generations of her family.

My family escaped from Hungary during the revolution in

1956. I was six years old at the time and my little brother was four. When we arrived in America, we had to live with relatives. My parents immediately went to work for a cousin in his fur business. My brother was cared for by an elderly aunt. I was sent to school to learn English and to "do well." I remember wishing that I could be at home with my little brother. But I was expected to work as hard as my parents, and so I did.

My parents moved us to our own home as soon as they were able to. They worked all the time. My father told us that everything he and my mother did was so that his children would have a better life than he had. I was supposed to be grateful. My sense of obligation was a heavy burden.

I went away to college, where I met my future husband, Jack. I loved being away from home and from my parents' ethic of all work and no play. I got married right after graduation, and although my parents were not thrilled with my choice of a husband, they offered him a job in the family business. Our marriage was not great, but it didn't really fall apart until after my daughter, Amanda, was born. As Jack started to drift away, I hid my hurt and disappointment by focusing on Amanda. He left for good when she was less than a year old.

I went to work in the family business, determined to make up to Amanda for not having a father. I made sure she had everything—private schools, summer camp, dancing and music lessons—whatever she wanted. I never missed a school play or a teacher's conference. I wanted Amanda to know what it was like to have a committed parent. We had a wonderful, close, and loving relationship.

When Amanda entered high school, she started running with a crowd of kids I didn't know. All we did was fight over what she was doing and who she was doing it with. She had no respect for my feelings. We would argue and then make up. I would take her shopping and we would be fine for a few days. Then it would start all over again.

Amanda wanted a car and I refused to buy her one unless I saw an improvement in her attitude. Furious, she packed up all her things and moved in with my mother and father. I felt devastated and betrayed by both my parents and Amanda. All my parents could say to me was, "She's our granddaughter. How can we not do what she wants?" I absolutely fell apart. A friend suggested that I go see a therapist. In therapy, I realized that we had all been operating under the same unspoken rule: "Do everything for your kids." I realized that, as much as I had chafed under this rule while I was growing up, I had re-created it in my parenting of Amanda.

When Rules Are Broken

Because these rules are unspoken, you may not be aware of the presence of one until you break it. When you do break a rule, you risk feeling uncomfortable, tense, and, at times, highly anxious. In fact, much of your behavior may be unconsciously controlled by your need to avoid those anxious feelings and, therefore, not to break rules.

Breaking rules also can trigger fears of arousing anger in the "rule giver." This fear, left over from childhood, dwells inside all of us. By the time we are adults, we have internalized the rules to such an extent that it doesn't matter whether the rule giver lives around the corner or has been dead for twenty years; the rule and the rule giver are still powerful forces in our lives.

For example, an African-American client of ours, Celeste, told us the following story.

The first time I went out on a date with a white man, I thought I was having a heart attack in the middle of dinner. All of a sudden my chest became tight and I couldn't catch my breath. I went to the women's room and tried to figure out what was happening to me. All of a sudden I could hear the voice of my mother in my head, angry and disapproving.

"The women in our family do not go out with white men." I felt like she was in the room with me, it was that intense.

What was so odd about this experience is that I don't remember her telling me directly that she would not approve if I dated a white man. I was just aware that it was something I "knew."

This was Celeste's first conscious recognition that she had broken her mother's rule. Not everyone has physical symptoms when they break a rule, but they do have feelings—powerful ones—that they have done something wrong.

And can a mother feel that she has broken a rule or crossed over a boundary set by her daughter? Yes, this phenomenon can work both ways. If you have an adult daughter, you know that familiar feeling of walking on eggshells around your child in order to avoid upsetting her. We will talk more about breaking rules, and the impact of this action on both mothers and daughters, later in the chapter.

Who Is in Charge Here?

As we've already suggested, mothers realize early on in the course of their mothering that they must convey to their daughters the rules about issues that are emotionally loaded for both of them: rules about love, work, self-image, marriage, parenting, sex, and money. In fact, when we first interview a woman, part of our work is to ask about the rules regarding these sensitive topics that she learned as a young girl. In our mother-daughter workshops, we always ask participants to share, not only the specific rules they learned directly from their mothers, but also the underlying unspoken rules that usually accompany them. Understanding how these rules, both spoken and unspoken, are affecting their lives today then becomes an important part of our work together.

What are some of the things we discover? Sometimes women learn that rules and how they are implemented have led to an unconscious power struggle between mother and daughter. Because unspoken rules have an enormous influence on our perception of ourselves and the world we live in, a woman may unconsciously equate her effectiveness as a mother with the way she passes on the rules to her daughter—and whether her daughter lives by them. Mothers can feel emotionally devastated when they perceive that their daughters may be going against the rules that they themselves live by.

For this reason, the role of rule giver can become an uncomfortable one for a mother. Quite often, it makes her feel trapped. Also, while she may feel confident about conveying rules to her children that are comfortable and familiar to her, what happens when she runs up against a rule that makes her feel uncomfortable? After all, not all of the rules she grew up with and lives by today have always met her needs; in fact, some of them may be in direct opposition to her current needs and wants. That's why a mother may feel uneasy and ambivalent about passing on rules to her daughter that arouse conflicted feelings in herself.

Getting Specific About Spoken and Unspoken Rules

In the next few pages, we want to share with you a sample of specific rules that women have revealed to us. In talking with them, the same four topics—*being a woman; men and relationships; work;* and *sexuality*—seem to appear again and again and generate the greatest amount of energy. Here are some of the spoken rules they have shared with us, followed by their unspoken counterparts.

Being a Woman

SPOKEN	UNSPOKEN
Do not express your true feelings.	It's dangerous to let anyone know what you're thinking.
This is what mothers do.	Take care of others first, like I did.
You need to be taken care of.	I need to be taken care of.
Be as attractive as you can be.	Men won't want you if you're not beautiful.
Be happy.	Don't be like me.
Women are responsible for relationship harmony.	Don't tell everything.
Women are not supposed to take care of themselves.	I don't know how to take care of myself.
Don't let anyone know how you feel.	Feelings are dangerous.

These rules reflect some of the differences between the generations that we wrote about in Chapter Five and mentioned earlier in this chapter. When we talked to a group of mothers, they confirmed that they were often tempted to justify the rules they live by because they were given to them by their own mothers ("This is the way we have always done it"). The social changes that have taken place in the course of their lifetime, however, may have left them feeling isolated and unsure about the rules—and their role as rule givers.

Here is the way that Evelyn, age sixty-seven, described the impact of rules on her life: *I was taught that it was important to be "ladylike"—soft-spoken, courteous, mindful of the needs of others. I didn't think about what I wanted, I thought about what my parents and sisters, and later my husband and children wanted.*

But I know that I am the product of my generation. When

I confronted my teenage daughters about their strident manner of speaking, they said they were only being assertive. I didn't know what to do. I felt somehow that I had failed them. They were so unladylike.

Evelyn felt caught between the rules that felt comfortable to her and the changing times in which she raised her daughters. But there is room for dialogue and Mending Moves here. The following are some of our suggestions if you find yourself in this situation:

MENDING MOVES FOR DAUGHTERS:

- You might begin by talking with your mother about how both of you interpret her rules. If each of you can listen carefully to the other's point of view, you will have accomplished something important. This does not mean you enter into a discussion with the expectation that she is going to change. The only expectation here is that you both will listen.

- If you find yourself feeling irritated at your mother, try to pinpoint what is triggering that feeling. Does it feel familiar? It might, because the imposition of rules takes us back to a time when we were little and helpless. To get back in touch with yourself as an adult, use a statement like: "Mom, I hear your point of view, but I'm an adult now and I'd like to make that decision for myself."

- Ask your mother how a particular rule has been useful to her. Has it served to protect her from feeling helpless or out of control? Then find out what her goal is for you. Without analyzing and blaming her, you can create an atmosphere where she can entertain the idea that her rule may not work for you.

MENDING MOVES FOR MOTHERS:

- Think about your internal response when your daughter either rejects or breaks a rule that is important to you.

Do you experience feelings of anxiety, anger, or fear? Does it feel like a personal rejection? If so, then you need to look at how you have used rules to define yourself as a mother and as a woman. If you believe that you have no value unless your daughter accepts your rules, then you need to acknowledge that not only to yourself, but at some point to her.

- Ask your daughter to tell you what you have contributed to her life that feels positive to her. You may find that you don't need to use all of your rules in order to maintain a connection with her.

- Your struggle with your daughter about rules may really be about the change in the balance of power in your relationship. Your daughter needs you in her life, but she probably doesn't need you in the same way that she did when she was growing up. Talking to her about ways you can relate to her, other than in the role of rule giver, can open up new opportunities for both of you to expand your relationship.

Men and Relationships

SPOKEN	UNSPOKEN
Always please your man.	A man's needs come first.
Do not ask for what you want.	Give yourself up, be taken advantage of, be what they want you to be.
You can change men.	Manipulate like I do.
Date and marry only perfect men.	Don't marry a man like your father.
Don't be assertive with men.	Be like me.
The women in our family don't marry those kind of people.	We are special.

Don't be smarter than men.	Men are threatened by smart women.
Hold on to any man.	It's better than being alone.

What strikes us as significant about these rules—and about many others that we have collected about men and relationships—is the aura of anxiety, self-protectiveness, and fear that permeates them. We recognize that many of these rules reflect unmet expectations and disappointments in love relationships that went awry. We are intrigued, however, by the lack of what we call "positive rules" received (or perceived) by daughters. We will talk more about positive rules and their creation at the end of this chapter when we address the issue of rewriting family rules.

By the way, whenever we introduce the subject of rules about men in our workshops, energy levels soar. We are always interested to observe a lot of laughter and nods of recognition as group members share with one another the rules that they learned about men as they were growing up.

Barbara's Note: *At one of our workshops on the East Coast, my youngest daughter joined us as a participant. She shared a rule with the group that I had forgotten (repressed?). I had conveyed to her: "Don't pay any attention to your father." I laughed and told the group I was "guilty." The memory and the power of that message really sent me back—back to my own childhood and my mother's attempts to protect me. I remembered how much I wanted to please my busy but rather distant father. When I felt I had disappointed or failed him in some way, my mother would intervene and reframe his response to me. She would tell me: "Don't pay any attention to what he says. He really loves you and he doesn't mean it."*

My mother's protective stance was exactly the one I took with my own children. Never mind that it wasn't relevant to my husband. For me, the best part of this exercise was the opportunity, after the workshop, to talk with my daughter about her memories of other rules. I highly recommend this kind of a discussion to everyone. It is the best Mending Move ever!

Work

SPOKEN	UNSPOKEN
Have a career.	But make sure you get married.
Be anything you want.	But don't be better than me.
It's not enough to be good, you have to be the best.	Otherwise I'm afraid you won't survive.
You'll be better off in a traditional woman's job.	It's dangerous to be different.
Women don't need to work.	Have a baby like I did.
Work hard, it will pay off.	Don't end up alone.
You have to work.	Because you don't have a man.
Don't worry about having a career.	Women aren't supposed to work anyhow.

Once again, we have a set of rules colored by ambivalence and distrust of the self. No wonder daughters feel confused when it comes to making life and career decisions. Rules are supposed to make us feel secure, to provide parameters. But the mixed messages in these rules can only muddy the waters of a daughter's decision-making process about herself and her life choices.

The concept of working outside the home is still new for a generation of women raised to be housewives. These women have had no applicable rules about work to pass on to their daughters. After all, they were raised in the decades before and immediately after World War II, when women were encouraged to train for a career (teaching, nursing, social work) but only as "something to fall back on" in case their husband became ill or they divorced.

No other generation can be compared, in terms of education, with the young women coming into the workforce today. They have more degrees, both undergraduate and graduate, than any of their predecessors. But they also have the highest degree of anxiety and confusion about the direction of their lives. They know that their mothers' rules aren't applicable to their life situations and yet they long for the stability and predictability that rules represented for their mothers and grandmothers.

For example, Dolores, age twenty-nine, felt confused and upset as she contemplated her career as an office manager of a large law firm.

I was the first woman in my family to graduate from college. All the time I was in school, my mother worried that I was spending too much time studying and was not meeting any boys. She was very proud when I graduated, but when I got my first job, all she wanted to know was if there were any nice men at the office. She is never interested in hearing what I'm doing at work. She only wants to know whom I am dating. It is so hard. She doesn't understand me or my life or what I'm struggling with. She only sees that I'm not getting married and having a family like she did.

Jocie, another client of ours, told us the following work-related story and its connection to her mother.

While working at my first job as a dental hygienist, I had several run-ins with my boss. I couldn't seem to please him, no matter how hard I tried. I loved my job, so I decided to make an appointment to talk with him about our working relationship. I felt sure that I could find a way for us to work together successfully. I started to tell him my concerns, but he cut me off almost immediately and began to defend himself and his behavior toward me. I could feel myself becoming less and less confident with each attempt I made to state my position. It was almost as if I was shrinking on the inside. My voice got smaller. My breathing became shallow. It was all I could do to hold back my tears.

I mustered enough dignity to walk out of his office without crying. But I kept thinking, "What happened to you in there? You had valid concerns. Why did you collapse?" The more I thought about it, the more I felt that this was a replay of something awfully familiar in my life. I realized how much I was experiencing my boss to be like my mother. And the more I experienced him as my mother, the more powerless I became.

Jocie is wrestling with a problem that has its roots in some early messages from her mother, Eileen. Jocie never received encouragement from her mother to do anything on her own. Eileen's word on any subject was the last word. Jocie learned never to openly disagree with her mother.

No wonder Jocie felt like she was falling apart when she tried to challenge her boss. In her interaction with her boss, she felt "one down" to him, as she once did with her mother. By reacting to her boss as if he were her mother, Jocie again experienced herself as little and powerless. In the process, she gave away her remaining sense of control, which reinforced her perception of herself as a helpless child.

Sexuality

SPOKEN	UNSPOKEN
Don't talk about sex.	It makes me uncomfortable.
You are responsible for birth control.	Don't trust a man.
Good girls don't.	I want you to stay a virgin.
All men want is sex.	I didn't have anything else to offer.
Masturbation is not okay.	I'm uncomfortable with my body.

Don't act or dress that way.	I am uncomfortable about my sexuality.
Reproduction is good.	Sex is not.
A woman must use sex to gain power.	Do what I did.

We have observed that most parents are either anxious or uncomfortable—or both—about teaching their daughters about sex. If this was the case with you, you ended up with two messages: the spoken information (or misinformation!), and the unspoken anxiety and discomfort, about the subject of sex. Mothers, as information-and-rule givers, find themselves in an awkward position: They have to overcome not only their own inhibitions and discomfort about a sensitive subject, but also the anxiety and restraints passed down to them by previous generations. It is a paradox, but a mother often feels caught in a no-win situation: If she encourages her daughter to value and enjoy herself sexually, she runs the risk of raising someone who is, at best, viewed as a "tramp" or, at worst, will contract a sexually transmitted disease.

And what about a mother who hides her beliefs and feelings about the pleasures of sex to protect her daughter in a world where everything from sexual harassment to AIDS is part of the daily equation? She dilutes her power as a role model. This is a real tragedy, because for a daughter, there is no more important model to have than a mother who enjoys and is comfortable with herself and her sexual feelings.

As a result, daughters often find themselves struggling to interpret their mothers' behavior. A daughter may feel that her mother is sending her "mixed messages": "It's okay to have sexual feelings—but don't act on them." "Sex is wonderful—but only after you are married." No wonder daughters frequently feel angry with their mothers for their lack of openness about dealing with sexual issues.

Nicki, age thirty-six, told us: *Sex was not talked about in our house when I was growing up. The slightest suggestion of anything sexual brought a look of tight-lipped disapproval from my mother. My first sexual experiences were awful. They made me feel ashamed and dirty. Where was the passion and the intimacy that I longed for? Fortunately, I was lucky enough to marry a man who wanted me to feel as good about my sexuality as he did about his.*

My biggest problem now is what happens to me when my children ask me questions about sex. I can feel my body literally begin to tighten up. It is all that I can do to stay in the room with them and answer their questions. I feel like my mother is looking over my shoulder.

Ironically, Nicki appears to be replaying her mother's role with her own children. What is most important, however, is Nicki's awareness of the impact of this issue on her interactions with her children. That awareness is the first step in moving toward a healthier, more open mother-daughter dialogue with her own daughter about sexuality.

Susan, age fifty-eight, told us: *I grew up in the days of the double standard—one set of rules for men and another set for women. We also grew up in a time when pregnancy, not sexually transmitted diseases, was the biggest fear. My generation was trained to guard our reputations at all cost. It was very confusing. We learned it was okay to flirt (in fact, our mothers encouraged it!) but it was not okay to be a "tease." We were supposed to "save ourselves" for our husbands. No wonder so many of us came back from our honeymoons disillusioned and feeling like failures. We were supposed to go from virgin to vamp after repeating some vows! Many of us never made the transition. I don't know if I have succeeded, but I've tried awfully hard to do it differently with my daughter.*

Many women would prefer to have root-canal work without anesthesia than talk to their mothers or daughters about sex. And yet, by addressing this subject, you and your daughter or mother can communicate and learn from one another, woman-to-woman. Imagine how different the stories of Nicki and Susan would be if they'd had open, honest dialogues with their mothers about sex and how it feels to be (or not be) a sexual woman.

Bear in mind that we are not *blaming* mothers for the lack of straightforward communication. As we have written repeatedly throughout this book, mothers are a product of their times and the culture they live in. Susan's story only hinted at the consequences facing a girl (and her reputation) who went against the prevailing belief systems of her generation. We truly believe that Nicki and Susan's mothers would have welcomed more open dialogue with their own mothers. In fact, we have never talked to a mother who, if she were being honest with herself and with us, did not express that desire.

Here are some Mending Moves for dealing with the topic of sexuality.

MENDING MOVES FOR DAUGHTERS:

- In your perception of yourself as a sexual (or a nonsexual) woman, make a list of the aspects of sexuality that are the most problematic for you today. Then make a list of the rules you learned about sex and being sexual. Do you see any connections?
- If the idea of talking directly to your mother about sexual issues is uncomfortable, you might consider asking her what she learned (or didn't learn) when she was growing up about being a woman and being sexual. What were the messages she received about sex from her mother and her culture during her youth? It is much less threatening to talk about a subject in a historical context. It can be a first step toward a discussion about her own personal attitudes about sexuality.

- Remember that conversations about sensitive topics take time. Allow yourself the luxury of dialogues with your mother at intervals that are comfortable for both of you.
- If your mother is no longer living, talk to family members or family friends from her generation about what they were taught about sexuality. It will help you flesh out the picture of what life was like for your mother, and help you make sense of some of the rules she communicated to you.

MENDING MOVES FOR MOTHERS:

- Think about how you learned the rules about being sexual and being a woman. Who was the person who gave you those rules? How did you feel about those rules at the time? Were they helpful to you as a sexual person? Did you do anything differently with your own daughter? By answering these questions, you allow yourself to "put on your daughter's shoes and walk around in them." You will gain insight into what it felt like for your daughter to grow up with your rules. If you can find areas of commonality in your experiences, you can begin to bridge the gap.
- While the idea of a dialogue with your daughter about sex may seem daunting, don't dismiss it out of hand. Your daughter may be struggling with some of the same issues that were problematic for you at her age. Even if her concerns and experiences are totally different from yours, the opportunity to share some of her fears and worries with you in a noncritical atmosphere can be growth producing for both of you. Be prepared to feel anxious. But, remember, no one ever died of anxiety—it only feels like it!

We have gathered pages and pages of rules that have the same flavor and feeling as those we have shared with you.

When we review them, we are struck by the sense of fear and defensiveness that seem to be a part of so many of them. True, the women who lived by them functioned, raised families, and had careers. Yet the feelings imparted by most of these rules is one of inadequacy and self-doubt. There is a sense of "I want to protect my daughter," "I want the choices that I made in my life to be validated," or sometimes, "I want her to do it differently." As a result, many of the daughters we have talked with believed that their only alternative was to pull away from their mothers and to reject those rules that felt so confusing and repressive.

"Guilt Trips"

Go back and take another look at the four groups of rules. Did you notice that the majority of them have a common theme—the capacity to produce guilt? Guilt is a common medium that family members use, and have used for generations, to keep other members of the family in line. One of the most common complaints we hear from clients is, "My mother is always trying to 'guilt-trip' me." (We also hear about daughter's attempts to "guilt-trip" their mothers!)

But using rules and their by-product, guilt, as a means of controlling a relationship creates hazards for both mother and daughter. Guilt-producing rules test the tolerance levels of their relationship, and can often lead to the following impasse:

1. A mother feels that when her daughter fails to comply with her rules, it is a repudiation of her as a mother;

    OR

2. A daughter feels that her mother's rules are a blow to her burgeoning attempts at independence.

We know that most mothers and daughters have a strong desire to relate to one another in an open and positive way.

(If you didn't, you would not be reading this book.) Neither wants to create a breach between them, yet each may find herself clinging to her entrenched position as if her life depended on it. Old rules have the potential to upset the sometimes fragile equilibrium of a relationship. When this happens, neither mother nor daughter can function effectively. For the most part, it is daughters who struggle under the burden of rules. And the major strain between the generations can erupt in heated battles fought over these rules.

To get beyond the problems that rules can cause, here are some additional strategies to try.

MENDING MOVES FOR BOTH MOTHERS AND DAUGHTERS:

- Spend some time by yourself, writing down lists of rules that you were given, using our four categories as a guideline (being a woman, men and relationships, work, and sexuality). If you want to include other categories that are applicable to your family system, that's fine, too.
- Meet with your mother or daughter at a mutually agreed-upon time and place to discuss your lists. As you look at the lists, try to find areas of commonality.
- If either of you begins to feel angry and/or upset, take a time-out and talk about what was just said that disturbed you. Allow the person who is upset to talk. You don't have to defend yourself or fix it; just listen to how the other person feels.
- Here are some other obstacles to watch for:
  Daughters: Be aware that you may have an unconscious need to protect your mother from your perceptions of her rules, which could get in the way of being open about sharing your lists with her.
  Mothers: You do not need to defend yourself over the rules your daughter learned. You did the best job you could in raising your daughter. Try to hear her experience of the rules as simply that—her experience— and not as a judgment of you as a mother.

This process is not easy. Be good to yourselves and recognize that you have taken on a tough assignment in service of your relationship.

Rules, Roles, and Maternal Ambivalence

Every one of the rules and vignettes we have presented is loaded with ambivalence for both mothers and daughters. As we wrote earlier, families use rules to keep behavior predictable and relationships in their place. If you are a mother, you know the discomfort you feel when your children begin to move beyond your orbit—beyond the reach of your rules. You watch them with pride, but also with fear ("Suppose something happens to them," "Suppose someone hurts them."). After all, your rules were supposed to be there to protect them. Rules are also there to protect *you* from experiencing the uncomfortable awareness of how very different your children are from you. These differences can create a sense of uneasiness in you.

Mothers, and society in general, have shied away from acknowledging the concept of maternal ambivalence. After all, our culture has, on some level, deified motherhood, yet at the same time we have relegated it to the status of second-class citizenship. Neither of these positions takes into account a mother as a woman and a human being. Mothers, like everyone else, want to be seen and valued for who they are, warts and all. Most mothers have learned, however, that the expression of ambivalent feelings about their role as a mother will fall on deaf ears.

For example, a mother who, after a long day of taking care of a sick or colicky infant, doesn't dare voice her fantasy of leaving on the next plane for Tahiti (sans baby) because someone will think she is a "bad mother." Worst of all, as a true product of her times, she then begins to think of herself as a bad mother. So here we have a tired, overworked, and often undersupported woman who feels that she is failing in the role of mother because of the very natural feelings of ambivalence that accompany exhaustion and overwork.

According to conventional wisdom, motherhood is supposed to come naturally to women. Nothing, however, could be further from the truth. Not all women are natural-born nurturers. Yes, they can learn to be nurturers and most do, but it doesn't always come easily or instinctively. Yet, as a culture, we turn a blind eye to this phenomenon and are quick to judge a mother whose attitude or behavior toward her child appears less than optimal.

In our own practice, many mothers who come to see us feel inadequate, helpless, and angry. They often feel misunderstood, not only by their families, but by society at large. They feel that they have not lived up to the ideal of being "perfect mothers"—they haven't played their roles properly. Sometimes just having the opportunity to talk with us about their angry or helpless feelings allows them to look at themselves as mothers more objectively. When we ask what they have done to help themselves overcome these distressing feelings, many say they have depended upon the power of rules to support them and keep their feelings of inadequacy at bay.

So rules do help mothers live up to their internalized ideals of what mothers "should" be and "ought" to do. No wonder they become upset when their daughters question their rules. It feels as if their daughters are questioning them in their roles as mothers. The shakier a woman feels in the role of a mother, the more threatening her daughter's challenge to her rules is going to seem.

As a daughter, you have a role to play, too. Perhaps you've made the choice to go along with your mother's rules because it's easier. Her rules, while not always comfortable, feel familiar. A significant part of going along with mother's rules means staying connected in ways that your family approves of, and not "making waves." But what about you as an individual under those circumstances? What if, by going along with the rules, you run into conflict with your own needs or dreams? At some point you will begin to chafe against the rules. Then they become part of the problem.

Rewriting the Rules

When mothers and daughters contemplate making changes in their relationship, they often think about these changes in terms of breaking and/or rewriting rules. But as rules are broken, it is often the "rule breakers" who suffer most as a result of their actions. As one young woman told us: *In order to make a point with my mother I used to, as my grandmother would say, "cut off my nose to spite my face." I was so busy taking a stand and trying to do things differently than everybody in my family, I wasn't aware that I was hurting myself more than I was hurting them.*

Rule breaking, for the most part, is not a measured response; it is a gut reaction.

There is a better way to make changes in your life and relationships, especially with your mother or your daughter. We want you to think in terms of rewriting some of the rules that simply don't work for you. Before you begin, however, let's add a cautionary note: Don't throw out the baby with the bathwater! In other words, we don't want you overthrowing rules indiscriminately. Some of them must be working for you or you wouldn't have gotten this far in your life. So what we suggest is that you make a thoughtful list of the rules that you would like to change. Then go through the list and check to see if they are reality-based. Ask yourself:

- Am I clear about which part of the rules are a problem for me?
- How have I been responsible in the past for keeping the rule in place?

- How will changing the rule affect me and my mother (or my daughter)?
- What do I want to accomplish?

To help you answer these questions, read and take some time to think about the following ideas.

Know Who You Are

In your own mind, be clear about what you want in your mother-daughter relationship, and what you are willing to do to get it. Be realistic. Don't set yourself up for failure by creating unrealistic goals for your relationship—i.e., "I'm going to change my mother (or daughter) if it kills me." It just might. Remember, the only person in this life that you can change is you. You can change how you respond to your mother or your daughter. It is *not* within your power to change them.

What if your mother or your daughter doesn't like who you are? In a nondefensive way, ask them what they don't like. You'll learn things about yourself that can really be useful. Listen without reacting defensively, but if it gets to be too much, suggest a time-out: "You are really saying some important things. I need some time to assimilate everything you've said."

This may sound like a difficult process, but it's not impossible. Armed with your new awareness, you can then decide if it would be in your best interest to change rules that pertain to you.

Reworking the Rules About Communication

Many women grew up with the admonition "Be nice." Our question, when we hear this, is always "To whom?" Very often, this is a directive meaning, "Take care of someone else's needs at the expense of your own." Of course we don't advocate going off and acting like a selfish boor in service of your own needs. We do suggest, however, that you look at your usual ways of behaving and communicating your needs to others. You may find you haven't communicated as well as you would like to or need to in order to accomplish the things you want.

When you are rewriting your rules, be clear about what rules you want to change, and what you want from your mother or your daughter. You also need to state your case and get your point across clearly to others. When you are clear about what you need or what you want to do, you are being responsible for yourself. On the other hand, communicating in an ambiguous manner, or hoping that the other person will "know" what you are thinking is not going to help you move in a new direction. Your mother or daughter may be able to do lots of things, but we bet that mind reading isn't one of them.

Also, make an effort to create "positive rules." They are based on a combination of self-awareness and life experience. Their foundation comes from realistic expectations of oneself and not infantile longings. These are the rules that are based not on tradition but on knowledge of yourself— your strengths and weaknesses as a woman, a mother, and a daughter.

The following are examples of positive rules that we have seen created and implemented by women we've worked with:

- I will do the best I can based on what I know about myself and the situation I am dealing with.
- I will give myself permission not to try to be "right" or "perfect" all the time.
- By taking responsibility for my mistakes, I can be the kind of role model I want to be for my daughter (or my mother!).

Hidden Pitfalls

You may find yourself running into hidden pitfalls as you attempt to rewrite rules for yourself. Change is anxiety producing—even change that you have initiated and that you believe to be in your own best interest. Change creates anxiety in others, too. When you change your behavior, you threaten the status quo of your relationship with your mother or your daughter. Don't forget, you both have been living by these rules for a long time.

So be prepared to meet with resistance and countermoves that send the message "Change back" and "Don't be different." You may even hear some of these messages in your own head. Take a deep breath and think about what you are trying to accomplish for yourself and your relationship. If you fall into one of the "pits," you can always crawl out again and start over.

A Willingness to Change

The impetus to change rules needs to come from a loving, not an angry, place. You and your mother or daughter cannot grow in an atmosphere where you are both struggling for control of your relationship. The changes you seek should enhance both of you. The goal here is to fine-tune family rules that are outdated or restrictive so that you can expand the repertoire of ways you interact with one another. A willingness to change, of course, is an important component of this process. In our next chapter, we will explore how the unconscious needs of both mother and daughter play a role in keeping this process from happening.

7 *Leaving Home—Can I Take My Mother with Me?*

Robin's dream:

> I'm in a subway station. The train is sitting at the platform.
> It is empty, except for my mother. She is sitting there, on
> the train, all by herself. I don't really want to get on with
> her. But I know that if I don't get on the train and accom-
> pany my mother, I will never see her again. I hurriedly get
> on the train—and kiss my mother good-bye. I then get off
> the train, and it begins to move. I wake up and I am feeling
> overwhelmingly sad and crying.

Robin, a native of the East Coast, had moved to California
a few months before she had this dream. She is a set de-
signer, and believes her move has been a positive one for
her career. But at age thirty-three, she never lived so far
away from her close-knit family—and asserting her autonomy has not always been easy.

The poignant imagery in Robin's dream captures the essence of the struggle that takes place as children naturally
move toward independence and begin the process of separation from their parents. While this process can be painful
for most parents and children, it is especially difficult for
mothers and daughters. For example, in her dream, Robin
is ambivalent about moving forward with her life and, sym-

bolically, "leaving mother." The picture of her mother going off on the train alone arouses feelings of sadness and confusion in her.

Why is this process of growing up, which ideally should feel natural and right, so difficult? Is Robin unique or does this happen to every mother and daughter? As we begin to explore this issue, let's look at more of what Robin told us about her history.

I grew up in a small town in Massachusetts. My dad was a police officer and my mother, Ruth, was a teacher. I am the middle child (I have an older brother and a younger sister). We had a typical small-town childhood.

While I was growing up, I was always closest to my mom. I adored my dad and I think he was a really good father, but sometimes he would get mad at us and stomp around the house (although we knew it wouldn't last long). My mother was the comforter—the one who soothed us and made everything bad go away.

When you have a mom like mine, you always want to show her how much you appreciate everything she did. She loved it when I would tell her about my day and my activities. She always had suggestions, good ones, about things I could do and how I could do them.

Occasionally, I became interested in something or someone (boys!) that she really didn't have any use for. We would talk about it, and while she never overtly disapproved, I could just feel that she wasn't happy. It was hard for me to put energy into something that upset my mother.

It wasn't until I went to college and decided to major in art and set design that she and I had our first major disagreement. She had always viewed my love of painting as a hobby. Art, for her, had nothing to do with the real world. I had very good grades and had received a scholarship to an Ivy League school. Looking back, I now realize that she had dreams of me going to law school or medical school. By focusing on the arts, I was really letting her down.

During my first semester at school I experienced a bout of depression, although I didn't know I was depressed at the time. I thought I was just homesick. What I really felt sick about was that I could not please my mother. Our weekly phone calls were punctuated by her sighs and silences when I told her about my classes and my work. I had gone from being her shining star to a lump of coal.

As Robin struggled with her dilemma—to please either herself or her mother—she became physically ill. She developed a severe case of mononucleosis that caused her to miss the second semester of her freshman year. When she went back to school the following fall, she changed her major to prelaw.

We asked Robin if she could remember her mother's reactions to her during that period. She told us that she recalled her mother telling her, *I only want the best for you. You are so bright. You can do anything with your life. I want you to take advantage of your education. I wish I could have had your opportunities.*

Then Robin became very quiet as she reflected upon her mother's words. *It's really so sad. To this day it feels as if I was going to school for her and not for me.*

We will come back to the story of Robin and Ruth later in this chapter when we discuss different ways daughters cope with the separation process—growing up and away from home.

The Process of Separation

Before we go further, let's define some terms. When we talk about separation and the growth process called *individuation*, what do we mean and how are these words relevant to your relationship with your mother or your daughter?

- *Separation* is the process of experiencing yourself as distinct from your mother or your daughter. This does not imply that in order to feel separate, you must physically remove yourself to another geographic location. Rather, it means that you feel okay about having your own feelings and making your own choices.

• *Individuation* is the process by which you create an internalized picture of yourself as an independent person. This is a lifelong process that allows you to become an autonomous individual. It also allows you to relinquish dependence on others while remaining emotionally connected to the important people in your life.

For most women, this process is much less difficult if their mothers were successful in their own attempts to become independent. If a mother had difficulty separating from her mother, her daughter's moves to separate can trigger an enormous amount of anxiety.

Changing Lives, Changing Roles

As women move from the role of child to adult daughter, both they and their mothers face a difficult adjustment. They have played their respective parts for so many years that on some level, they really don't know any other way to be. A mother, for instance, has to be in charge in order for her baby to grow safely from infancy to childhood. It is her job to set boundaries, model behavior, and instill values. Her "on-the-job behavior" becomes problematic, however, when her daughter reaches young adulthood. Because her daughter is still her child, a mother may find it difficult to see her offspring as an adult. For most mothers, the feeling that their daughters are still unformed, and that they need advice and protection, dies hard. Letting go isn't easy.

"I'm Only Trying to Help"

While most mothers pay lip service to the idea that they want their daughters to be independent and autonomous, many adult daughters have heard the following kinds of questions and advice from their mothers: "Honey, don't you think you ought to get your bangs trimmed?" "Have you made an appointment to get your teeth cleaned?" "Don't forget to call your grandmother before you leave town."

From a mother's point of view, these statements are simply attempts to be helpful. They are her way of showing love and concern. From a daughter's point of view, however, they can feel judgmental and controlling. She doesn't hear her mother's comments as loving because she is too busy struggling to become independent.

Meanwhile, if the mother in this scenario fails to recognize how challenged her daughter feels in her own search for independence, she may feel hurt by her daughter's inability to understand her. At that point a mother may find herself wanting to distance herself from her daughter to protect herself from feeling rejected.

Clear Communication: A Two-Way Street

How can mothers and daughters successfully weather this developmental storm? Both sides need to make some shifts in perspective and clearly communicate them to one another. As a daughter, for example, you need to be able to hear and understand that your mother is *not* trying to control your life. This is not easy, however, because you've spent most of your young life being told what to do. Why, at this point, should you begin to experience your mother any differently? The answer is simple: because you still need your mother. You just need her differently than you did when you were a child.

As a daughter moving out into the world, you need a sense that your mother believes in you—that your mother will validate your attempts to fly even when you fail to get off the ground. You don't need your mother to "fix" things for you, but you do need her to listen to your fears and to your dreams.

At the same time every daughter needs to take a good look at the messages *she* sends to her mother. For example, are you proclaiming to your mother, "I want to be independent"? Or are you sending the unspoken message "Rescue me, because I'm afraid I can't do it myself"? If a daughter can learn to acknowledge her own ambivalence about letting go, then she can feel better about asking for help in situations where she really needs it.

If you're a mother, what do you need to do at this point in the mother-daughter relationship? You need to trust that you have done a "good enough" job with your daughter. You probably weren't perfect. But you did your job well enough so that your daughter wants to move out into the world in a healthy and appropriate way. If you want your daughter to recognize that you have done the best job that *you* could, then you will have to acknowledge that your daughter is doing the best job that *she* can. In the process, you may have to literally, sit on your hands as you watch your daughter take the steps necessary to assume her place in the adult world.

Some mothers, of course, *can't* let go. They try to smooth the way for their children, but in doing so, they are sending their daughters the message "I don't really believe that you can do it . . . You can't make it without my help." But a mother needs to remember the look of triumph she saw on her daughter's face the day she first learned to walk—the look that says, "I can do it myself!" Her adult daughter needs to hear, "I believe in you . . . you can do it"—not, "Do it my way or you are sure to fail."

There is a great deal of truth in the old adage "There are no mistakes, only lessons." Mothers have spent a lifetime learning lessons. They need to give their daughters the same opportunity, even if some of those lessons hurt. Daughters don't want to be treated like they are a piece of fine porcelain; they want to know that it is okay to live their lives the way they want to, even if it is different from the way their mothers lived theirs. We'll come back to this complex issue late in this chapter.

In the Beginning . . .

To put this transition period into perspective, let's take a look back at the entire process of gender separation from its beginning. As a toddler, a little girl never has to experience the break from her mother that little boys must on their road to becoming men. In order to make a positive gender connection and identification with father, boys begin a mini-separation from mother at about three years of age—a process that continues until about age five. This process is vital for their personal and social development into adult men. At the same time their ability to make this shift and to identify with daddy serves as a training ground for their later important separation from *both* parents, which takes place at adolescence.

But girls are different. The mother-daughter relationship is unique in that the daughter's sense of relatedness and connection with her mother has been in place since birth. This gender-based difference has a critical impact on a daughter's future ability to separate from her mother.

Author Carol Gilligan wrote in *In a Different Voice*, "For girls and women, issues of femininity or feminine identity do not depend on the achievement of separation from the mother." Gilligan continues that while separation is crucial to the development of a healthy sense of *male* identity, a young girl's sense of herself as a woman is linked to the quality of her attachment to her mother. Yet even though girls have never had to withstand the early pain of switching allegiance away from their mothers, they are suddenly confronted with this monumental task of separation at a time when they are most vulnerable: adolescence.

Perhaps you recall saying to your own mother: "When I grow up, I'm going to be just like you!" As a daughter, this quest for relatedness stems from the recognition of yourself as a female person, like your mother.

But there is a flip side of this process of recognition. Long before adolescence, you became aware that you and your mother were not the same person—which may have felt frightening. After all, if you and your mother were different people, then you might have asked, "Who am I?"

Was Freud Right?

In his essay "Femininity," Sigmund Freud addressed his earlier view on the nature of the mother-daughter relationship: "We knew, of course, that there had been a preliminary stage of attachment to the mother, but we did not know that it could be so rich in content and so long-lasting, and could leave behind so many opportunities for fixations and dispositions."

Historically, a daughter's process of separation from her mother has been recognized as an action potentially studded with pitfalls. As we've suggested, it can be a source of fear and apprehension for both. Their unspoken fears sound and feel like this:

> Daughter's Fear: "I need to move on but I'm afraid—afraid that something bad might happen and that you won't love me if I leave. Will you feel hurt and abandoned? Who will take care of you? *Who will take care of me?*"

> Mother's Fear: "I really don't want you to move away from me. I'm afraid that you will move beyond me. I'm afraid that something might happen to you. I'm afraid that something might happen to me. *Your leaving feels like a kind of death.*"

The power of these fears resides in the fact that, while both mother and daughter are aware and feel them, neither one dares to talk about them openly. As we've pointed out, communication is crucial, but mother and daughter seem to be in collusion to avoid dealing with the underlying question aroused by these fears: "Who are we without each other?"

If mother and daughter were to address this question openly, they would face the terror that without the other, each may cease to exist. A mother may have defined herself for so long by her role as mother that her daughter's growth feels like a threat to her existence: *I have shaped you and molded you. I have cared for you and watched over you. Now you want to do life your way. Your questioning of me makes me question myself.*

A daughter, who of necessity has been dependent all of her life, now finds herself stepping into unknown territory as she begins to assert her autonomy: *It would be so easy to run home, to never leave your side. I feel torn. I hear the siren call of independence and yet I long for the comfort of what I've always known.*

The following story of forty-two-year-old Karen, an attractive, divorced lawyer, and her fourteen-year-old daughter, Laura, illustrates how this dilemma is played out. Karen and Laura had a very close relationship. Laura, a bright, sweet girl, had always been a fearful child, and her fears were compounded when her parents divorced. Her intimate relationship with her mother, however, seemed to soothe her many anxieties.

As Laura approached adolescence, Karen, both consciously and unconsciously, began to relate to her daughter more as a girlfriend than a mother. For example, she encouraged Laura to dress and act in a way that could be described as pseudomature. Karen gave Laura her clothing to wear, while she began to wear clothes that looked like Laura's.

Laura began to blossom physically. But Karen's awareness of her daughter's beauty aroused feelings of conflict in her. Here was her daughter, unfolding like a flower, at a time when Karen believed that her own beauty and options had reached a plateau.

Karen began to develop another conflict as well. On the one hand, she complained that Laura was never home and was neglecting her schoolwork. On the other hand, she bragged about how popular Laura was, with both boys and girls. Laura was running with a very fast crowd and appeared to be obsessed with her appearance. Not surprisingly, by the time she was a junior in high school, she had developed an eating disorder.

When Karen discovered Laura's illness, she went into a tailspin: *We have always had such a perfect relationship. How could something like this happen without my knowing it?*

Karen's definition of a "perfect relationship"—where mothers and daughters have no secrets and no separate selves—was the core of Laura's problem. They went into therapy together, and by the time Laura graduated from high school, her eating disorder was under control.

What can we conclude from this story? Laura's illness created a crisis that ultimately broke the chain of her mother's overinvolvement in her life. Laura had to become ill before she could openly acknowledge her discomfort and fear at being prematurely thrust into the role of an adult by her mother. Laura's greatest fear was that if she did not conform to her mother's expectations, Karen would no longer love her and she would be emotionally abandoned.

But as both mother and daughter confronted her eating disorder and its underlying issues, Laura was finally given the opportunity simply to be a teenager and not the end product of her mother's fantasy. Karen, meanwhile, began to understand that her obsession with Laura's life and appearance was a way of keeping her own fears of aging and inadequacy at bay.

Painful Truths

In order for both mother and daughter to begin the process of separating from one another, each has to acknowledge the necessity and consequences of such a step. Both must also confront the often painful truth of their similarities and differences. The differences may be particularly unnerving in that they can lead to a change in the status quo—and that change, like most change, can feel frightening.

As a mother, you look at your growing daughter and realize that she is becoming a distinctly separate person. As with Karen, this can be a source of pride—but it can also instill feelings of envy, fear, and sadness. Watching your daughter make her first forays toward autonomy, with the freshness of youth and a long future ahead of her, may arouse painful feelings in you. Like many mothers, your awareness of time passing and memories of missed opportunities may create internal conflicts that are expressed as ambivalence about your daughter's attempts to separate.

A daughter has a different but nonetheless difficult dilemma. She needs her mother's love and support so that she can feel secure in her efforts to go out and find a place for herself in the world. To gain her mother's approval, she may "give in" or conform to something important to her mother, just as Laura did. Every girl (and for that matter, most adult women) wants to feel valued and appreciated by her mother, but sometimes the price that she pays for being valued is the suppression of her own needs.

Consider the story of Alex, a high-energy, forty-year-old executive. She told us about the time that she ran for president of her junior high school. She was in the eighth grade and was running against two ninth graders. Alex recalled that this was a very exciting time for her. She had many enthusiastic supporters among her friends and teachers. She remembered, however, that her mother, Gwen, was worried. *What if you lose?* she asked Alex. *I don't want to see you hurt.*

Alex assured her mother that she would be fine. She was enjoying this process and felt that she had a good chance to win, even though she was younger than the other candidates. She spent a lot of time and energy reassuring her mother.

Election day arrived, and by a very narrow margin, Alex won. She came flying home, wreathed in smiles and confetti. Gwen congratulated her and said how proud she was. But although Alex heard her mother's words, she vividly recalls that through voice and body language, Gwen appeared anything but pleased. Her mother seemed distant. Her voice was cool. Alex felt sick. *What's wrong? Why isn't she happy for me? What have I done to displease her?*

In looking back, Alex speaks sadly about her relationship with her compliant and unassertive mother. *I was always looking to her for approval. I realize now that it must have been overwhelming for her to have a daughter like me. It didn't matter to me that we weren't alike. She was my mom and I loved her. I realize now that she wasn't worried about me being hurt. She was terrified because I was different from her.*

At this very young age Alex found herself between a rock and a hard place. On some level, Gwen experienced her daughter's running for office and winning as an invalidation of her as a mother and a role model. In order for Alex to obtain her insecure mother's wholehearted approval, she would have had to deny her own needs to assert herself—a truly no-win scenario.

As an adult, Alex still feels the grief and some of the guilt of that period in her life. She recognizes that her election was a turning point—the beginning of the separation process from her mother.

Just suppose, however, that Alex had been less confident or less ambitious. Would there have been a different ending to her story? Would she have eventually risen to the executive ranks in her career? Perhaps not.

"Why Don't I Feel Successful?"

Women sometimes come into our offices and say to us: *Look at me from the outside. Most people would probably describe me as successful. Why don't I feel successful? What will it take for me to become comfortable in my own skin?* These kind of statements make us take a hard look at the issue of women and success, and the way that women themselves define it.

For the women we have worked with, success means something broad and personal. For them, success means the capacity to be separate and functional while also *maintaining positive connections* to the important people in their lives. One of their most important relationships is, of course, with their mothers.

Recent research shows that women have a much greater emotional investment than men in maintaining relationships. This investment in relationships occurs not only in their personal lives, but in the workplace, too. For most women, just "doing a good job" is not enough. Their definition of success is being both competent on the job *and* working to maintain positive connections.

How do we define a positive connection?

- A *positive* connection means that you can maintain yourself and a relationship in emotionally charged situations. Your sense of self does not get lost in "hot button" issues or in unresolved emotional history.
- A *negative* connection means the inability to keep your perspective as an individual when confronted with people or situations that have been problematic in the past.

So how does the history of the way a mother relates with her daughter affect the younger woman's sense of feeling successful? To answer that question in your own life, you need to look at those elements in your relationship with your mother that are keeping you (or have kept you) from fulfilling your ambitions. Dr. Ruth Moulton, in her article on the effect of mothers on their daughters' success, wrote: "If the mother does not encourage and reinforce her daughter for fear that she herself may be surpassed and feel superfluous, the resulting discouragement can undermine the daughter and result in extreme anxiety and a tendency to fail."

The unconscious push-pull between you and your mother (or daughter) may feel something like this:

Mother: "Be successful . . . but don't be better than me."
Daughter: "I can do it alone . . . but don't leave me."

These mixed messages can leave both you and your mother (or your daughter) feeling frustrated and possibly alienated. The underlying tension created by these messages has the potential to shatter your relationship. This rupture is what mothers and daughters fear most. Every daughter wrestles with this issue: Must I lose my relationship with my mother in order to gain my heart's desire?

A Daughter's Greatest Fear

Like many of the women we work with, you may be operating under the influence of an unspoken fear: If I become successful, I'm afraid my mother won't love me, or that she will abandon me. What is the origin of this fear? Very often, it began with a mother's relationship with her own mother. If, for example, Alex's mother, Gwen, had difficulties, for whatever reason, establishing her independence from her own mother, she is going to have trouble either acknowledging or accepting Alex's attempts to do something differently—becoming an individual in her own right. When Alex won her election, Gwen experienced a profound sense of anxiety. It felt as if her daughter's victory was a move away from her. Alex had no idea how her mother was reacting emotionally to her success; she only knew that something had shifted between them.

Continuing to use Alex and Gwen as examples, let's take a closer look at why a daughter's success produces anxiety in her mother. Gwen, like many mothers, may be unaware of how deeply she is impacted by her daughter's accomplishments. Let's suppose that Gwen, as a young woman, had to stifle her own need to be assertive in order to maintain a harmonious relationship with her mother. If that scenario fits, then Alex's drive and aspirations have the power to rock the foundations upon which Gwen has built her life.

In an interview with Gwen, we asked her to think back to the time when Alex was growing up and tell us what it was like to be her mother. She responded, *Being Alex's mother was unlike anything I could have predicted. In fact, that was my problem. She was so unpredictable.* Gwen laughed, and then added, *I guess she wasn't really unpredictable. She just wasn't like me.* Gwen had very neatly summed up the essence of her relationship with her daughter.

So what happens when a mother has a daughter who is "not like me"? According to Gwen, *My mother would never have let me assert myself the way Alex did from the time she was a very little girl. My mother would not have approved of that kind of behavior. It wasn't ladylike. You have to understand, I am a product of my time. Women of my generation just didn't go against what we were told to do. My mother would have disapproved. To this day it is unthinkable that I would do something that she did not deem fitting behavior for a woman. Her approval was the most important thing in the world to me. I think, perhaps, it still is.*

This is an example of a daughter who, by repressing her longings to be assertive, assured herself that she would never be threatened by the loss of mother's love. By not breaking any family rules, she bought emotional insurance that she would not be abandoned. At the same time, however, she may have forsaken some of her own dreams for success.

The Development of Success Phobia

Let's go back specifically to the issue of why many women aren't more comfortable with the idea of success. As we have already written, we believe that a mother's values and beliefs have a powerful influence on her daughter's approach to competitive situations and relationships in which she needs to be assertive. For example, singer and songwriter Carly Simon, in an article about her relationship with her mother in *Vanity Fair* magazine, traced her difficulties in performing in public directly to her mother's withholding of approval.

Studies have shown that both mothers and fathers tend to validate and reward their sons' efforts in the arena of competition and achievement more frequently than they do their daughters'. Even in nursery school, little boys are rewarded for their attempts at mastery, while little girls are rewarded for being quiet, compliant, and obedient.

The implied message that many little girls receive from both parents is: "If you are good and sit quietly in the corner, one day your Prince Charming will come and you will be happy forever." Cinderella is alive and well even today. Cinderella, by our definition, would be designated as a "submissive daughter." Of course, in the fairy tale, by suppressing her own needs, sitting by the hearth and being good, Cinderella ends up with the prince. Unfortunately, this does not happen in the lives of most people. So if a daughter buys the myth and sits and waits for a prince to arrive and make her happy, this will only compound her difficulties in finding her own voice, and achieving the success that, on some level, she may desire.

While the message in Cinderella may sound farfetched, it has been assimilated by and strongly influenced generations of women. If a daughter grows up seeing her mother being passive and dependent, what does she do with her own impulses to be assertive? She may experience a great deal of anxiety that her outgoing behavior will not be tolerated. And what about the intelligent daughter who doesn't trust her intellectual gifts because they haven't been validated by her mother? She may legitimately fear that her intelligence and her work will move her beyond her mother's orbit and cause a rupture in their relationship.

There are times when a daughter's need to please her mother is so great that it stops her from functioning in important areas of her life. The intensity of her need for her mother's approval creates a situation where instead of performing successfully, she "freezes." Her fear of being unable to satisfy her mother—either her actual mother or her internalized mother—creates a state of panic, which in turn keeps her from doing things that she normally knows how to do. The following story of our client, Hailey, age thirty-four, is a good example of this process.

When I was a kid, my mother wanted me to be the best at whatever I did. She was determined that I be the best student, the best athlete, the best dancer in my ballet class. She made it clear that she was there to help me. All I had to do was listen to her, to follow her lead, and I would be successful.

My life felt like torture. School was painful because I knew I wasn't the smartest student in my class, and how disappointing this must be to my mother. I wasn't particularly athletic and my attempts to excel fell far short of her expectations. I had to report all of this back to her at the end of the day. As I talked, I could see the disappointment in her face. It was so painful to let her down. Afterward she would regroup and say, "okay, let's get to work." Out would come the flash cards with math problems on them. She would quiz me until I felt like my mind was fried. Then we would go out into the yard and she would throw a baseball with me or have me shoot baskets, whatever sport we were doing in physical education at the time. I hated the fact that I wasn't good and I think I hated her for not accepting me for what I was.

As an adult, whenever I am called upon to perform, either at work or in my personal life, I freeze. I feel like a deer caught in the headlights of a car. I know that I'm going to let someone down. I feel like a child again, realizing that I'm going to disappoint my mother and not being able to do anything about it.

The irony of this situation is that Hailey's perception of her mother's expectations, and those of others that she imbues with authority, may have no grounding in reality. Like most of us, as a small child, she experienced her mother as both commanding and invincible. She acknowledges that her mother may simply have been attempting to help her—and Hailey admits that she really did need assistance. But whatever the reality, the end result is that Hailey's early interactions with her mother have kept her from experiencing herself as a competent person.

The Experience of Being Separate

In order for you to make the transition from dependent child to autonomous adult, you need to experience yourself as an individual, separate from your mother. For this process to take place smoothly, you must have some sense of feeling right about what you are doing—which relates back to the way you, as a little girl, were perceived and validated by your mother.

Think back to Chapter Two and the discussion of the early lessons of our attachment experience. A woman's ability to separate successfully is directly linked to a solid attachment relationship with her mother. So for emotional separation to take place, a daughter must truly believe that she not only has her mother's support for such a move but that her mother validates her efforts and *approves of who she is.*

As we have written, a daughter's moves to separate can be very threatening and anxiety producing for her mother. This is especially true if her mother's attempts to become independent from her own mother were not successful. If a mother's own efforts to create a separate self resulted in frustration and dead ends, she may cling even more tightly to her daughter. The following vignette about our client Bonnie poignantly illustrates this scenario.

Bonnie, a young professional, has always had difficulty asserting herself, both personally and in the business world. Her insecure and self-involved mother, Nora, felt that she knew best how Bonnie should live. According to Bonnie, *My mother has all the answers, including how I ought to live my life.*

When Bonnie began to take more responsibility with her career and her living circumstances—taking out a home loan, buying a new car—Nora became highly anxious. Rather than being proud of her daughter's efforts to become more self-sufficient and less dependent, she reacted with a barrage of criticism. *You don't know what you've gotten yourself into,* Nora said. *You'll end up saddled with debt. Don't come to me when you're in trouble!*

Nora had an intensely conflicted relationship with her own mother, Sheila. She grew up feeling overcontrolled and "smothered." Her response to her mother's intrusiveness was to run off and marry at nineteen. Like many women of her generation, Nora went from her mother's home to her husband's home. She dropped out of college and had two children, Bonnie and her sister, in quick succession. She never had the opportunity to live on her own or feel independent.

Bonnie understands that her own priorities and options are different from her mother's. When she told her mother that she had decided to go back to school to get a master-of-business-administration degree, Nora erupted once again. Bonnie told us, *My decision to pursue an advanced degree, to do my life differently, feels like an attack and a betrayal to my mother.*

When Bonnie pointed out to her mother that she saw a pattern of overly involved mother/daughter relationships in their family, Nora told her in no uncertain terms, *I have no idea what you are talking about. Whether or not I had problems with my mother, I'm certainly not overly involved with you.* Bonnie, as a result of this conversation, has been left feeling guilty and ambivalent. She asks, *How am I supposed to feel good about myself when my choices are so threatening to my mother?*

For Bonnie, the dilemma and source of her fear is how to create a separate sense of herself, without her mother's acceptance. Bonnie longs deeply for her mother's support. She sadly told us, *I don't think my mother is capable of giving me that kind of approval. She acts as if my wanting to do something different from her is a referendum on her life.*

In this brief, powerful vignette, you can see how difficult it is to feel empowered and successful if you are feeling insecure and anxious about being different—or, in other words, separating—from your mother.

We wondered what was lying beneath the surface of Nora's attacks on Bonnie. So we asked Nora to tell us her version of the story.

I don't understand Bonnie. According to her, I don't know anything and I can't do anything right. Doesn't she see that all I want to do is help her and keep her from making mistakes?

I never got along well with my mother and I wanted things to be different with Bonnie. I remember promising myself that if I ever had a daughter, we would have a warm and loving relationship. Now I'm terrified that I'm losing her.

Nora wants a close relationship with her daughter. But she doesn't understand how her ambivalence about Bonnie's life choices are affecting her daughter. She is so afraid that Bonnie is leaving her behind and that she is actively, and unknowingly, pushing her away.

The following are some Mending Moves that we suggested for Bonnie and Nora. Perhaps some of them might be helpful to you and your mother or daughter.

MENDING MOVES FOR BONNIE:

- Take some time to create a dialogue with your mother. Talk about your relationship in terms of how you feel—

"I would like . . ." "It makes me sad when . . ." "I feel confused when I hear . . ." Do your best to be nonjudgmental. Analyzing and blaming only create more distance.

- Try putting yourself in your mother's shoes, and think about what it would be like to have *you* for a daughter.
- What would you do differently if you were your mother?
- Take responsibility for yourself. If your mother is not emotionally available or capable of giving you the support you need, find other people and/or groups who can (church groups, women's groups, work-related groups, therapy groups). You do have choices.

MENDING MOVES FOR NORA:

- Take a long look at the history of your relationship with your daughter. When she says something that upsets you, are you reacting to her as your daughter or because she reminds you of some other important person in your life, past or present?
- Try to be as candid as possible with yourself about the role you play in creating conflict between you and your daughter. Are you being honest with yourself about your expectations of your daughter? You might find it useful to make a list of the expectations you have of her, both realistic and unrealistic. You may find that you are expecting her to do things for you that you are either unable or afraid to do for yourself.
- Seek out support systems for yourself. A parent who depends on her child to meet her emotional needs is going to be disappointed. Creating a circle of support for yourself can give you some needed perspective on your relationship with your daughter.

Styles of Separation

Next, let's get more specific about the process by which mothers and daughters separate. As a daughter, the way you go about separating from your mother is strongly influenced by the following issues, all of which we have previously touched on:

- the quality of your attachment process
- the style of mothering you experienced
- whether your family was enmeshed or disengaged
- the makeup of your family rules

Because everyone comes from a family with its own distinctive style of relating, each person approaches the process of separation in a very unique way. We want to acquaint you with a few of the methods utilized by various women at this crucial point in their lives.

The Submissive Daughter

Throughout this book, you have read the stories of women described, by themselves and by their daughters, as compliant. These are the "good girls," who never questioned their parents, especially their mothers. These passive and unassertive daughters have been like reeds growing on a riverbank—bending whichever way the wind blew in order to survive within their families.

Very often we see these women in our offices with symptoms of depression or anxiety. Some have been on the edge of addiction to alcohol, prescription medications, or inappropriate men. These are daughters who gave away the essence of themselves in exchange for approval from their mothers.

Forty-six-year-old Suzanne told us, *I was the youngest of three. My mother always told me I was the intuitive one. My older sister was the smart one and my brother was the dreamer. Because I was intuitive, her expectation was that I would know what everyone wanted, especially her. Well, she was right. I became really good at figuring out what every-*

body needed in my family. The problem was, I never was able to figure out what I needed. I still can't. Here I am, four years away from fifty, and I still don't know who or what I want to be when I grow up!

Then there is Penny, who married at age seventeen in order to get away from home and from her mother. Penny told us, *I wasn't thinking about my future or whether I really wanted to be married. What I saw was that marriage to Mike was my ticket out of that house—and I took it.*

We have also seen a particularly compliant daughter who we call the "time bomb." This is a woman full of longing and frustration. She is not seen or heard in her family for who she is, but rather for who they need her or want her to be. When she does try to separate, she acts out because there appears to be no suitable alternative available to her.

Does any of this sound like you or your daughter? If so, here are Mending Moves that you can take:

For Daughters:

- If you are still living at home, seek out women mentors at school or work—women who are interested in you, and from whom you believe you could learn. Join an organization where you have the opportunity to meet women of different ages. By expanding the number of supportive women in your life, you can increase your opportunities to make positive choices for yourself.
- Take an honest look at yourself and your relationship with your mother. Are you still playing the role of "good girl"? If so, what are the payoffs for you? If you feel more like the "time bomb," be honest with yourself and think about the kinds of feelings you have been sitting on. You also might want to talk about them—with a friend, a counselor, or better yet, your mother, if she's willing—before you act on them.

For Mothers:

- Create a list of the ways that you and your daughter are different from one another. Next to each of these differences, make a note, describing how this particular dissimilarity makes you *feel*. Next, look at this list of feelings. Whether you are experiencing fear, anger, frustration, or sadness in reaction to these differences, think of other people and situations with whom you have felt the same emotions. What did you do to make yourself feel better in those situations?

- Think about your relationship with your own mother. Make two lists, one of similarities and one of differences between you and your mother. How did your mother reinforce or encourage similarities between the two of you? What are the differences that you would have liked for her to acknowledge? Can you find similarities between you and your daughter in your list of differences?

The Rebellious Daughter

The rebellious daughter is a "little girl lost." She is crying out for attention and permission to be herself. The only way she gets the recognition she craves, however, is by hurting herself. As therapists, we frequently see this young woman when she is still an adolescent. She often has a history of running away from home. Most important, however, she always comes back. What is she attempting to communicate with this type of behavior? Usually, it is something like this: "Notice me, listen to me, pay attention, *I am here!*"

A daughter whose needs for validation have either been ignored or distorted by her parents is going to have a hard time finding herself as a separate individual. How can she leave when she hasn't gotten her necessary supply of recognition and nurturing from her family, especially her mother? This daughter can't move forward because to do so would mean giving up the hope of being acknowledged and of feeling special. In this kind of situation, acting out or "rebellious" behavior is common.

The rebellious daughter frequently engages in self-defeating behavior, such as failing in school, driving while intoxicated, engaging in unsafe sex, using drugs, and forming relationships with inappropriate and/or dangerous men. Her impulsive and erratic behaviors are most often motivated by her need for attention from her mother. Unfortunately, she usually ends up attracting the attention of another sort of authority—the police, a school counselor, emergency-room personnel—before her mother becomes involved. This vulnerable daughter is also a prime candidate for recruitment by a cult. As one young woman told us, "At least the cult wanted me and made me feel that I was lovable."

The rebellious daughter commonly has a mother whose style of mothering we discussed in Chapter Three—the Supermother—whose self-involvement takes precedence over the reasonable needs of her child. Thirty-seven-year-old Nina told us, *My mother didn't care what I did as long as I didn't interfere with her lunches and her tennis games. My classmates all had curfews and were grounded for coming in late. When I started coming home stoned, just to see if she noticed, she just looked at me and asked me if I'd had a nice evening. I could have lain down in the middle of our street naked, and she would have driven right by me.*"

Does any of this sound like you or your daughter? Here are Mending Moves that you can take:

For Daughters:

- Self-destructive behavior is often a cry for help. If your mother can't hear you, run—don't walk—to someone who can. If you are in school, talk to a counselor and get a referral for individual or group counseling. If you are employed, find out what kind of assistance is available through your company's human-resources department. Talk to your minister, rabbi, or priest. Join a self-help group. At the same time stop the behavior and look at your underlying feelings (anger, need for attention, revenge).

- Be a good "mother" to yourself; don't let yourself get hurt.

For Mothers:

- If you think that you have done everything you can to reach out to your daughter (making yourself available to listen to her, suggesting family and/or individual counseling) and she is still acting out (dropping out of school, consistently showing up late and/or missing work) or exhibiting self-defeating behavior (using drugs or alcohol, having affairs), your best alternative may be to let go of the fantasy that you can fix her problems. Your daughter will, ultimately, have to take responsibility for her actions, and you can't do it for her.

- Many mothers feel that it is their "duty" to go in and pick up the pieces for their adult children. Take a step back and stop telling your daughter what to do. By letting her take responsibility for her own actions, you may be doing the best thing you can for her.

The Frustrated Daughter

To illustrate the frustrated daughter, here is what twenty-nine-year-old Wendy told us about growing up with her mother: *I think I spent most of my childhood feeling confused. I never knew what to expect from one day to the next. I guess you could say that I learned to expect the unexpected.*

My mother was a puzzle to me. One day she would be angry and volatile. I never knew why. The next day would be like sunshine after a thunderstorm. She would hug me and put me on her lap for a story. She was wonderful, like nothing had happened. But I guess it really wasn't so wonderful. I had stomachaches all the time.

Wendy's mother is reminiscent of the mothers of the anxious and ambivalent children we described in Chapter Two. She was emotionally uninvolved with her daughter while Wendy was growing up. As a result, Wendy felt lonely and frustrated, as her mother alternated between periods of responsiveness, followed by neglect.

According to Wendy: *When my mother was attentive to me, I couldn't get enough. Those times were few and far between, however. I sometimes thought of myself as a rat running through a maze. I could run until I was exhausted. All I needed to keep going was that little intermittent reward every once in a while. I couldn't look anywhere else to get my needs met. If I took my eye off my mother for a minute, I might miss one of her good moments.*

Today, Wendy's ongoing sense of frustration and longing is compounded by a great deal of anxiety. She feels insecure in most of her relationships, with both men and women, and finds it very difficult to assess her own self-worth. Nothing and no one in her life feels reliable. As we wrote earlier in this book, a growing child needs to feel secure that the adults around him or her are available and dependable. But because her mother was so unpredictable, Wendy never had the opportunity to experience that feeling.

Wendy vacillates between feeling intense love and intense anger toward her mother. *I don't trust her, yet I keep returning to her. I make trips home, hoping that maybe this time things will be different. Most of the time I end up furious with myself. I'm trying to get water out of a dry well.*

How do you "leave home" if you have spent a childhood dining on emotional crumbs? If you're able to try out your wings, this indicates that somewhere you learned that taking risks was okay. But for Wendy to move out into the world, she needs a foundation—a sense that she is strong enough, secure enough—to sustain herself. It is too risky to leave, either emotionally or physically, if you don't know where your next "emotional feed" is coming from. Even crumbs are better than nothing. So Wendy waits for something from

her mother—something that her mother may not be emotionally equipped to give. According to Wendy: *It is so frustrating to watch other people moving ahead with their lives,
when I feel stuck in the same old place in mine.*

If this sounds like you or your mother, here are some
Mending Moves that you can take:

For Daughters:

• Let go of your blaming stance. Yes, it was difficult for
you while you were growing up and you were "shortchanged" by your mother's unavailability. Don't use this
as an excuse, however, not to get on with your life. Anger can feel empowering but only momentarily.

• It's hard to let go of the dream of an all-nurturing and
readily available mother. For an adult daughter whose
mother was available only intermittently to her as a
child, it can feel like a kind of death. Make a resolution
to yourself to make connections with nurturing women.
They are out there—at work, at church or synagogue,
in organizations, in support or therapy groups. You can
begin to feel empowered when you allow people into
your life who validate you. Start looking outward, instead of toward your mother.

For Mothers:

• Let's assume that due to some life circumstance—physical or mental illness, financial difficulties, divorce, cus-
tody arrangements—you were unable to provide
emotional sustenance for your daughter while she was
growing up. She is still your daughter and it is never too
late to try to form a relationship with her. Contact her
and ask if the two of you can meet, either in person or
on the phone. Go slowly and don't push. Like you, she
probably has a lot of mixed feelings about your rela-

tionship. Let her hear that you are sincere about opening up new lines of communication with her.

- Learning about yourself is the best foundation for a relationship. Understanding what was going on in your life during your daughter's childhood and how it affected you can be crucial to your efforts to reconcile with your daughter. Professional or pastoral counseling might be a good place to start.

The Parentified Daughter

I think I was born an adult. That is what Lise told us at age twenty-four, appearing competent and mature as she spoke. *I can't remember a time when I wasn't making sure my mother was happy or at least okay, and that everything in our house was running smoothly.*

Lise, the oldest of four children, was more than her mother's helper while she was growing up. She was her mother's caretaker. Her father was a very demanding man, so between her husband and her children, Lise's mother was simply overwhelmed.

Lise never had what might be called a "normal" childhood. Her responsibility was to meet her mother's needs. Lise not only had to help take care of her brothers and sister, but she also had the job of reassuring her mother that she was a wonderful mother. The parental system in her household was completely reversed. There was no room for the needs of the children because the needs of the parents were so formidable.

Lise shared with us a vivid memory of what happened when she was elected president of her junior class in high school. She knew it would be a lot of work, but she was sure she could manage while juggling her responsibilities at home. Her biggest problem was the weekly class meeting that was held every Tuesday after school. That meeting meant she would be late coming home to watch the children and start dinner for her mother. She made arrangements for a friend to walk her brothers and sister home from school. She told her mother that she would be home at six on the dot to start dinner.

The evening after her first meeting, Lise returned home to absolute chaos. Her siblings were in their rooms crying, her father was yelling at her mother, and her mother was in the kitchen mopping up the ingredients of a spilled casserole from the floor. She turned on Lise in a fury and said, *How could you do this to me? You know how your father loves my casserole. Why weren't you here on time to make it for him?* Lise was stunned. She had never seen so clearly how her mother simply could not see her, Lise, as someone separate from herself, someone who had their own needs and feelings. There wasn't any room for anyone's feelings but her mother's.

Children gain a sense of who they are by seeing themselves reflected in the mirror of their parents. When that parental mirror reflects back that they are doing fine, that they are loved and valued, a child internalizes that reflection and allows it to become a positive part of the way they see themselves. When Lise looked to her mother for validation, however, she saw only her mother's needs. Lise was left feeling inadequate and flawed. There was no affirming mirror available to her.

A parentified daughter like Lise grows up with a very skewed view of the world. While she seems independent and self-confident on the outside, on the inside she is distrustful of the world and her ability to function in it. According to Lise: *I'm still living at home and taking care of my mother. I moved out for six months last year, but I came back. I'm not sure why. It's just so hard to leave. I keep feeling that something is missing in me and the only place I'm going to find it is there.*

Lise is right. She finds it very hard to leave, because she didn't get what she needed while growing up. Remember, in order for a daughter to separate, she has to feel that she is doing the right thing for herself. This is easier said than done. After playing the role of caretaker for many years, a daughter is going to feel tremendous guilt when she gives up the role of "parent." She's also going to feel a sense of loss because there was a "payoff" for meeting her parent's needs. The payoff was that she felt important and, in some ways, powerful in her role of caretaker.

Does any of this story sound like you or your daughter? Here are Mending Moves that you can take:

For Daughters:

- Make a list of all of the things that you want or might have wanted from your mother while you were growing up. Go over the list and check off the things that you believe you are not capable of getting for yourself. Then review the list again. Spend some time researching resources—people or organizations—that can help you meet your unmet needs. Use them!

- If you believe that you have always been an adult or that you never had a childhood, then it's time for you to create one. Have some fun! Do something silly that you have always wanted to do. Organize a game of "Capture the Flag" on the beach with friends, spend an hour finger painting, stroll through a toy store, and make up a wish list. Allow yourself to let go of your adult persona for an hour or two. You might get in touch with that inner capacity for play that we are all born with.

- Give yourself permission to rest, to receive, and not take care of everyone.

For Mothers:

- If you were or are overwhelmed by the job of being a parent, you are not alone. No mother deliberately sets out to rob her children of their childhood. If you looked to your daughter for support while she was growing up, you need to acknowledge that fact, both to her and to yourself. Talk to her, without excuses or rationalizations, about what it was like for you as a young mother. Acknowledging that you would have done things differently if you could have allows her to see you as vulnerable and human.

- Tell your daughter about your relationship with your own mother. Did you long for things from your mother that she was not able to give you? You and your daughter may have more in common than you think.

Back to the Beginning

We began this chapter with Robin's dream, and the early history of her struggle to move out of her submissive role and experience herself as separate from her mother, Ruth. Robin became depressed and then physically ill in response to her inner struggle to try to please both her mother and herself.

To satisfy Ruth, Robin spent a miserable semester as a prelaw major. At the end of that time she finally realized that it was not enough to please only her mother. By doing so, she felt like she was destroying herself. Robin gave up her scholarship and dropped out of school. She moved to New York and took a job in the garment industry as a design assistant. Her parents were horrified. Ruth begged her to return to school. Robin told her that she wasn't ready yet. But this was not quite true.

Robin had already started taking classes in set design at night and on weekends, without telling her mother. She was excited to be back in a creative atmosphere, but she was also scared. Robin was, after all, breaking a family rule ("We are a close family and we don't have secrets"). One of her instructors, a woman, was very supportive of her work. She became a mentor for Robin, and Robin thrived under her encouragement.

At some time during this time period, Robin had another dream:

> I'm standing offstage, ready to go on for a performance. I'm wearing a diaphanous costume that shows off my new slender, tight body. My mother is pulling at me, saying that I cannot go out there dressed like that. I move out onto the stage and I am flying. I feel free.

Right after having this dream, Robin knew that she had to create a Mending Move to deal with the breach between herself and her mother. She asked Ruth to come to New York to spend a weekend with her. This was not an easy task, however. In fact, Robin reported: *I was scared to death to face my mother. But I knew I didn't want to lose her either.*

Robin's last statement is a crucial point about the process of separation. Separation is not about emotional cutoff. As we said earlier, separation is about feeling good about yourself as a person separate from your mother AND, at the same time, maintaining a relationship with her.

ROBIN'S MENDING MOVES:

- During their two days together, Robin explained to her mother how she felt about what had happened between them, and what she would like for herself and from her mother in the future.
- She told her mother that even though it would be difficult, she would like to feel that her mother respected her decisions about what she was doing with her life.
- In turn, she told her mother that she would not ask her to validate or agree with everything she did.
- Robin said that she would like to spend time sharing with her mother how she felt about her work and her

ambitions. She hoped that by doing so, Ruth would not feel so removed from her.

- She said that she would like to talk to her mother about Ruth's feelings about the two of them and the creation of a different kind of relationship.

It takes courage to take the kinds of risks that Robin took in her conversations with her mother. We all know that good intentions are not enough, and her encounter with her mother could have been a disaster. Ruth, according to Robin, had courage, too, and was able to listen to her daughter. The situation was not entirely comfortable for either of them, but it was in service of their relationship; on that front, they were both totally united.

It takes two to make the separation process work well. It takes strength on the part of both mother and daughter to enter this kind of uncharted territory. For Robin and Ruth, the rewards were worth it. Their story illustrates what happens when mothers and daughters can look at each other from differing points of view. As they each begin to appreciate their differences, they can find themselves at the cusp of a new kind of relationship.

8 Sticking Points and Immovable Objects

While we have discussed many issues up to this point in the book—attachment, styles of mothering, family history, and family rules—you may still feel that the obstacles that stand in the way of a good relationship with your own mother or daughter have not been dealt with. We know it is impossible to address all of the roadblocks that can arise between a mother and daughter. Yet we find that there are some issues of the heart that seem to hinder the kind of progressive growth that we have been talking about throughout this book. In this chapter, we'll talk about some of these difficult sticking points.

In recent years, for example, we have spoken to numerous women who, for very legitimate reasons, cannot accept or tolerate *any* contact with their mothers. Their feelings of hatred and resentment are so powerful and overwhelming that they find it easier to avoid dealing with their mothers entirely. Yes, these daughters often feel a sense of guilt for not dealing with or confronting their mothers, but this emotion is often less intense than their rage and resentment.

Nevertheless, when a deep-seated resentment is left untreated over time, it can alter the life course of the person involved. Unresolved pain and resentment associated with the trauma of your personal history with your mother, daughter, or family is very real, and the process of exploring emotions like this, buried deep inside the heart, may feel like walking barefoot on a bed of hot coals. But true personal growth and a clear sense of yourself has to include this type of uncomfortable exploration. Your goal here is not to blame or point fingers. The purpose is to find emotional relief and the ability to move forward in your life.

The Limited Value of Defense Mechanisms

Have you ever been in the middle of a discussion with someone when, suddenly, you remember a frustrating, painful event that happened fifteen, twenty, or thirty-five years ago? You can feel the emotion as strongly today as you did then. The discussion ends and the feeling passes. But the respite you feel is only temporary. In fact, you may experience some constant and nagging anxiety, knowing that it is always there—right below the surface of your awareness—waiting to be sparked by a similar theme. It can and will happen again, anytime a related issue is raised. Eventually, you will find yourself avoiding any discussion, activity, event, or person that triggers your painful associations.

This avoidant style of self-protection, however common, is of limited usefulness. At best, it is a defense mechanism that is a Band-Aid approach to dealing with vulnerable issues of the heart. Strong feelings are suppressed. A very restricted range of emotional expression becomes the norm. And while the original intent of such a measure probably made sense at one time, eventually you may find yourself stuck with a defense mechanism—supported by overwhelming feelings, memories, and resentments—that no longer fits your life.

No amount of time or denial can erase the painful and, for some women, the horrible events of their past. However, these disturbing elements from the past can become the starting point for the creation of a new self. Our history is part of what makes each of us unique, and it can be used as the motivation for change and growth. As you will discover in this chapter, emotional clarity is the key to creating an understanding of the powerful resentments that feel unchangeable. The more clarity we have about our wounds, resentments, and history, the greater our impetus to move out of our painful ruts.

Sticking Points

As we've already noted, there may be things in your life that feel like "immovable objects" or "sticking points." It may seem as though no Mending Move could possibly resolve them. Some of these issues that are intensely problematic for many mothers and daughters are the following:

- child abuse—sexual, emotional, and mental
- substance abuse—drugs and/or alcohol
- sexuality—lifestyle differences, lesbianism, guilt
- adoption—secrets and guilt
- abandonment—daughters who have been literally left, through divorce and second marriages

If your personal issue or concern is not mentioned above, add it to the list. Each of these issues is powerful. The worst-case scenario for any mother and daughter is that they both have intense feelings of hatred toward one another. Hatred is a very difficult emotion to experience and discuss because of the raw energy that surrounds it, but it demands our attention here. Let's begin our discussion on immovable objects with the role that hatred plays between a mother and a daughter.

The Taboo Issue of Hatred

In our culture, there is such a taboo about expressing hatred that it is often seen as a character flaw rather than a reaction to previous or ongoing emotional wounds. But we believe that no one makes a conscious decision to hate someone. Rather, for some people, hatred becomes a powerful, protective coat of emotional padding. It is the flip side of love, but with much different reactions and consequences. It takes courage to admit that your life contains elements of hatred. It takes even more courage to admit that your mother or daughter is the object of that hatred.

The real problem with hatred is what it does to the holder of these feelings. Hatred does not know limits or boundaries. Thus, much like cigarette smoke, it fills an entire room with its smell. So if you have intense feelings of hatred for your mother, for example, it will be very difficult to keep those feelings from spilling onto others—and onto yourself.

The reality of human nature is that emotions, like the blood in our veins, circulate throughout our body. Whether this emotional circulation is a problem or a blessing depends largely on the emotion itself. When you are feeling happy, for instance, you experience a sense of well-being and exhilaration. You feel energized and empowered, with the capacity to accomplish the things you want to do. However, if you spend your life immersed in feelings of hatred toward your mother, it will be almost impossible to limit it only to her. Hatred will spread as far as it can go, and has the potential to color and contaminate your outlook, beliefs, and sense of self.

If hatred can be likened to a raging fire, then resentment is the gasoline poured onto it. Hatred is a very strong emotion, and resentment is its best friend. Resentment, if left unchecked, can evolve into a global kind of hatred toward others and yourself. Hatred also has the capacity to keep you on a circular track of "stuckness," with little chance for personal growth or change. The act of hating a mother or daughter keeps both of you stuck in a rut, with no new input to bring relief to the situation.

In therapy, we give daughters and mothers a chance to explore their deepest feelings. The goal is to uncover the secrets of the heart, and that includes elements of hatred— resentment, anger, mistrust, and self-hatred. In order to illustrate our point, let's introduce you to Carla and her mother, Berinda, who migrated together to the United States from Eastern Europe in 1967. Their relationship is an example of the development of hatred between a mother and daughter, and how they handle—and avoid—it.

We first met Carla seven years ago. She came to see us for help in trying to understand why she had suddenly chosen to stop working as a freelance photographer. She had worked very hard since coming to this country, getting an education and developing a meaningful career. She had developed contracts with a number of corporations to do all of their photography. But she gave up her very productive career, and we wanted to find out why.

Carla, who was forty-two years old when we met her, told us: *I just don't have the energy to work. I have been going at a hundred miles an hour for the last few years. My mother complains that I am a workaholic. That's ironic because I have supported that woman since we got to this country. My mother is mean and has taught me to hate myself. I try to be patient with her, but we always end up fighting.*

My mother is the most disagreeable person I have ever met, and I hate to be around her. Whenever I begin to pull away from her emotionally, she has a medical crisis. This causes me to feel guilty for not being there for her, so I come back to help her. It may take a few weeks, but eventually she will do or say something cruel to hurt me. For instance, she reminds me over and over about what a disappointment I have been to her and that I have done nothing to "earn" her love. This type of remark makes my blood boil, and I find myself hating her all over again.

Several years later we worked with Carla again. At that time she said, *I still have so much hatred toward my mother and I can't get past it. Now she has throat cancer and I am consumed with feelings of hatred and, at the same time, longing for her love.*

These feelings of hatred for my mother have touched

everything in my life. I have got to find a way to put them aside and live my life properly. I have not worked seriously in several years, and have lost most of my professional contacts. I find myself blaming my mother for that, and for having to be in therapy to deal with our relationship.

I feel guilty and hopeless when I think of my life without my mother in it. She has been such a part of my daily existence that it is beyond me to think I might not be consumed with her or something she said to me.

We should note that Carla is an incest survivor, a recovering alcoholic, and an abandoned daughter. She knows that her alcoholism has been a cushion for the painful feelings she has about her mother and her own life. Carla met her father only once, at the age of eight. Painful experiences like this have further fostered her deep dislike of her mother and herself. Carla is struggling to find her place in life. There is a part of her that longs to mend her relationship with her mother. The secret to her emotional growth and mending, however, is to start with herself and not with her mother. Intellectually, Carla knows this is true, but she has not come to terms with it emotionally. The "immovable object" that has paralyzed Carla's life might be changed if she could alter her focus—shifting her energy from the horrible things her mother has done to her to dealing with her self-hatred. This Mending Move will create room for her to see herself and her mother differently.

If you're feeling stuck like Carla, change is possible. Toward that end, let's look more closely at some of the most problematic "sticking points" between mothers and daughters.

Abuse: Sexual, Emotional, Physical, and Mental

One of the most devastating effects of the abuse of a daughter is the psychological damage that it does to her sense of self. Most of the time the abuse began long before she had developed a sense of herself and the inner personal strength to stop the abuse. A young girl is in no position to resist a parent who is unable emotionally or physically to control his or her impulses. The need to please her parent makes a daughter vulnerable to the exploitation of abuse.

When a daughter is abused, she is left with a distorted picture of what she is worth and what she is capable of doing with her life. And she finds herself asking two very problematic questions: Where was my parental protection? Did anyone care enough to protect me from the abuse? If you have been abused, the answers to these questions can be disturbing. But they need to be asked and answered so you can move past this part of your history.

As a daughter, your core reaction to abuse is a sense of betrayal and difficulty in being able to trust parental figures. Having been misled and misused by a parent who was supposed to provide protection, you will find it almost impossible to learn to trust adults. If the abuser was your father, you might understandably test any and all of the men who come into your life to see if the abuse or betrayal will happen again. Another reaction is to avoid men altogether.

If you feel this need to test men or other adults, it can lead to a pattern of unconsciously but deliberately damaging your relationships. This, in turn, reinforces your sense that something is wrong with *you*. We find that, very often, the victim of abuse feels as if her core sense of self is flawed and, therefore, she is responsible for what happened to her. If she were a "good girl," she reasons, maybe she would not have been abused. Her feelings of "ugliness" and "badness" are part of the powerful distortions and emotional fallout of abuse. In a sense, these negative feelings about herself can become the continuation of childhood abuse.

And how does her mother fit into this scenario? In many cases, key questions about her are never asked: What was Mom doing when the abuse occurred, and how could she have allowed it to go on? We have often heard from daughters that their mothers did not believe them when they were told about the abuse. This kind of "empathic miss" by a mother sends her daughter the message that she is either lying or in some way to blame for what transpired. As this happens, the denial creates a distorted reality for both mother and daughter. The mother takes no responsibility for her role in the abuse, placing all of it on her daughter. When this occurs, the daughter is left with no maternal support and the belief that she was at fault.

How can the healing process begin? To recover from any type of abuse, you need to correct those internal beliefs and feelings that you are "damaged goods" and a bad person. An important Mending Move is to go beyond the neglect of your mother and family, and take care of yourself. This means that you no longer have to listen to those old tapes in your head that do not nurture you. Also, you need to give yourself permission to move beyond the abuser and the power he or she had in your life. As an adult, you do control your life. By making your own choices, you'll take a giant step toward healing yourself and coming to terms with your mother.

Substance Abuse

If you're the daughter of a substance-abusing family, you are at risk for repeating two destructive patterns: You may become a substance abuser yourself or you may turn into a "parentified child" (see Chapter Seven).

Frankly, the emotional damage that occurs in children living with an alcoholic parent has no limits. One of the primary casualties among these daughters is a matter we've already discussed: their inability to trust people. Rather than developing a core sense of trust as they grow up, they instead have an intense need to make sure that things and/or people are safe.

Life in an alcoholic home feels unpredictable and unsafe. Many times an alcoholic parent will, while intoxicated, say and do things to a young child that are extremely damaging. For example, our client Patty was raised by Enid, her alcoholic mother. Enid, was sober until five P.M. every day; but after a few glasses of gin and tonic, she would become a monster. This drinking pattern and the behavior that followed were the norm for Patty while she was growing up. Years later, as an adult, she has struggled to develop a sense of self that is neither influenced nor controlled by her mother's mood swings. Patty is also dealing with the old belief that if her mother loved her, she would have stopped drinking. This is a common scenario for children raised with alcoholic parents.

We want to share more of the story of Patty's struggle to develop a positive sense of herself. If you had or still have a substance-abusing mother, you will identify with the unique history that Patty is trying to make sense of now.

Patty told us: *My mother would get so drunk that, on a regular basis, she would threaten to kill herself. Unfortunately, I was totally controlled by the fear that she would kill herself. I did everything I could to make sure I was perfect so that she would not have to drink or feel hopeless any longer.*

My father, whom my mother taught me to hate, left us when I was three years old. That was when I began to learn to manage my mother and take care of her. By age six, I knew how to cover her up with a blanket when she passed out in the hallway or on the floor. The only bright spot in my relationship with my mother was when we did drugs together, during my middle-to-late teens. Now that I am leading a drug-free life, we have nothing in common.

Patty looked at us, her eyes welling with tears, and in a very sad voice, she said, *What do we have in common? My deepest fear, if I am completely honest, is that I really don't have a mother in the emotional sense of the word.* I do not have a mother. *My reality is that I am related to a woman in her sixties who gets hysterical and maudlin every day after a few drinks.*

I do not live with my mother anymore, and I cannot tolerate her late-night phone calls, threatening to kill herself. It is too painful for me to deal with her after she drinks. I have tried to accept the harsh reality that my mother has chosen the bottle over me. No matter what I try to do to please her, the alcohol always wins out. As foolish as it may sound, I still hope, deep in my heart, that someday things might be different. Then maybe I will finally have a mother who cares more about me than drinking.

Patty explained that, finally, at age thirty-five, she was becoming an emotionally independent adult: *I never learned how to say no to people. If I dared to have a different opinion than my mother, I was treated as if I had committed an act of treason. It's understandable that I never learned to think for myself; I only learned to think like her.*

I never got to be a child. I was an adult woman in a little girl's body from the age of three. I vacillate between feelings of rage and of longing for a mother. But neither extreme leaves me feeling very good. I have so much to learn about being me, my own person, and not just the caretaker of my mother and every other lost soul.

Patty is well aware that her life has been shaped by her mother's drinking and unpredictable behavior. Early on, she learned to be a compliant person so she would not have to risk facing her mother's wrath. The task of developing a sense of self, with her own thoughts and opinions, is now her challenge as an adult.

Like many daughters of alcoholic parents, Patty feels guilty when she speaks critically about her mother. She is also troubled that she sees so much of her mother in herself. For instance, Patty, in those moments when she starts to feel out of control, panics. She grew up watching her mother kick holes in the door and punch holes in the wall. As a result, she fears any degree of strong emotion in herself and others.

Of course, that's not surprising, since all daughters have so much of their mothers in them, which makes for conflict as well as comfort. The question for Patty and for all women, is: What do I keep of my mother's and what do I let go of?

What Mending Moves are appropriate here? To move beyond an abusive mother, you need to confront a number of emotional, mental, and physical challenges. First, you need to separate out the useful things you learned from your mother from the harmful ones. That isn't always easy, however. The issue facing Patty is how to keep *anything* from her mother without continuing to be the daughter of an alcoholic parent. Can she define herself as a woman without having to disown every aspect of her mother?

The turning point for Patty will be to recognize that her life and development do not depend on her mother's involvement. She will continue struggling if she looks to her mother as a crucial part of her movement forward, and if she remains in a blaming frame of mind. There is a cultural belief that a daughter's recovery is dependent on the abusing parent's confession of past transgressions. However, that belief is simply not true, and sometimes it creates only more damage in those relationships. In Chapter Nine, we will discuss this issue of parental acknowledgment of wrongdoing as part of the healing process. But for Patty, the emotional rubble that remains in her life, as a result of her mother's drinking, is now *her* responsibility to resolve.

A crucial Mending Move for Patty is to truly assess the baggage that she carries from her relationship with her mother. She needs to let go of the unrealistic expectation that her mother will become the mother she has always wanted. Patty's mother is who she is, and that will probably not change, nor will it repair the past. The ability to accept her mother for the person she is will allow Patty to accept who she herself is, too.

In a sense, Patty has to become her own mother and take care of herself. Yes, it is difficult to relinquish the dream of having a mother who is healthy and sober. But with the support of friends, Al-Anon, therapy, and her own will to re-parent herself, Patty has begun to move beyond the alcoholic pattern of neglect, despair, and irresponsibility that is her legacy from her mother, into a healthier way of living her life.

Another Side of the Story

Patty's issues are not much different than those of a mother trying to relate to her substance-abusing daughter. We encountered this situation in the lives of Roberta and her alcoholic daughter, Shelley. Roberta is fifty-five years old and Shelley is thirty-two. We also got to know a third generation in the family—Shelley's daughter, Mandy, who is twelve. In fact, Roberta initially came to therapy with Mandy, because of her concerns about Mandy's poor school attendance.

Roberta told us that Shelley would disappear for months at a time, and leave Mandy with her. All three of them agreed to this arrangement. Mandy has lived with her grandmother on and off since she was born, as Shelley would disappear on drug (heroin) and alcohol binges. Now that Mandy was becoming a teenager, she was living with Roberta full-time.

When we first saw Roberta and Mandy, Shelley's current binge had been going on for six months, with no attempts to communicate with her daughter or her mother. Roberta and Mandy talked very matter-of-factly about Shelley's erratic behavior and, at least initially, neither of them appeared as upset about Shelley's chronic substance-abuse pattern as you might expect.

But when Mandy left the room, Roberta told us: *I am so scared about Shelley. I don't know what I did wrong as a mother to have a daughter who could abandon her child. Mandy and I both worry about Shelley, although we rarely talk about her. I find myself hoping that Shelley will reach the end of her rope and begin to lead a sober, productive life. Mandy is the victim in all this craziness. She has no drive or energy to attend school. She has been threatened with expulsion from the district if she doesn't go to class. I try hard to suppress my rage about this whole situation, but I have developed colitis, and Mandy has problems with overeating.*

The more Roberta talked about her situation, the more overwhelmed she sounded. Her panic about her daughter and granddaughter filled the room. Then, when we asked her about her feelings about herself, she said, *I am most definitely influenced and controlled by my daughter's drinking and drug abuse. I never drank, and I'm so puzzled about where her behavior comes from. I took Mandy to live with me because Shelley threatened to put her up for adoption. I just couldn't let my granddaughter go to strangers.*

I have no savings left because I have spent all my money on Shelley, trying to get her help. Shelley tells Mandy that I am a bad grandmother and that she shouldn't listen to me. The last time we spoke, Shelley was drunk and asked for money. I told her I had given her everything I had. She hung up and has not called since. My feelings of guilt about this whole situation are enormous.

We asked Roberta how much she blamed herself for what has happened to Shelley. Without pausing, she replied: *I am one hundred percent responsible for this mess. If I were a good mother, Shelley would not be an alcoholic or a drug addict. I feel very much like a failure and I am trying to make things different with Mandy.* At this point Roberta hung her head and started to sob.

After six months of working with Mandy and Roberta, their lives are beginning to turn around, and they are developing some sense of stability at home. In an important Mending Move, Roberta is attempting to let go of her illusion that she will, someday, have a perfect relationship with her daughter. She accepts the fact that Shelley has a substance-abuse problem that is beyond her control. Roberta is also less critical of herself. She is spending less time focusing on why this is happening, and more time on how to make things work for herself and her granddaughter. In the process, her own sense of hopelessness, anger, and responsibility are easing.

And what about Mandy? She is going to school regularly and is attempting to deal with her feelings about her mother. She and Roberta are beginning to talk about the loss of Shelley in each of their lives. This is particularly helpful for Roberta, who is grieving over the loss of her daughter and the unrealistic expectation of having a "perfect" relationship with her. Roberta is very aware that she has the opportunity to do it differently in raising Mandy.

There is no candy-coating the fact that these three women have suffered. Roberta and Mandy, however, have stopped their irrational pattern of denial, unpredictability, and irresponsibility. These issues were once immovable objects in the lives of all three women. But now Roberta and Mandy are developing a secure sense of self, in spite of Shelley's behavior.

One final point: Shelley has yet to come to terms with her self-destructive use and abuse of alcohol and heroin. However, she has made an agreement with her mother that she will not attempt to take Mandy away from her until she is sober. The process of mending these fragile relationships will require many more years of healing.

Sexuality: Issues and Orientations

If there were ever a topic that most mothers and daughters would just as soon avoid, ignore, or simply overlook, it is the emotionally loaded subject of female sexuality. As we discussed in Chapter Six, the topic of sex is burdened with rules, as well as strong feelings and attitudes. No one is neutral about it. Every woman has opinions about the right way for her to express her sexuality. Each mother and daughter have their own comfort level with the topic and their expression of sexuality.

Conflict arises when a mother and daughter do not see eye to eye about what sexuality means to them, and how to express their sexual feelings. Unfortunately, their differing points of view can cause a major breach in their relationship. A daughter who ventures too far away from her mother's sexual ideals will encounter either disapproval or disappointment. Yes, there has been a growing tolerance for sexual differences and choices in our culture during the last decade, yet we still see many women caught up in a battle between how they feel internally (their inner selves) and who they are "supposed to be" (their outer selves). The inner conflict, or guilt, that many women feel about their sexuality is in part a reflection of their relationship with their mother or daughter. If the relationship can tolerate degrees of difference, then one's sexuality can be expressed openly; otherwise, it may go underground.

An important issue, the role of lesbianism in female sexuality, can cause enormous strains between a mother and daughter, depending on the rules that a family (particularly a mother) had about sex. The gay daughter or mother has to confront and deal with the beliefs about sex that both she and her daughter were raised with. Going against the family norm requires a lot of courage. If lesbianism is an issue in your life, the key Mending Move in dealing with your family is, first, to give yourself permission for this lifestyle choice. Next, by accepting your sexual preference, you can loosen the grip that guilt has on your life.

Guilt is a controlling emotion that prevents women from following their deepest desires. Guilt can serve a purpose, at times, in helping us identify right and wrong behavior. But it is problematic when it comes to issues of the heart and becoming a complete person. The ability to understand guilt and its associated emotions—shame, low self-esteem, fear— is critical to the development of a complete sense of self.

Learning to cope with guilt will allow you the emotional room to move beyond major differences with your mother and with yourself.

The next Mending Move in sexual-identity development is for both mother and daughter to deal with the grief that goes along with unmet expectations. As a mother, you may have to put aside your own beliefs about what constitutes a loving relationship in order to encompass your daughter's sexual and emotional preferences. You may fear that you will never have grandchildren, and you need to take time to mourn that loss. And if you are a daughter who has learned that your mother is gay, you may have to readjust your belief about who your mother is in order to preserve your relationship.

In this situation, the family rules that you were raised with will make an enormous difference in your (or your mother's or daughter's) ability to "come out" successfully. If there is a lack of support or empathic understanding, it probably has its roots in your family history. The degree of acceptance you can expect from your mother or daughter is directly correlated to the degree of acceptance she has experienced, in the context of the family, for her own individual preferences. Mothers and daughters who become bogged down by this issue of lesbianism, regardless of whether it is the mother or daughter who is coming out, may have spent most of their lives acting under the belief that differences should be avoided. If you come from this type of family, attempting to win a daughter's or mother's approval for lifestyle differences can feel like running into a brick wall.

Our client, Cassie, picked the day she graduated from college to tell her mother, Joan, that she was a lesbian. But Joan was no more ready to hear this announcement than she was to fly to the moon. Joan asked her daughter, "Are you trying to kill me by embracing a gay lifestyle?" Cassie's anxiety had been so focused on getting her mother's acceptance, she was simply not prepared for that kind of response.

Ten years later, Cassie still feels compelled to be secretive about the permanent relationship she has with a woman. She is still waiting for her mother to give her permission to be who she is—a gay woman. She and her mother never talk about her relationship or lifestyle. As a result, Cassie feels torn between her desire for an open, committed relationship with the woman she loves, and her sense of guilt for disappointing her mother. She vacillates between the need to please her mother and her sadness and rage at her mother's lack of support.

At times, Cassie's guilt feelings are so profound that she goes out and has random sexual encounters with other women. By indulging in this type of impulsive (and dangerous) behavior, she is able to displace her feelings of guilt onto her random sexual liaisons. Putting her relationship in jeopardy keeps her from dealing with the deeper issue of her mother's lack of approval.

Cassie is also fearful that her partner will find out about her secret sexual life and leave her; this fear reinforces her feelings that she is worthless and fundamentally flawed. This cycle of guilt and self-defeating behavior keeps her from ever getting to the core of her relationship with her mother, and prevents her from working toward reaching a common ground between the two of them.

We find Cassie's story particularly powerful in the way it illustrates her profound lack of self-acceptance. She comes from a family with very rigid beliefs and a strong religious influence. Her family does not view lesbianism or a gay lifestyle as a viable option or choice. The gay culture, according to Cassie's family, is "sinning against God." This belief is the immovable object wedged between her and her mother. Cassie is faced with the choice of developing her new self or continuing to ignore her deeper feelings while playing out the family script. For Cassie, adopting a gay lifestyle means she has chosen to leave her family and God.

The challenge that Cassie faces is like that of any daughter who takes a position vis-à-vis her sexuality that is not only different from her mother's, but perceived as threatening to their family values and their relationship. Rather than lesbianism, the subject could be about abortion, living with a partner prior to marriage, having a child outside of marriage, or any of the myriad ways that sexuality can be expressed. When issues like these are a source of discomfort for either mother or daughter, they present potential problems for their relationship.

Is there a solution or Mending Move? Any discussion of sexuality can be tricky, but you need to make the effort to develop a more meaningful dialogue with your mother or daughter. Allow room for flexibility in thought and opinion. When your respective beliefs about sexuality can be discussed in a rational way, in an atmosphere of openness, acceptance, and respect, you can avoid placing unnecessary strain on your relationship.

Adoption: "Whose Little Girl Am I?"

Over the years we have discovered that daughters who have been adopted have a wide range of feelings about the adoption process, not all of them positive. If you were adopted, the responsibility for your feelings about this momentous event has rested mainly in the hands of your adoptive family. During the course of your childhood the issue could have been moot, or a point of contention and strife, depending on how your adoptive parents handled it.

Difficulty most often arises when an adoption becomes public knowledge after years of secrecy. If you were adopted into an existing family, and not told of your adoption, you may feel a real sense of loss when this knowledge comes to light. Your siblings who were not adopted may seem to belong to the family in a deeper way, even though you have found a loving place there. You may have the lingering feeling that, somehow, you do not completely belong. This sense of being an outsider, no matter how strongly your family embraces you, is something you need to resolve.

The dilemma experienced by an adoptee can become even more complicated if she also has strong feelings of abandonment. We frequently hear adopted daughters ask, "Why did my natural mother give me up for adoption?" Answering this type of question goes a long way in helping daughters to resolve their primary sense of abandonment. They may feel rage and resentment that their natural mother gave them up. But by confronting and moving beyond these painful feelings of abandonment and not belonging, they can begin to develop a new sense of self.

And what about the mothers who put their babies up for adoption? Let us introduce you to Stacy. When she was twenty-one years old, she turned over her newborn daughter to an adoption agency for placement with a new family. When we met her, she was ten years older, and was still questioning her decision to give up her child. During that decade she had developed strong feelings of resentment toward her own mother. Simultaneously, she had become angry with herself for not doing what she felt had been right—keeping her daughter. These are the issues that brought Stacy to our office.

Stacy's story began when she became pregnant by a man she was dating from her church. The religious organization that she belonged to at the time had a program designed for unwed mothers. The church, as well as her mother, strongly advised Stacy to give her daughter up for adoption. Two years later, doubting her own decision, Stacy stopped attending church.

She told us: *Because of my family's religious beliefs, abortion was not an option for me. It wasn't even a topic that could be discussed in our house. I was living with my parents when I became pregnant, and my mother, Nancy, was dead set against me keeping the baby. She got the church to support her in persuading me to put the baby up for adoption.*

The minister and other leaders convinced me to give up my baby. It became an issue of good and evil for my mother. In her eyes, good won. But in my eyes, evil won!

I had a beautiful baby girl, and I named her Danielle. I gave her to the adopting family when she was three days old. This family was from Arizona. I felt like I was in a daze when it was time for me to give them Danielle. We met in a neutral location in Phoenix. I remember that, before I even had my car door open, my mother already had Danielle out of our car and into theirs.

The people who adopted Danielle were from the same church organization as us. During the first year, with help from the church, I was able to keep in touch with the family and see pictures of Danielle. I then found out that it was the policy of the adoption agency to recommend that the adopting family change the name of their child. I was struck, for the first time, by the reality that Danielle would never be a part of my life. I remember feeling enraged and thinking I had lost my baby to an "organized smuggling racket." I realized that my little girl would never have the opportunity to know me until she was at least twenty-one years old.

For the next two years I was depressed and miserable. I broke off the relationship with Danielle's father, stopped going to church, and went into seclusion. At the same time families from our church were all having babies and I couldn't stand seeing the painful reminders of my loss. All I did was exist and wonder about my baby girl. My heart ached. There were many times that I went to bed at night hoping that I would never wake up.

Stacy seemed to stare right through us as she spoke: *I have never become pregnant again, and I don't know if I ever will. My sense of guilt and regret for giving Danielle away is always with me. There is never a day that goes by that I don't think about her and wonder "if only . . ." I do not know how other women give their children to adoptive or foster families. It is beyond my understanding. I look at ten-year-old*

*girls in the mall and wonder, "What does Danielle look like?
Is she happy? Would I have been a good mother?"*

*I can't contact her or write to her until she is an adult. I
blame my mother for being so rigid in her beliefs and I blame
myself for being weak in going along with them. I swore to
my mother that she would never have to worry about another granddaughter because I would never have another
child. I know that sounds pretty strong, but that is how I
feel. I tell the men I date now that if they want children,
they better date somebody else. I am done with having children.*

Stacy's plight is the tale of a mother grieving the loss of
her dream of raising a daughter. Her strong reaction to what
she now feels to have been an impulsive decision to give up
Danielle has caused a permanent rift between her and her
mother. Their relationship has never been the same since
the adoption; in fact, they no longer speak to one another.
Stacy also lost her church and its support. She has felt unable
to go back to church because of the lingering memories of
being told to give up Danielle.

Stacy no longer blames the adoption agency that found
Danielle a home. She knows that the people there were doing the job she and her mother had asked them to do. But
she continues to hold herself and her mother responsible for
what she believes was an impulsive, shortsighted act. Stacy
believes that her inability to say no to her mother, and to
break away from her family rules, has caused irreparable
damage in her life. She would like to move forward in her
life and, perhaps, give herself permission to think about
having a family. She knows, however, that this will be a long
time in coming.

We want to share with you another story about the impact
of adoption on a family. Susan is a forty-three-year-old attorney, and was adopted as a child. Today she is married and
the mother of two children, Jessica, age twelve, and Ted, age
seven.

Susan did not meet her biological mother until she was thirty-seven years old. She grew up knowing that she and her two sisters were adopted and that all of them had come from different families. Neither she nor her sisters felt different because they all shared the same background—they were adopted.

During a therapy session Susan told us that six years earlier she had received a phone call at work from a woman who claimed that she was her birth mother. The woman said that she wanted to meet her. Susan was startled by this phone call. In the back of her mind, she had always believed that her mother was dead. It had been easier for her to think that her birth mother was not alive than face the fact that she had been given up for adoption.

With some understandable anxiety, she agreed to meet the woman for lunch. Shortly after that meeting, she told us the following: *I could not believe how nervous I felt, sitting there, waiting for her. The woman had told me that her name was Linda, and she described what she would be wearing so that I would recognize her. I knew I was feeling off-kilter when I didn't tell my sisters or my parents about what I was planning to do.*

Linda drove up to the restaurant in a late-model, convertible Mercedes. My immediate, cynical thought was, "Thanks for supporting me all these years." I could not believe the hostility that suddenly welled up in me, all directed toward this stranger who claimed to be my mother. She was an attractive women, in her late fifties. We were both nervous as we began to exchange niceties. Each of us had a glass of wine to break the tension.

I asked Linda why she decided to contact me now, after thirty-seven years? She told me that the decision to give me up for adoption had been the low point in her life. She was twenty years old at the time, unmarried and scared. She also knew that she didn't want to have an abortion.

Linda told me that she had now been married for over

thirty years, and has three grown children. She wanted me to meet them and become part of their family. For years Linda had contemplated contacting me and decided finally to do it. She seemed as unsure as I did about starting a relationship. I got the impression that just seeing me was very healing for her.

As we continued to speak with Susan, she appeared to become angry at the thought of involving herself with this new family. We asked her if she had any desire to incorporate her biological mother into her own family.

Without pausing, she replied, *I don't want to start a relationship with Linda. There is no place for her in my life or in the lives of my children. Naturally, she was someone I had wondered about as a child, but now it feels too disruptive. My children know who their grandmother is and that woman is my adoptive mother, the woman who raised me.*

We then asked Susan if she had told her family about her meeting with Linda. She replied, *Yes, I finally told my mother and sisters, after the fact. My mother didn't say so directly, but I could see that she was upset. My sisters were very irritated with me for keeping it a secret and not telling them sooner. Neither of them has ever been contacted by or met her biological mother. It took a little time before things with my mother and sisters felt normal again. I think they were concerned that I would leave them and go off with Linda. At my son's birthday party, I told my mother and my sisters that I had no intentions of pursuing a relationship with Linda. No one addressed it directly, but I could tell that they were all relieved to hear my decision.*

In both of these stories, Susan and Stacy are attempting to find ways to cope with the impact of the immovable object—adoption—in their lives. Every day, Stacy is confronted with her strained relationship with her mother, and the loss of her daughter. As for Susan, she is faced with literally saying no to her biological mother, and finally acknowledging her ambivalent feelings toward her. Of course, unlike Susan, many adopted daughters actively seek out their biological mothers. But Susan does not have any desire to have a relationship with hers.

Both Susan and Stacy have been greatly impacted by the adoption process, and are attempting to put it in perspective for themselves. As they grapple with the issues surrounding their adoption, new opportunities for resolution will be created for them. Their decisions will allow each woman to experience more personal fulfillment in her own life and in her relationship with her mother.

Keep in mind that being adopted, or of putting a child up for adoption, is a life-altering event. If it has happened in your own life, you need to show compassion and understanding toward yourself in order to mend the situation to any degree. The goal of this Mending Move is not to deny that the adoption is part of your life, but rather to fully incorporate it into who you are. You need to demonstrate self-acceptance for being adopted, or for giving up a daughter for adoption. Resolving whatever guilt, resentment, or anger surrounds your adoption experience is a necessary part of the process of accepting yourself as a fully complete person—one who just happened to be adopted. No one can second-guess your circumstances—and most of all, neither should you.

Abandoned Daughters

Are you an abandoned daughter? This is a woman who has been left, ignored, or replaced as a result of a parent's remarriage. Every child's deepest fear is that she will somehow be forsaken by the people who love her, especially her parents. There are few circumstances in life more harmful to a young child's self-image than the threat or the reality of being abandoned this way.

Just consider how your entire sense of trust and your ability to function in life has its beginnings in the emotional safety of a nurturing parental relationship. When the emotional, physical, and mental pillars of caring and love are lost, you are immediately at risk for severe problems.

A child's reactions to the loss of the primary relationship with her mother or father can vary. Of course, the immediate outcome of abandonment is neglect, which is the variable that is the gasoline, so to speak, on the fire of anger. The degree of emotional and physical neglect experienced by a daughter is directly correlated to the amount of anger that she feels toward the abandoning parent.

For example, a common scenario is the daughter who lived through her parents' painful divorce, and then who suddenly finds herself left alone, being cared for by baby-sitters when her mother begins dating. We have seen this pattern of neglect culminate when a mother remarries and sends her daughter to live with her ex-husband because her new spouse does not want children around. This same mother then wonders why her daughter, as an adult, wants nothing to do with her.

The following story involves Lucy, age thirty-four, who asked us for help in resolving the anger she feels toward her mother who left her.

Lucy is a very thin, attractive woman, with an edge of hostility in her voice. She told us: *My parents divorced when I was seven years old, and my mother, Helen, never seemed to want me around after that. My dad was a nice guy, but he could not deal with my mother, so he just backed away from both of us. I had always been a very shy child. After my father left, I became more withdrawn. My mother remarried when I was twelve years old. Her new husband, Hank, did not like children, and I was sent to live with my father.*

My dad rose to the occasion. He literally saved me because he paid attention to me. That was something my mother had never done. The "sticking point" with my mother, other than the fact that she didn't want me to live with her, was finan-

cial. She was an executive in the entertainment industry, and after she remarried, she began to make very good money. My father was and still is a frequently unemployed actor, with no money.

I wanted to go to private school and I begged my mother to send me, but she refused. She wouldn't spend any money on me other than my child support. By the time I was ready to go to college, my mother was richer than God. She told me she could not pay my tuition because Hank, her husband, thought I should work my way through college. Hank has never worked, and is completely supported by my mother. When my mom told me she wouldn't give me money for school, I thought I would lose my mind with anger. I did not know who to be more angry at—Hank for controlling my mother, or my mother for allowing him to do this to me.

Lucy was moved to tears as she continued with her story of neglect and despair: *My mother deserved to have anything she wanted, after all, she worked very hard. Yet she was always threatening to cut me off financially and would get very angry if I did not call her regularly. I am an only child and my mother really resents the fact that she has to spend time or money on me when it is not on her terms.*

I finally told my mom off when I was a senior in college. She was shocked that I was angry at her for the horrible choices she had made in our relationship. I was really awful, because I confronted her in her office, where her staff could hear me screaming that she was a "no-good loser of a mother." Since then, my mother has continued to be very tightfisted with her money, although she does give me extra money about four times a year behind Hank's back. We are very cool toward one other. We talk very little about our relationship and what has happened between us.

Lucy's story is a powerful example of the long-term damage of parental neglect on a daughter's relationship with her mother. Lucy was clear with us that her issue with her mother revolves around her mother's abandonment and neglect. She recognized that Helen's constantly leaving her with baby-sitters before and after the divorce was in part due to her mother's desire to develop a relationship with her new husband. Lucy says that she never wanted to be a burden in her mother's life, particularly after the divorce. But even with Helen remarried and Lucy painfully feeling her absence, they never discussed the situation. Now they can barely be in the same room together without arguing about the past or present problems in their relationship.

Lucy would like to move beyond the immovable object of her feelings of abandonment, but her unfinished business with her mother keeps getting in the way. Their current relationship illustrates how these two women feel strongly for each other, but are unable to settle their painful history. Their anger toward each other actually unites them quite powerfully. Lucy has enough insight to know that her anger is the way she stays connected with Helen, and that anger keeps her hooked into her mother's need for control. Both women are stuck together in a situation that neither one can break out of to mend and heal.

We had the opportunity to meet Helen when Lucy brought her to a joint therapy session. Helen, like her daughter, is an attractive women, who looks fifteen years younger than her age. She sat down on the couch next to Lucy and immediately told us the following.

I love my daughter. I never intended to cause her so much pain. I don't agree with her about Hank—that I chose him over her. Lucy did not want to live with me when I remarried. She is a very headstrong young woman, who has had a chip on her shoulder toward me since she was three years old. I would not be here if I did not care about her. She means so much to me, and she makes me feel like such a lousy mother.

At this point Lucy sighed loudly, moved off the couch, and threw herself into a nearby chair. We asked Lucy what was bothering her. She replied: *My mother always plays the victim in front of strangers. She takes no responsibility for the crap that she pulled on me while I was growing up. Now she says how much she regrets the things that happened, but she still keeps doing the same things, every day of every week. My mother is very self-absorbed and is concerned only with how other people see her. The issue between me and my mother is how I am always second or third on her list. Whatever makes her feel good or look great always wins out over me.*

As she talked, Lucy became more upset. She continued to be verbally aggressive toward her mother and threatened to leave the meeting. We redirected the focus back to the issue of mending their mother-daughter relationship. We asked both women to describe their feelings, without blaming or accusing one another of foul play. Lucy listened to our request, and then got up and walked out of the room, without saying a word.

Helen started to cry and said: *It is no use. We will never have a relationship. I've blown it with Lucy, and she will never let me forget it. Lucy does not believe how guilty I feel about the things that happened at the time of the divorce and about Hank. The toughest thing I have ever faced as a woman is having my daughter tell me that I am a horrible mother and that she hates me.*

Unfortunately, we see many women like Lucy and Helen, who have had traumatic events occur in the course of their relationship and who do not know how to move beyond them. For Lucy, her mother's physical and emotional abandonment continues to be the immovable object in her life. Helen does not know how to move beyond her mistakes with Lucy. The historical events that happened many years earlier between them now seem impossible to overcome. For both women, it feels as if they can do nothing but blame each other. But although the past did happen, it can—and has to be—put aside. It will take a tremendous amount of risk taking for both Lucy and Helen to move toward each other without throwing up the past as a protective shield against any real, intimate connection. But that is exactly what they need to do to mend.

The issues discussed in this chapter are just a few of the many complex matters faced by many mothers and daughters in the course of their life together. No one would willingly submit herself to the emotional pain and damage that we have recounted here, yet there are countless women who have similar stories.

After reading this chapter, can you think of the emotional roadblocks in your own life? This is a difficult question for many women to answer, because self-reflection is sometimes limited by our unwillingness to examine the painful and frightening events of our pasts. Nonetheless, the power of your own self-disclosure and insight is the healing ingredient to move you forward in your life and mend your relationships.

Your goal should be to mend yourself so your relationships and life can thrive. The process of becoming a complete woman and emotionally connected to your life requires that you push out of the way the issues that block the direction in which you want to move. This may mean that you need to get out of your own way and let go of the elements of your past that hold you back.

Sometimes we reach places in our lives where it is not so much a matter of recognizing that "I don't know how to do that," but rather, "I can't do any more and I have to move on." Each of the daughters and mothers described in this chapter has reached such a place. They have tried, without success, to bring about changes in their relationships with one another. They have raged. They have wept. They have tried being proactive. They have tried being detached. Now they need to grieve the loss of their dream about the relationship they wanted with their mother or their daughter, try to heal, and move forward with their lives.

Like many of the women in this chapter, you may need

to take the time to grieve for your lost relationship. When someone we love dies or we lose something that is precious to us, we experience different stages of grief—denial, anger, bargaining, depression, and finally acceptance. You need to experience all of these stages; there is no way to cut corners. And by experiencing each stage, you can reach the goal of acceptance. When we arrive at acceptance, we are ready to move on.

Grieving means letting go not only of unrealistic expectations, but of realistic ones, too. The women we have seen confronted with this situation find themselves not hysterical, but unflappably rational. They realize that if they keep attempting to create a relationship when there is no hope of one, they will have sacrificed their lives on the altar of an unworkable dream.

We all know that it's difficult to accept a very unpleasant situation in a key relationship in your life. You may feel, "If I give up, I won't survive." But Mending Moves are not always possible. And the paradox is that by giving up, you may find the road to survival. By surviving wounds that are painful and circumstances that feel unfair, you can find a path on which to move forward, which is a cornerstone of human growth. There is a sense of wisdom that comes from accepting the following "unacceptable" ideas:

- "I cannot make my relationship with my mother or daughter work."
- "I cannot make it into something that it's not."
- "I cannot mend it."

These simple statements may be the greatest gift that you take away from your relationship with your mother or daughter. This type of deep emotional recognition points you in the direction of a more fulfilling and satisfying life.

9 The Psychology of Mending Moves: Moving Beyond Diagnosing and Blaming

I've always had dreams about flying, and in my dreams, I'm usually showing others how. In my dreams, flying was always so easy and effortless. I could just do it. The feeling was one of incredible freedom and control—to be able to will myself to fly. Now that I look back at it, I see that it was indeed a freedom of sorts. But more than that, it was an escape—I could feel free from whatever danger I perceived. This was how I lived. It was the only way I knew to survive.

DIANA'S DREAM

I'm walking toward a caged area, carrying the key to unlock it. This area is old, dingy and dreary, filled with lots of boxes and old things of my mother's. I'm going there to find my mother's purse, which has her credit card in it. I need to use the card so that I can fly to the store and buy a gift. My mother is dead but I know that I can go to this secret, locked place and use her card. I know she won't mind. I reach into her purse and get the card. Then I begin to fly, effortlessly, rising up, moving in between the telephone wires. I know I must get high enough above the wires so I don't get caught or tangled up in them and electrocuted. I do this easily and I find myself at the store, walking from counter to counter, trying to decide what gift to buy. I can't find anything and so

I fly back. I return to a place where my sisters are gathered, and they tell me that I must go back and buy a gift. I reluctantly agree, and I try to fly back to the store. But this time I can't get off the ground. I try and try, but I can't fly! I can't fly! Oh no, I can't fly!

I woke up feeling sad, as though I'd just experienced a great loss. While I was dreaming, I knew in my heart it was probably a good thing that I couldn't fly anymore, but I felt the loss just the same. After all, I've been flying all my life. (Diana, age 45)

This is the last in a series of dreams about flying that Diana shared with us. It is a dream about movement and change and letting go. Diana dreamed it after several years of exploring her family relationships, especially the one with her adored mother. While she had a close and loving mother-daughter relationship, her mother had not protected her and her sisters from their abusive father while they were growing up. Diana's denial of her mother's inability to protect her and her sisters has kept her from forming, as an adult, intimate relationships with both men and women.

We interpreted this dream with Diana. The dingy, dreary caged area represents her past, specifically the part of her past that embodies her mother. The purse with the credit card is the essence of her mother, and because it is in a place that only Diana has access to, it is all the more valuable. It is the symbol of her very special relationship with her mother.

In her dream, Diana must rise above the wires in order to feel safe. These wires represent the reality of her everyday life (ex-husband, adolescent children, career struggles). As long as she can fly, she never has to deal directly with these issues. The gift she is seeking is, ultimately, for herself. But when she can't find it, she is quick to give up. Giving up easily is a familiar pattern of behavior in Diana's family. Even with the encouragement of her sisters, she is still reluctant to go back. When she does decide to move, she finds she cannot fly. Her inability to fly, while feeling like a loss, is really a sign of maturity—she can no longer avoid her life and her feelings.

Diana's ability to "fly" is a crucial metaphor in her dream. Instead of dealing with her relationship problems directly, she loses touch with her body—she flies away—when presented with the opportunity to form an intimate relationship. Many of the daughters in this book created their own means of flying away from their unpleasant realities and relationship failures. Change isn't easy, and most of us don't change unless we have to.

In her dream, Diana sees herself wanting to buy a gift, and in order to do this, she must go into her mother's purse to find her credit card. Going back to the past and using something of mother's is the way many women get through their lives every day. Using "mother's things" (rules, styles, behavior) in combination with "flying away" (lack of awareness and denial of feeling) can keep a daughter from taking action and using her own power.

One of the powerful images for growth in this dream is Diana's awareness that she has to fly above the telephone lines or she might die. This is a completely new concept for her. Until this particular dream, she had experienced flying as safe—there was no danger. Now she sees the potential for self-destruction if she flies.

In all of the relationships we have written about, there came a point where either the mother or daughter, or both, questioned the direction in which they were moving. It was at this moment that their awareness of their abilities to make choices became a part of the mending process. Your capacity to mend your relationship with your mother or your daughter is contingent upon your ability to be in touch with yourself, and not to fly off into denial and rationalization.

Diana needs to buy a gift, but she cannot get "off the

ground"—she cannot fly. The gift, of course, is herself. But in order to purchase the gift, she will have to take some action. Her old way of dealing with the world and relationships no longer works. Naturally, she has a sense of loss. As she said, "I have been flying my whole life." But Diana's dream is a vital message to herself that she is indeed moving beyond the world of her mother—a world where safety was paramount, and taking action was viewed as a threat. And while this feels scary to her, this is how she will find the gift of herself.

The task of transforming the critical tie between yourself and your mother or daughter is the focus of this chapter and the heart of Diana's dream. How many of you can read about Diana's dream and not recognize that we spend a great part of our lives weighed down with old baggage that we tell ourselves and others we have dealt with years ago? The primary message of this book, like the message of Diana's dream, is that we have the ability to set those emotional and mental burdens down and move toward the goal of mending our lives.

Moving Beyond Blaming

The basis of all moral, psychological, and educational teachings lies in the fact that any degree of significant personal change starts with you. The most valuable prerequisite for self-discovery is a nonjudgmental and openly curious state of exploration, and a level of insight that goes beyond finger-pointing and accusing. It would be easy for Diana to feel sorry for herself and blame her mother for all the difficulties she has experienced in her life. But Diana, with her new level of awareness, has moved beyond that position, as her dream clearly demonstrates.

Throughout this book, we have discussed the need for mending and healing our ties to ourselves and to our mothers. Diana is taking steps to move forward and see her life as it really is, and not as a reflection of her and her mother's painful past. By doing so, she is, paradoxically, creating an atmosphere where she can be more understanding and accepting of her mother's failings.

To help you move toward the goal of healing your ties to yourself and your mother or daughter, this final chapter will present a very pragmatic step-by-step way to enhance your own life and all the relationships connected to it. There are six stages of Mending Moves that can assist you in moving beyond emotional roadblocks and developing the kind of life that you desire:

- *Stage 1:* finding and accepting your sense of self: "This is me!"
- *Stage 2:* acknowledging your emotional "hot spots"; what are they?
- *Stage 3:* removing roadblocks—abandonment, anger, and depression
- *Stage 4:* moving beyond blame and taking responsibility
- *Stage 5:* forming new attachments and relationships
- *Stage 6:* finding resolution—with yourself and with others

Let's discuss each stage, and how to deal with the related issues that arise between a mother and a daughter. We will also explain what is involved in the complete process of implementing the Mending Moves that can strengthen the mother-daughter bond.

Stage One

This stage is about taking a nonjudgmental, introspective look at your sense of self. For example:

- How do you really feel about your true self?
- How well do you relate to your personal history?

- Are there things in your past that feel very raw and off-limits for discussion?
- Can you take an objective, nonjudgmental look at events in your past that have been troubling you?

These questions are difficult because they force you to look at how you truly feel about yourself. Having a secure sense of self can offset the troubled history from which you evolved. The ability to give yourself permission to be a competent and empowered woman, regardless of what your family has or has not done, is the beginning of true personal growth.

The cornerstone to the formation of a cohesive self is owning your present, past, and future. When you define and acknowledge who you are, you will begin to develop a sense of inner security. You have the capacity to feel secure about what you feel and think, which is a hallmark of personal growth.

Another marker of personal development is having the inner confidence that your opinions about yourself are important, and that you believe them. For instance, it is always interesting to hear women say that they do not care what their mother or daughter thinks of them. Usually, quite the opposite is true. Of course, they *do* care deeply, but when faced with a painful situation, they feel at a loss. But they need to acknowledge that the key to feeling their own personal power doesn't exist outside of themselves, but within themselves. No one's opinion of them is more important than their own.

When you were a child, if your opinions and thoughts were acknowledged and valued, then your core self was being nurtured. The recognition of who you are as an individual today is directly correlated to the amount of nurturing you received. But even if you are a product of a chaotic, dysfunctional family, you can still learn to nurture yourself now as an adult woman.

When we use the word *nurture*, we are referring to the loving attention and involvement that a parent gives a child. Here are some examples:

- the welcoming smile on your mother's face when you brought home your first finger-painting project
- the nod of approval and the hug from your mother when you learned how to tie your own shoes
- the inner confidence that no matter what happened at school, you knew that your mother would be in your corner
- your mother always finding a way to make you feel better, no matter how badly you felt about yourself or what you did
- knowing your mother would be at your seventh-grade play, no matter how boring it was
- your mother's willingness to find time to talk to you, even when she was busy
- knowing you were valuable because whenever you cried out for comfort in the middle of the night, your mother would come. It did not matter how tired she was or if you had six brothers and sisters, your mother knew that you needed her and she was there.
- the feeling that you could do and try things, and your mother would be supportive. You knew that this support was there for you, even if the two of you did not agree about the activity or task.
- growing up knowing that your opinions and feelings mattered to your mother
- the unspoken support she gave you when you decided to pursue a professional career
- the feeling that your opinions and choices are important to your mother today, whether she is living or not
- knowing that your mother wants you to be everything you can possibly be, even if it means surpassing her own accomplishments

These traits of nurturing are examples of how a girl's development, from infancy through adulthood, is mirrored by her mother's unconditional approval. This approval allows the daughter's self to unfold like a flower. She learns, before the age of four, that her life is either of great value to her mother or a burden. In your own life, acknowledging the kind of mothering and nurturing you received will help you create a stronger sense of self. Most of us have had the experience of falling between the extremes of being completely nurtured and having had no nurturing or attention. As an adult daughter, your task is to fill in the emotional gaps in your perception of yourself and allow your inner self to develop like a rose, thorns and all.

To repeat, in order to mend your relationship with your mother (or daughter), the mending has to start with you. The first step in this process is to ask yourself if you can tolerate being in your own skin and thinking your own thoughts. Is there a sense of acceptance of yourself, including all of your ideas, feelings, and perceived strengths, shortcomings, and weaknesses?

Women frequently ask us, "Are there tangible ingredients I need for fully developing this sense of self?" Here are some important questions to help you address this issue and the growth of your emerging sense of self. Answer them yes or no:

1. Do you find yourself being too suggestible and/or easily influenced by others?
2. Do you consistently use your physical appearance to draw attention to yourself?
3. Do you spend a considerable amount of energy and time concerned with the fear of abandonment?
4. Do you have chronic feelings of emptiness?
5. Do you have feelings of persistent insecurity in your professional, personal, and family relationships?
6. Do you need constant reassurance about yourself and approval for any or all your decisions?

7. Do you feel worthless and depressed when someone does not agree with you?
8. Do you spend considerable amounts of emotional energy worrying about what other people think of you?

These questions highlight the power that you give to others to define who and what you are. The key here is to work toward answering the above questions with an unequivocal no. All of us have self-doubts from time to time. But those uncomfortable moments of insecurity are normal and are very different from having an underdeveloped sense of self. Your task is to recognize in which areas your power is—and is not—functioning. The more you are emotionally aware of your personal power and value, the more you can do to lead a fulfilling life. Developing the freedom of not having to look to others for approval can become the foundation for important changes not only in your relationship with your mother or your daughter, but in all of your relationships.

Stage Two

The process of developing a strong sense of self entails knowing where your emotional "hot spots" lie. These hot spots are wounds that have never been treated or cared for. They are the issues, actions, expectations, and behaviors of your mother or daughter that are guaranteed to set you off like an unguided missile. The problem with being set off is that in those moments of pure emotionality, you are not in control.

Let's suppose that your significant other is late for an important date with you. You feel upset and you explain to him that, in the future, it would be better not to plan such a tight timetable. However, if at the same time you find yourself feeling enraged to the point of wanting to break up or divorce your partner over this event, it is a clear signal that something from your past is operating in the present.

When your rage is triggered by some present-day event

or relationship, your ability to feel under control is greatly diminished. The problem is that you don't usually have the emotional clarity or insight to understand where the rage is coming from. All you know is that you feel angry and uncomfortable. In these moments you are no longer thinking and feeling as a responsive adult.

After this kind of emotional outburst, you may find yourself filled with an enormous sense of guilt. You can apologize for what you said and did during the outburst, but the core issue is still not addressed. And unless the underlying issue is dealt with, the same behavior will occur again. The potential, long-term effect of such emotional outbursts is the loss of important relationships, accompanied by guilt and shame for your behavior.

Why do you blow up over some things and not others? The answer lies in your expectations. What do you expect from your mother, daughter, partner, best girlfriend, co-workers, or supervisors? It would be a mistake to assume that you have no expectations of these significant relationships. We all have expectations, and the more you know about them, the less likely you are to fall into old, destructive behaviors.

Expectations have their roots in your childhood, and can explain both your present-day disappointments and your personal victories. The emotional outbursts that leave you feeling out of control tend to come from unrealistic expectations that have not been met. For example, it is unrealistic to expect that everyone you meet will like you; this erroneous belief can lead to the conclusion that if someone doesn't like you, then there must be something wrong with you. This expectation may be a reaction to an earlier time when you might have felt that you were not lovable or valuable unless you were perfect, and that the only way to get your mother's attention was to be a perfect daughter. Now, as an adult woman, you may find this same unrealistic expectation still operating in the important relationships in your life. If someone does not respond to you in a positive manner, then you automatically assume that the problem lies with you.

The constant disappointment of not having your expectations met can trigger a rage response. Unfortunately, rage wipes out all memory or insight into the problem and focuses only on the immediate disappointment. As we've written, it is extremely difficult, if not impossible, to have any insight into what you are doing when you are feeling enraged. In order to examine this rage, you need some emotional distance from it in order to recognize that you are actually responding to something old that is impinging on your present life. There is nothing more frightening than being blindsided by a flood of rage, and not knowing why it is happening. Your goal is not to eliminate these strong feelings, but to understand and control them.

Rage and unrealistic expectations are really just layers covering over sadness, depression, loss, and a lack of self-awareness. Too often, you may manifest these powerful feelings in old, repetitive responses—such as feeling rejected if your mother or daughter does not immediately return your phone call, or feeling paranoid that no one likes you.

Even as a rational adult, it's sometimes difficult to comprehend that someone's lack of response to you may, indeed, have nothing to do with you. Perhaps your mother or daughter simply did not get your phone message. If you can create the mental and emotional space to explore how a certain behavior might *not* be directed at you, that is the first Mending Move toward changing your style of responding. Behavioral patterns and relationship choices that constantly expose your emotional hot spots are something that you *can* take control of and begin to transform.

You will probably find that old styles of relating are not quick to change because they feel reliable, comfortable, and familiar, even though they are nonproductive. Until you can take control of them, these habits of reactivity will impair your ability to enhance your relationship with your mother or daughter.

So allow yourself some time to think about what feels like emotional unfinished business from your childhood, adolescence, and adulthood. What emotional issues still feel incomplete and never really very far away? What is it about those early years or later teens, for instance, that seem so scary? The answers to these questions may help you fill in some of the emotional gaps in your self-awareness and heal those old wounds.

Stage Three

In Stage Three of the Mending Moves, you need to explore the roles of depression and the sense of abandonment as roadblocks to secure self and fulfilling relationships. Often deeper feelings of helplessness and despair are also interwoven with this depression and fear of abandonment.

Many times, in order to avoid periods of depression, people create a personality style of anger and rage. However, there are systematic stages of these angry responses that evolve into rage and, ultimately, to the very depression they were trying to avoid. The following sequence of emotions is common, and can occur in a moment, activated by an important life event. The power of these emotional responses can direct and control the course of all of our relationships, particularly those with mothers or daughters:

- no anger: you feel neutral about the situation; you have no feelings either way.
- mild anger: you have opinions, but also the objectivity to hear other sides; you feel secure in your relationship.
- moderate anger: you have a strong opinion; while you are still objective, your sense of security is decreasing and your insecurity is increasing.
- extreme anger: your ability to be objective is not func-

tioning; you are flooded with old feelings of abandonment, and feel trapped by your emotions and the situation.

- self-hatred: you become stuck in this pattern when assailed by strong feelings; you blame yourself for everything, and feel worthless.

- rage: you feel as if you could kill the person who has provoked your feelings of abandonment; you are not rational.

- self-mutilation: you turn the emotional explosion you feel onto your body by binge eating, drinking excessively, and behaving recklessly.

- suicidal behavior: you feel hopeless, extremely anxious, and see no solutions; death seems to be the only alternative to your misery. This stage feeds into the deep, dark feeling of complete abandonment.

- fear of abandonment: you feel depressed, lonely, and scared of being so disconnected from yourself and your world; you have no insight into this repetitive cycle. This period can last from a few hours to several weeks. You might terminate relationships, quit your job, and withdraw from your social support network. The fear is so overwhelming that it is the bottom of your emotional cycle.

These nine sequences of emotions can short-circuit your ability to create a more fulfilling relationship with your mother, daughter, or anyone else in your life. It is impossible to function if you are falling apart emotionally. When these patterns are in operation, you'll experience a lack of emotional stability and an inability to trust yourself and the people in your life.

The cycle of abandonment and depression can be triggered by many things, any one of which might be a milestone event in your life—marriage, graduation, moving out on your own, the birth of a child, or death of a close friend or a family member. And its roots may go back to childhood fears of being abandoned by your parents. What you did with those feelings then is relevant to your feelings of abandonment as an adult.

As a daughter, answering the following questions can start the healing process by evaluating the strength of your mother's attachment to you and your fears of abandonment:

1. Can you recall crying when your mother left you at kindergarten class or with a baby-sitter?
2. Can you recall ever worrying that your mother would not come home, and you would be left alone?
3. Can you recall how much you worried about your mother's safety when she was not with you?
4. Can you recall worrying about your mother dying?
5. Did you constantly worry about losing your mother more than your siblings did?

If you answered yes to three or more of these questions, then it is fair to conclude that you had childhood fears of abandonment. But these childhood anxieties can be resolved today as an adult.

To mend this part of your life you need to acknowledge how feelings of abandonment have affected you in the past. For example, Janet, age fifty, is still in denial about her divorce that took place fifteen years ago. She speaks about her ex-husband as if he had just left town for a business trip. Janet's mother died suddenly of a stroke when Janet was twelve. She lived with her father and two older brothers until she was eighteen, when she eloped with her now-ex-husband. As a result of her mother's death and her profound feelings of abandonment, Janet was unable to deal with the fact that her husband had left her. Denial was a way to bury her enormous sense of pain and emptiness.

It is one thing to grieve over the loss of a close friend or a loss of a job, but these feelings are very different from those generated by the cycle of abandonment. Remember, part of the problem may be a very strong but unrealistic expectation—perhaps you may believe that no one should ever leave you. This belief may not even become conscious until someone or something moves out of your life. This leave-taking can rock your equilibrium to the point that your ability to think rationally and your capacity to stay objective are gone. It takes a lot of emotional discipline to increase your tolerance for feelings of abandonment, but the more you are able to identify your fear of abandonment and the associated depression, the more readily you can maintain your emotional balance.

As part of this process, you also need to clarify the realistic and unrealistic expectations you have of yourself, your relationships, your mother or daughter, and your significant other and family. Unrealistic expectations set you up for disappointment, and it is this disappointment that activates old feelings of abandonment.

What are other examples of unrealistic or distorted expectations? Many women believe that everything their mother does is an attempt to keep them under her control. While it may be true that a mother has difficulty with control, if all her daughter sees or feels is her mother's claws in her back, then it will be hard to relate to her other than as a threat.

You might also have another common unrealistic expectation—namely the belief that your mother or daughter will not love you if you become an independent woman, making your own decisions. While it may be quite realistic that your mother or daughter will begin to feel insecure if you do not have a lot of time for her in your new life, this is not necessarily a threat to the love she feels for you.

How about the expectation that if you get a new job, a new house, a promotion, or a boyfriend—that if you find happiness in your life—your mother will not be excited and supportive? For some women, this scenario may be true. If this sounds familiar, the reality is that your mother may never be the mother you long for. But she is who she is, and other people in your life—friends and colleagues—can be excited and happy about your accomplishments. It is a very big step to accept your mother's limitations realistically and stop trying to make her into something she will never become. However, this is what you need to do. Allow yourself to honestly accept that your mother is who she is; by doing so, you will stop the cycle of abandonment from controlling your life.

Ultimately, all of your expectations, realistic or not, are about you and how you feel about yourself. The more time you put into knowing how you feel about who you are, the more quickly you can control your feelings of abandonment, depression, and fear.

Stage Four

If there is one factor that interferes with a woman's potential and dreams, it is the role of blame in her life. Thus, any effort toward personal change, growth, and mending of relationships must address the emotional and feeling components of blame.

Blaming or accusing is a frequent reaction to wrongs that we have suffered at the hands of another person. As children we learned to blame our brothers and sisters for things that went wrong, even though we were at fault. Our fear of being caught or found out was a strong deterrent to admitting that we had a role in a given incident. The need not to be exposed, punished, or wounded was a strong motivator, and blaming others enabled us to protect our core self.

The power of blaming increases with age, as does its negative effects on the formation of our sense of self. When you engage in a blaming type of relationship with your mother or daughter, the relationship becomes stalled. Both of you are on constant alert to protect your position and argue that the other person is at fault. Nothing constructive, supportive, or positive can come out of that kind of connection. Both of you are left feeling emotionally starved. It is impossible to have an adult relationship with your mother if you are still blaming her for all of the things that make you unhappy or that you can't control. This includes blaming her for events that happened in the past.

Blaming is also a symptom of unresolved personal issues. For instance, if you have had difficulty making use of the opportunities in your life, it might be much easier to blame your mother than yourself for your lack of success. According to your belief, if you had an emotionally stronger, smarter, and more sensitive mother, then your life would be more fulfilled. This kind of reasoning can be very seductive because it completely ignores your own responsibility for your present-day difficulties. This leads to the "ultimate victim" scenario, where you have nothing good in your adult life because your mother screwed up your childhood. While this may seem exaggerated, we, unfortunately, hear highly capable women blaming their lack of growth and adult development on their mothers. If these daughters moved forward and pursued their own dreams and desires, who could they blame if they failed? Here is the truth of the matter: If you make the effort to pursue your own dreams and desires, then you are successful, regardless of the outcome. The process of taking full responsibility for your decisions should be your goal.

We also hear mothers blame their daughters for derailing their lives. Many mothers gave up their dreams and careers in order to raise their daughters. Twenty-five years later, with their daughters grown and out of the house, these same mothers have still done nothing to further their dreams or aspirations. In both of these cases, the mother or daughter has to take responsibility for her choices and shift from a place of blaming to one of personal acceptance of her choices.

In your own life, there may be many short and long-term

emotional payoffs to blaming and accusing your mother for messing up your life. You may believe, for example, that she is not loving or supportive of you but, rather, is critical of your every move. But blaming is a sure way to stay emotionally connected to her even though you do not get what you want or need. In the process, the underlying issue of the need for love and support is never addressed and is buried under the rubble of blame and accusations, and the core issues between you and your mother or daughter are never clarified or adequately addressed.

Another payoff of blaming is never having to face the challenge of becoming an adult woman. Either consciously or unconsciously, you may be reluctant to take on this role and become, to some degree, like your mother. This hesitation is understandable, especially if you perceive your mother as competent and powerful. You may wonder if you can measure up to her achievements and successes. On the other hand, you might feel that your mother is powerless and scared. In either scenario, you are faced with becoming an adult woman in the light of your mother's influence.

The fear of success goes hand in hand with the act of blaming. If a daughter can point to her mother's shortcomings, then she can avoid dealing with her own anxiety about the future. It is much safer to focus on the past and what your mother did *not* do to prepare you for being an adult woman than to focus on what *you* are not doing today. Blaming stalls you from taking the next step in your life and serves the purpose of keeping your fears buried. It also drains you of your personal strength and drive, and puts you back in the past, where you were powerless.

Going beyond blaming means stretching your emotional muscles and maturing. It is deciding to take a different path without having to drag your mother along. When you develop the ability to stop yourself from automatically blaming your mother for your difficult childhood or your adult struggles, you will be on the road to the development of a more defined sense of self.

The ability to take responsibility for your present-day actions and choices is a major step toward improving the relationships in your life. The goal is not to forget the difficulties in your past, but rather make them a part of the fabric of your life. By taking responsibility, you will feel empowered and autonomous. As a result, your own process of personal growth will always look forward, not backward with a finger pointing at your mother.

You can diminish the impact of troubling issues such as rage, abandonment, and fear of success when you are willing to take full responsibility for your actions, choices, and dreams. There is nothing more growth producing than stopping the cycle of blame with the words "That's not my mother's fault; I take responsibility for that"—and feeling good about doing it.

Stage Five

In the previous four stages of Mending Moves, we discussed how to change your expectations, develop your true self, mature emotionally, and stop your old habit of blaming. As you make these changes, they will force you to examine how you form relationships. They will also raise the issue of Stage Five: how to develop deeper, more meaningful connections and attachments. Let's begin with the following questions:

- Can you tolerate the anxiety of being an independent woman with opinions and choices that differ from those of your mother or daughter?
- Can you connect to your mother or daughter without having to repeat your old patterns of relating (blaming, rage, abandonment)?
- How much does your anxiety or depression keep you from forming the relationships that you desire?

Through these questions, you can see that your personal growth and change are tied to your emotional connections with your mother or daughter. But your own individual thinking and acting, without your mother's or daughter's approval, is the key to developing new relationships with others and yourself.

By creating a new kind of connection with your mother or daughter, you can have more fulfilling relationships with the other adults in your life. These "complete relationships" are the type of friendships and associations that foster all aspects of your personality. Whether professional, romantic, or family-oriented, they do not hinder your evolving sense of self. Yes, by letting down the walls of defensiveness and blame, you will increase your capacity for vulnerability; but being vulnerable is an important aspect of complete adult relationships, and a step toward greater intimacy.

Thus, the goal of this Mending Move is to form attachments that empower you to express the full range of emotions. The ability to express yourself freely in a relationship creates a sense of completion and fulfillment. By contrast, the problem with insecure attachments is that, as a child, you learned to withhold certain aspects of yourself. Depending on your type of family, style of mothering, and level of emotional functioning, these factors (along with how you feel about yourself) determined your attachment style and the parts of you that were withheld. Your goal now is to *stop* withholding parts of yourself with other people.

For instance, let's say that you came from a family that was rigid and dictatorial. It would follow that you would expose only those parts of yourself that fit into that framework. Other parts of your personality that did not fit the family norm would be buried, suppressed, or simply ignored. If your family rules demanded that you act submissively, then your role in relationships would tend to be passive. You could have rebelled and become angry and hostile in relationships, in an attempt to offset the subversive style in which you were raised. But in either case, your thoughts and opinions were not nurtured in your family relationships.

Another common scenario may have occurred if your

mother was depressed. The energy needed to nurture a depressed mother came at the expense of your own developing self-image. If your focus was on making your mother feel better, the connection between the two of you was disrupted and you were left feeling responsible for your mother's well-being. This is a classic way that women get into the habit of "fixing" other people and ignoring their own needs. How you feel about yourself in your adult relationships is greatly influenced by these mother-daughter dynamics.

Take a few moments to think about the issues, behaviors, and emotions that make you uncomfortable when you are in an intimate relationship. What feelings, thoughts, and memories—all of which are directly connected to your sense of self—are stirred up when you become emotionally close? If, for instance, you tend to feel insecure about becoming emotionally intimate with others, you need to ask yourself, "What am I afraid that this person will find out about me?" Your need to distance yourself from another person and create walls of defensiveness directly correlates with how comfortable you are with yourself. So what are the old fears of relating and the beliefs that keep you from being vulnerable and more open?

The above question is not an easy one to answer; it is related closely to your personal history. But the more clarity you have about yourself, the better able you will be to connect to the people in your life on all levels. Any degree of personal growth and change starts with how you connect to your own strengths and weaknesses. The key to the creation of a sense of self is accepting *all* parts of yourself. Coming to terms with who you are, and knowing your capacities and limitations, are crucial to the foundation of a complete self.

For example, if you think and feel that you are not smart and intelligent, but you believe you are attractive, your focus in relationships will be on your appearance. You will stay away from relationships based more on an intellectual connection than a physical one.

Or if you think you are smart but not physically attractive

or desirable, you might dress, behave, and act as if you have no physical self. Your self-doubt might hinder you from pursuing romantic interests and, instead, lead you to focus almost exclusively on work. It is very difficult to be involved with other people and reject a part of yourself. This sense of self-rejection will filter into all the attachments that you attempt to create.

Of course, the best style of relating incorporates your mental, emotional, *and* physical qualities. It is a problem to focus too much on one quality and, out of insecurity, ignore others. Women need to allow an adult body image of themselves to develop, learning to tolerate the anxiety of being aware of their body and the possible feelings that might emerge from this new connection. In fact, a balance of all parts of yourself will actually foster and develop your self-perceived "weaker" qualities. It requires that you let go of old insecurities and negative messages in your head about yourself, and connect more completely to your mother or daughter, and to other people in your life. Allowing your close friends, both men and women, to see all the parts of you is very empowering.

So by forming new attachments with yourself, you can learn to connect differently with the important people in your life—including yourself and your mother or daughter. To promote this process, answer the following questions, which are a summary of Stage 5 and a way of gauging your adult attachment progress:

1. What person or persons in your life would you like to be emotionally closer to, without fear of losing yourself in the relationship?

2. Why do you want more closeness with this(these) person(s)?

3. What steps do you need to take in order to achieve a complete connection with the person(s) in question one?

4. Do you have any fears about becoming closer to this (these) person(s)?
5. What strengths do you have that would benefit your relationship?
6. What are your weaknesses?
7. Are you prepared to deal with emotional discomfort if this person does not want a closer relationship with you?
8. How much of your sense of well-being is connected to whether this(these) person(s) want a closer relationship with you?
9. What kind of new patterns of behavior and connection do you want to create with this(these) person(s)?

These questions point out how much control you can have in your adult relationships. If one of the people you desire to have a relationship with is your mother or daughter, you need to remember that this connection starts with you. Do not let your mother's or daughter's lack of response to your overtures diminish your moves toward personal growth and development. The most powerful changes that take place between you and your mother or daughter happen inside of you. If your mother or daughter is unable to move forward with you or relate to you, your attempts to change are still important and productive. Don't give up on your goal of creating personal intimacy and connection with others. It is your source of strength and hope.

Stage Six

This last stage—finding resolution with yourself and others—is where all the concepts discussed throughout this book come together to create new actions and experiences. The bottom line to the personal histories of all of the women we have discussed is ACTION. There is no substitute for doing things differently and creating a new model for one's life.

A question that so many women ask us is: "How do I live my life and, at the same time, have my mother come with me—the mother who lives inside my head and heart?" We have never met a woman who truly doesn't want her mother to smile, hug, accept, and love her. No matter how painful their relationship, no woman wants to live her life without her mother's love and approval. It is in our genetic wiring to crave our mother's approval and acceptance.

The entire purpose of this book has been to help you create new ways of connecting, first with yourself, and second with your mother or daughter, on whatever level is possible. We want to share one woman's poem, which poignantly articulates her feelings and thoughts about her mother and the power of her memories, past and present:

SADIE, SADIE
by Judi Kaufman

My mother didn't work at my schools.
My mother invited my teachers for dinner.
My mother was sleeping when I walked to school.
My mother knew I would cook my own breakfast.
My mother gave me hand-me-downs to wear.
My mother gave me sewing lessons.
My mother didn't plan my birthday parties.
My mother knew my sister would.
My mother yelled at me.
My mother never spanked me.
My mother didn't believe in a lot of toys.
My mother knew I loved my only doll.
My mother did not make my bed or clean my room.
My mother knew I would.
My mother didn't take me to Disneyland.
My mother read to me.
My mother didn't have parties.
My mother made love to my father.

My mother didn't invite my friends to our house.

My mother was a friend.

My mother didn't ask me what I was thinking.

My mother let me think.

My mother never just bought a pair of shoes.

My mother's shoes were forty years old.

My mother wasn't fit or trim.

My mother had polio.

My mother didn't visit the neighbors.

My mother believed in integration.

My mother didn't celebrate the Jewish holidays.

My mother was a social worker during the Depression.

My mother chose a man who didn't finish elementary school.

My mother graduated from UCLA in the 1920s.

My mother didn't drive carpools.

My mother had a drive to learn.

My mother didn't take me shopping.

My mother took me to concerts.

My mother didn't give me many presents.

My mother gave me love.

My mother worked forty hours a week.

My mother had two self-sufficient daughters.

My mother suggested that I become a teacher.

My mother supported me when I became a home economist.

My mother didn't watch soap operas.

My mother cried when Roosevelt died.

My mother went through many crises.

My mother said, "Roll with the punches!"

My mother made mistakes.

My mother admitted them.

My mother never saw my house.

My mother knew Roy.

My mother wanted me to become pregnant.

My mother was proud when we adopted.

My mother didn't have a drawer full of diamonds.

My mother was rich.
My mother didn't light Shabat candles.
My mother lit candles in my heart.

This poem illuminates the myriad different facets of the mother-daughter relationship, and the complexity in which it exists. Even though the mother in the poem has passed away, she is alive and well in her daughter's heart and mind. How this daughter proceeds forward in her life will, to a large degree, be based on how she deals with the messages, rules, goals, feelings, and dreams of her internalized mother—the mother whom she carries with her everywhere.

Each one of us carries a portion of our mother's being inside of us. This is not a sign of a mental disorder, but rather an acknowledgment of the different pieces that make up our lives. The more you understand and have insight into the parts of your mother that you possess, the easier it will be to separate your life from hers. The more focus you have on your internal feelings and thoughts, the more decisions you can make based on your own opinions and wishes. The importance of making your own decisions is to complete the cycle of growth and to develop into an independent, thriving woman. The process of gaining a deeper understanding of yourself and your mother or daughter is the key to maximizing your potential. The female power that you can tap into, with your own awareness of your potential, is unlimited.

As we have written, how you deal with the many facets of your mother-daughter relationship will greatly impact your potential and the evolution of your life. Since the experience of being a woman starts with this relationship, it influences what it means to you to be a woman. It affects what you want to accomplish as a woman—professionally, in relationships, and as a family member.

As you think about yourself as an adult woman, you may find, as in the poem above, fifty-four different descriptions of yourself. The more personal information you have about yourself and your mother, the more you will understand the things that make you thrive. You have worked very hard to find out what is going on between you and your mother or daughter; now it is time to put your insights into action.

Ultimately, you have control over your life, in spite of how you may feel at times. The awareness that you control and are responsible for what you do with your life can be a staggering one. Your mother cannot take away the past or erase her mistakes any more than you can. But by accepting the truth about the past and what you can do in the present, you can become more of the woman you want to be. The freedom to love yourself and put aside old behavior patterns and reactions is the ultimate Mending Move. No other step, thought, or action will access your potential and deepest desires. Your life and your decisions are yours—not your mother's or your daughter's.

The resolution to develop yourself begins with knowing where you and your mother begin and end. As you develop an understanding of the cycle of your emotions, find out what triggers your anger, comprehend your fears, and know who you are, this will become your core self. These insights are the ingredients of a flourishing life. No amount of therapy, thinking, or waiting will ever replace the powerful experience of doing what you need to do. Nothing will ever replace the role that action has in helping you make the necessary changes in your life. The commitment to live your own life, while understanding the role of your mother in it, creates new opportunities for choice and action.

From time to time, look back at the chapters in this book and these six stages of Mending Moves to answer your questions about a particular issue that arises between you and your mother or daughter. Take the information, knowledge, and personal histories, and create new experiences for yourself in your relationships—with family members and with your mother or daughter. No matter what the response from the important people in your life to the changes you create, you will be a stronger, more complete woman as a result of this process. Remember, becoming the woman you have always wanted to be starts with taking action—action that creates opportunities for you to express your thoughts and feelings in new and different ways. The saddest thing we see in our practice is a woman who has never experienced her own personal power and potential. It would be a tragedy to let your life slip by, and not take control of your destiny.

You would not be reading this book if you weren't interested in maximizing your potential and changing your destiny. It is never too late or too early to find out who you are and where you are going. The journey will always have parts of your mother or daughter in it, and that can be a source of new movement and energy. The road map that you design is yours and we encourage you to go to places in your life, literally and figuratively, that might have seemed impossible at one time. Your gift to yourself is the creation of a meaningful life, which will positively affect all the people around you. Let your legacy to the next generation of women be one of courage and hope for all mothers and daughters to build on.

Bibliography

Ainsworth, M., and C. Eichberg (1991) "Effects on Infant-Mother Attachment of Mother's Unresolved Loss of an Attachment Figure or Other Traumatic Experience." In *Attachment Across the Life Cycle*. Tavistock/Routledge: London.

————, M. C. Blehar, E. Walters, and S. Wall (1978) *Patterns of Attachment: A Psychological Study of the Strange Situation*. Hillsdale, NJ: Erlbaum.

Bassoff, E. (1991) *Mothering Ourselves: Help and Healing for Adult Daughters*. New York: Dutton.

Beavers, W. R. (1977) *Psychotherapy and Growth: a Family Systems Perspective*. New York: Brunner/Mazel.

Bergman, Anni (1987) "On the Development of Female Identity: Issues of Mother-Daughter Interaction During the Separation-Individuation Process." Psychoanalytic Inquiry, 1987, v 7(n3): 381–399.

Bernstein, D., N. Freedman, and B. Distler (eds.) (1993) *Female Identity Conflict in Clinical Practice*. Northvale, NJ: Jason Aronson.

Bly, R. (1996) *The Sibling Society*. New York: Vintage Books.

Boszormenyi-Nagy, and Ivan and G. Spark (1973) *Invisible Loyalties: Reciprocity in Intergenerational Family Therapy*. New York: Harper & Row.

———, and D. Ulrich (1981) "Contextual Family and Therapy." In A. Gurman and D. Kniskern (eds.) *Handbook of Family Therapy*. New York: Brunner/Mazel.

Bowen, M. (1978) *Family Therapy in Clinical Practice*. New York: Jason Aronson.

———. (1980) "Key to the Use of the Genogram." In Carter and McGoldrick (eds.), *The Family Life Cycle: A Framework for Family Therapy*. New York: Gardner Press.

———. (1988) "The Use of Family Theory in Clinical Practice." In M. Bowen, *Family Therapy in Clinical Practice*, 2d edition. Northvale, NJ: Jason Aronson.

Bowlby, J. (1988) *A Secure Base*. New York: Basic Books.

———. (1969) *Attachment and Loss*. New York: Basic Books.

Brenner, M. (1995) "I Never Sang for My Mother." *Vanity Fair*, August, 96–112.

Caplan, P. (1989) *Don't Blame Mother: Mending the Mother-Daughter Relationship*. New York: Harper & Row.

Carnovan-Gumpert, D., K. Garner, and P. Gumpert (1978) *The Success Fearing Personality: Theory and Research with Implications for Social Psychology of Achievement*. Lexington, MA: D. C. Heath.

Chernin, K. (1986) *The Hungry Self: Women, Eating, and Identity*. New York: Perennial Library.

Chodorow, N. (1978) *The Reproduction of Mothering*. Berkeley: University of California Press.

Clance, P., and S. Imes (1978) "The Imposter Phenomenon in High Achieving Women: Dynamics and Therapeutic Intervention." *Psychotherapy: Theory, Research and Practice (15:3)*.

Cohn, D., P. Cowan, C. Cowan, and J. Pearson (1992) "Mothers' and Fathers' Working Models of Childhood Attachment Relationships, Parenting Styles, and Child Behavior." *Development and Psychopathology*, 4.

Crittenden, P., M. Partridge, and A. Claussen (1991) "Family Patterns of Relationship in Normative and Dysfunctional Families." *Development and Psychopathology*, 3.

Donaldson-Pressman, S., and R. M. Pressman (1994) *The Narcissistic Family.* New York: Lexington Books.

Dowling, C. (1988) *Perfect Women.* New York: Summit Books.

Edelman, H. (1994) *Motherless Daughters: the Legacy of Loss.* Reading, MA: Addison-Wesley.

Eichenbaum, L., and S. Orbach (1983) *Understanding Women: A Feminist Psychoanalytic Perspective.* New York: Bantam Books.

Embelton, G., D. Axten, V. Blandford, and L. Lavercombe (1996) *Freeing Ourselves from Our Family of Origin.* Northvale, NJ: Jason Aronson.

Finzi, S. V. (1996) *Mothering: Toward a New Psychoanalytic Construction.* New York: Guilford Press.

Freud, S. (1933) *Three Essays on the Theory of Sexuality.* In Strachey, (ed.), *The Standard Edition of the Complete Psychological Works of Sigmund Freud,* vol. 7, 576–599. London: Hogarth.

Gilligan, C. (1982) *In a Different Voice.* Cambridge, MA: Harvard University Press.

Greenspan, M. (1983) *A New Approach to Women and Therapy.* New York: McGraw-Hill.

Grossman, K. E., and K. Grossman (1978) "Attachment Quality As an Organizer of Emotional and Behavioral Responses in a Longitudinal Perspective." In *Attachment Across the Life Cycle.* London: Tavistock/Routledge.

Guerin, P., and E. Pendagast (1976) "Evaluation of Family System and Genogram." In *Family Therapy: Theory and Practice.* New York: Gardner Press.

Hedges, L. (1994) *In Search of the Lost Mother of Infancy.* Northvale, NJ: Jason Aronson.

Herman, N. (1989) *Too Long a Child: The Mother-Daughter Dyad.* London: Free Association Books.

Holmes, J. (1996) *Attachment, Intimacy, Autonomy.* Northvale, NJ: Jason Aronson.

Jacobvitz, D., E. Morgan, M. Kretchmar, and Y. Morgan (1991) "The Transmission of Mother-Child Boundary Disturbances Across Three Generations." In *Development and Psychopathology*, 3.

Kaufman, J. (1997) *Poetry to Go!* CA: Palato Press.

Kobak, R. R., N. Sudler, and W. Gamble (1991) "Attachment and Depressive Symptoms During Adolescence: A Developmental Pathways Analysis." In *Development and Psychopathology*, 3.

Kohut, H. (1984) *How Does Analysis Cure?* Chicago: University of Chicago Press.

Krueger, D. W. (1984) *Success and Fear of Success in Women.* New York: Free Press.

Lerner, H. (1985) *The Dance of Anger.* New York: Harper & Row.

———. (1988) *Women in Therapy.* Northvale, NJ: Jason Aronson.

McGoldrick, M., and R. Gerson (1985) *Genograms in Family Assessment.* New York: W. W. Norton.

———, C. Anderson, and F. Walsh (1989) *Women in Families.* New York: W. W. Norton.

Mahler, M., F. Pine, and A. Bergman (1975) *The Psychological Birth of the Human Infant.* New York: Basic Books.

Miller, J. (1976) *Toward a New Psychology of Women.* Boston: Beacon Press.

Miller, M. V. (1995) *Intimate Terrorism: The Deterioration of Erotic Life.* New York: W. W. Norton.

Minuchin, S. (1974) *Families and Family Therapy.* Cambridge, MA: Harvard University Press.

Moulton, Ruth (1985) "The Effect of the Mother on the Success of the Daughter." *Contemporary Psychoanalysis*, Apr., V21(n2) (21:2).

Parkes, C. M., J. Stevenson-Hinde, P. Marris, (eds.) (1991) *Attachment Across the Life Cycle.* London: Tavistock/ Routledge.

Parker, R. (1995) *Mother Love/Mother Hate: The Power of Maternal Ambivalence.* New York: Basic Books.

Pipher, M. (1994) *Reviving Ophelia: Saving the Selves of Adolescent Girls.* New York: Ballantine Books.

Rowe, C., and D. MacIsaac (1989) *Empathic Attunement.* Northvale, NJ: Jason Aronson.

Rutter, M. (1981) *Maternal Deprivation Reassessed* New York: Penguin Books.

Scarf, M. (1995) *Intimate Worlds: Life Inside the Family.* New York: Random House.

Scharff, D. (1992) *Refinding the Object and Reclaiming the Self.* Northvale, NJ: Jason Aronson.

Secunda, V. (1990) *When You and Your Mother Can't Be Friends.* New York: Delacorte Press.

Skynner, R., and J. Cleese (1983) *Families and How to Survive Them.* New York: Oxford University Press.

Slipp, S. (1991) *Object Relations: A Dynamic Bridge Between Individual and Family Treatment.* Northvale, NJ: Jason Aronson.

Surrey, Janet, (1991) "The Self-in-Relation: A Theory of Women's Development." In Jordan et al, *Women's Growth in Connection.* New York: Guilford Press.

Wachtel, E. (1982) "The Family Psyche over Three Generations: The Genogram Revisited." *Journal of Marital and Family Therapy* 8, 335–343.

Walsch, N. D. (1996) *Conversations with God: An Uncommon Dialogue.* New York: G. P. Putnam's Sons.

Winnicott, D. W. (1988) *Human Nature.* New York: Schocken Books.